Praxis® 5624 Principles of Learning and Teaching (PLT) Grades 7-12

How to pass the Praxis® PLT by using effective test prep, proven strategies, and relevant practice test questions.

By: Kathleen Jasper, Ed.D.

kj | Kathleen Jasper

Kathleen Jasper LLC
Estero, FL 33928
http://www.kathleenjasper.com | info@KathleenJasper.com

Praxis® 5624 Principles of Learning and Teaching (PLT) Grades 7-12: How to pass the Praxis® PLT by using effective test prep, proven strategies, and relevant practice test questions.

Printed in the United States of America
ISBN: 9798582386100

LIMIT OF LIABILITY/DISCLAIMER OF WARRANTY: Publication of this work is for the purpose of test preparation and related use and subject set for herein. While every effort has been made to achieve a work of high quality, the authors of this work do not assume any liability in connection with this information.

Kathleen Jasper

Thank you for taking the time to purchase this book. I really appreciate it.

Would you mind leaving a review?

Did you purchase this book on Amazon? If so, I would be thrilled if you would leave an unbiased review at your convenience. Did you purchase this book from KathleenJasper.com? If so, you can leave a review on Facebook, Google, or directly on our website on the product page. Thank you for using my products.

Visit my Facebook Page.

I post videos, practice test questions, upcoming events, and other resources daily on my Facebook Page. Join us every Tuesday at 5 P.M. ET for our Facebook live math help session. https://www.facebook.com/KathleenJasperEdD.

Check out my other products.

I have built several comprehensive, self-paced online courses for many teacher certification exams. I also have other books, webinars and more. Go to https://kathleenjasper.com and use offer code **PLT20** for 20% off any of my products.

Join my private Facebook group.

Are you trying to become a teacher and are you looking for a community? Share insights, strategies and connect with other prospective teachers.

Go to: www.facebook.com/groups/certificationprep/ to request access.

Subscribe to my YouTube channel

Check out my enormous video library with tons of interesting and insightful content for teacher certification exams and more.

Subscribe here https://www.youtube.com/kathleenjasperedd.

If you have any questions, don't hesitate to reach out. It will be my pleasure to help.
Good luck on your exam.

–Kathleen Jasper, Ed.D.

This page intentionally left blank.

Table of Contents

Quick Reference Guides

How to Use this Book

Often people will purchase a study guide and become overwhelmed with the amount of information and tasks within the guide. Below is a suggested way to use the book.

Step 1: Use the practice test at the end of the guide as a pretest. Do this first to measure your skills. This will be a baseline score.

- Take the practice test.

- Mark the ones you get incorrect, but DO NOT look at the correct answers or explanations. That way you can reuse this test later.

- Record your score. This will be your raw score out of 70 because there are 70 questions on the practice test.

- Determine the subareas and objectives in which you are low.

Step 2: Begin your studies with your strengths and weaknesses in mind.

- Start with Content Category I.

- Read the information under each section. That information is very important.

- Work through all the information in the sections in the guide.

- Complete the 10 practice problems at the end of each content category. If you get less than 80% correct, go back through and review content category.

- Do this for all sections of the book.

Step 3: Once you've worked through the entire guide, take the practice test again.

- Work backwards starting with the answer choices first. Eliminate bad words, focus on good words. Then read the question stem.

- Check your answers and read ALL the answer explanations. There is a ton of information in the answer explanations, so even if you get the answer correct, read the explanation.

- Review information as needed.

Step 4: Focus on the constructed response.

- Work through the constructed response prompts.

- Check your writing against the rubric provided.

QUICK TIPS: These tips are represented with a megaphone and include tips and vocabulary you need to know or strategies for answering questions for a particular skill or content category.

 TEST TIPS: Test tips are represented with a light bulb and are specific test taking strategies that can be, and should be, used while taking the exam.

 THINK ABOUT IT: These tips are not necessarily tested concepts, but they provide background information to help make sense of concepts and give necessary information to help answer questions on the exam.

 CAUTION: Caution tips explain what to avoid when selecting your answer choices on the exam. Test writers are very good at creating distracting answer choices that seem like good options. We teach you what to watch for when it comes to *distractors* so you avoid these pitfalls.

Don't forget to look over the reference pages

I have included a Good Words List before practice test one. This is a list of words, terms, and phrases that are typically in correct answer choices on this exam. There is also a Bad Words list, which contains words and phrases to avoid. Use the list to ***think like a test maker***, ***not a test taker*** and to be strategic on the exam.

I have also included a reference sheet that includes eminent authors, major works, and dates. This will help you with questions that are specific to certain authors included in the literary canon.

About the Test

The Praxis® Principles of Learning and Teaching (PLT) 5624 is designed to assess standards-based knowledge of skills and competencies of all high school teachers. The assessment is comprised of 5 content categories and a constructed response section. The following table provides an overview of the assessment.

Test at a Glance	
Test Name	Principles of Learning and Teaching: Early Childhood
Test Code	5624
Time	2 hours
Number of Questions	70 selected-response questions 4 Constructed Response (essays)
Format	Selected response; constructed-response questions related to two case histories.
Test Delivery	Computer delivered

Content Category	Approx. Number of Questions	Approx. Percentage of Exam
I. Students as Learners	21	22.5%
II. Instructional Process	21	22.5%
III. Assessment	14	15%
IV. Professional Development, Leadership, and Community	14	15%
V. Analysis of Constructed Scenarios	4	25%
A. Students as Learners	1-2	
B. Instructional Process	1-2	
C. Assessment	0-1	
D. Professional Development, Leadership, and Communityy	0-1	

This page intentionally left blank.

CONTENT CATEGORY

I

Students as Learners

This page intentionally left blank.

A. Student Development and the Learning Process

1. Theoretical frameworks for student learning

2. Contributions of foundational theorists to education

3. Learning theories

4. Stages of human development

5. How learning theory and human development impact instruction

1. Theoretical frameworks for student learning

On the PLT, you are expected to understand the prevailing theories and research on how students learn. Many factors contribute to a student's learning and development. You need to understand and be able to differentiate between various theories on learning processes, cognitive processes, learning experiences, and the impact of a student's learning environment (Donovan et al, 2000).

Construction of knowledge and acquisition of skills

The environment, experiences, and meta-cognitive processing of a child's education impact the speed and efficiency of their growth. Learning theorists differ in their ideas of how knowledge is acquired. However, their overlapping ideas and research inform the development of curriculum and instructional design used in schools today. On the PLT, you will see the theorists and foundational concepts for behaviorism, cognitivism, constructivism, and social learning theory. Later in this text, you will examine how these theories influence instructional design in the classroom.

Cognitive processes and how they are developed

The development of cognitive processes is ongoing and influenced by the students' learning experiences and environment. Students' ability to process information is critical to their growth and development. Cognitive development happens at the intersection of information processing, intelligence, reasoning, language development, and memory (Encyclopedia.com, 2020).

Here are nine cognitive processes that are generally associated with academic learning:

1. **Critical thinking.** To apply, analyze, evaluate, compare, and synthesize information.

2. **Creative thinking.** To create, develop, and understand new perspective.

3. **Questioning.** To ask why, how, where, what, or when.

4. **Inductive reasoning.** To reason by working from a specific concept to a general topic. For example, a lesson starts by exploring Earth and then moves to Earth's place in the Solar System.

5. **Deductive reasoning.** To reason by working from a general topic to a specific concept. For example, students are exploring ecosystems and determining how evolving ecosystems result in evolving species natural selection and species' evolution.

6. **Problem-solving.** To use a variety of thinking strategies to generate or evaluate solutions.

7. **Planning.** To prepare.

Quick Tip

The difference between inductive and deductive reasoning is simple:

– Inductive works from the specific to the general.

– Deductive works from the general to specific.

8. **Memory.** Working memory is used to process the current task or situation; descriptive memory is used to carry out a procedure or remember information over a long period of time.

9. **Recall.** To retell.

These processes build on one another and are useful to design instruction for various stages and types of learning.

Example question

A high school teacher facilitates a learning project where students work together to design and create rocket boosters. Through her instructional design, what cognitive process is the teacher expecting students to use to complete the task?

A. Inductive reasoning

B. Creative thinking

C. Recall

D. Memory

Correct answer: B

Key words from the scenario are *design* and *create* because these are mentioned in the definition of creative thinking. While the students will use a variety of thinking skills to collaboratively design and create their rocket boosters, creative thinking is the dominant cognitive thinking process from this list.

2. Contributions of foundational theorists to education

Relationship of theorists to educational contexts

On the PLT, you will be asked to identify influential education theorists and the foundational theories that govern the profession of teaching. In most cases, these questions will be presented in scenarios, and you will be required to identify the theorist or theory that aligns with the scenario.

Jean Piaget. Piaget is widely known for his stages of cognitive development. This is a framework for how students develop intellectually through various stages. Piaget asserted that cognitive development was a reorganization of mental processes resulting from biological maturation and environmental experience (1972).

The table below provides an overview of Piaget's 4 stages of cognitive development.

Stage	Age	Description
1. Sensorimotor	0–2 years	Children at this stage figure out the world through sensory and motor experiences. Object permanence and separation anxiety are hallmarks of this stage.
2. Pre-operational	2–6 years	Children at this stage identify and use symbols for objects but do not have the ability to apply logical reasoning. They know how to play pretend and are egocentric.
3. Concrete operational	7–12 years	Logical reasoning about concrete objects kicks in during this stage. Conservation, reversibility, serial ordering, and understanding cause and effect relationships are hallmarks of this stage, but thinking is still limited to the concrete.
4. Formal operational	12 years–adult	Abstract thinking such as logic, deductive reasoning, comparison, and classification are demonstrated by the individual in this stage.

(Piaget, 1972)

John Dewey. Dewey is one of the most influential theorists in education. Dewey believed that students learn by doing through hands-on, inquiry-based learning. This was revolutionary in the 1900s when schooling consisted mostly of the teacher standing in the front of the room giving students the knowledge. Dewey asserted that it is more effective for students to learn by interacting with their environment, relating the learning to real-life, and learning together with the teacher.

Jerome Bruner. Like Dewey, Bruner believed that learning is an active process. Like Piaget, Bruner believed learners construct new ideas or concepts based upon their current and past knowledge.

Fundamental concepts of Bruner's philosophy:

- Curriculum should foster the development of problem-solving skills through the processes of inquiry and discovery.

- Subject matter should be represented in terms of the child's way of viewing the world.

- Curriculum should be designed so that the mastery of skills leads to the mastery of still more powerful ones.

Erik Erickson. Like Piaget, Erickson believed that students pass through definitive stages. However, Erikson focused on psychosocial stages. According to Erickson, socialization happens in 8 stages:

1. Learning basic trust over mistrust 0-1.5 years

2. Learning autonomy versus shame 1.5-3 years

3. Learning initiative versus guilt (purpose) 3-5 years

4. Industry versus inferiority (competence) 5-12 years

5. Learning identity versus identity diffusion (fidelity) 12-18 years

6. Learning intimacy versus isolation (love) 18-40 year

7. Learning generativity versus self-absorption (care) 40-65 years

8. Integrity versus despair (wisdom) 65+ years

Lev Vygotsky. Vygotsky's theories stress the fundamental role of social interaction in the development of cognition. He believed strongly that community plays a central role in the process of making meaning. Vygotsky is most widely known for the zone of proximal development (ZPD), which he asserted is the distance between the actual developmental level as determined by independent problem solving and the level of potential development as determined through problem-solving under adult guidance, or in collaboration with more capable peers (Vygotsky, 1978).

Helping someone move through the ZPD depends on the following:

1. Presences of a more knowledgeable person

2. Social interactions

3. Scaffolding or supportive activities developed by the educator (ZPD is discussed in more detail below).

Albert Bandura. Bandura is best known for his social learning theory on modeled behaviors or observational learning. He believes that students learn from what they observe and that teachers can be proactive about how they demonstrate and promote behaviors. He argues that students are more likely to emulate a behavior if they value the outcome and admire the modeler. His theory builds on the central elements of Vygotsky's learning which also emphasize social learning. Bandura's social learning theory has four stages:

1. Attention (observation of modeled behaviors)

2. Retention (memory)

3. Motor reproduction (practice and replication of behaviors)

4. Motivation (self-efficacy and personal motivation to use new behaviors)

(Bandura, 1972)

Lawrence Kohlberg. Kohlberg built on Piaget's research to explore the development of morality. He created a set of moral dilemmas to present to a group of boys. The boys were interviewed to determine how they made their decisions. He continued to interview the boys over a 20-year period. Kohlberg came up with 3 levels of morality with two stages at each level. He argued that everyone works through the stages sequentially but at varying rates and not everyone reaches the highest stages.

Level	Stages	Example
Level 1: **Preconventional morality** Behaviors are based on perceived individual consequences. Ages 5-10+	**Stage 1: Punishment and obedience orientation** A child's incentive to obey is to not be punished.	Did my mom say this is ok? What will happen if I take this cookie?
	Stage 2: Instrumental purpose orientation Behavior based on receiving rewards or satisfying personal needs.	Is this self-serving? Can I do this without an adult knowing?
Level 2: **Conventional morality** Behaviors determined by the rules of adults, peers, and government. Ages 10-15+	**Stage 3: Good boy/nice girl orientation** Behavior based on social approval.	Am I following the school rules? Will my peers and teachers be happy with my actions?
	Stage 4: Law and order orientation Behavior based on laws and social rules.	Children begin to look beyond their own ties to the abstract, "greater good." They are more aware of laws and social norms of society.
Level 3: **Postconventional or principled morality** Behaviors based on abstract principles and values. Age 15+	**Stage 5: Social contract orientation** When the individual feels conflict between personal rights and the law, exceptions are made.	Laws are not always clear-cut. For example, my father had a heart attack. I needed to rush him to the emergency room, so I broke the speed limit.
	Stage 6: Universal ethical principal orientation Behaviors based on abstract ethical principles which take in multiple differing perspectives simultaneously.	Person acts to defend principles of equality, justice, equity. Personal conduct, intentions, character all play a role in decision making. Not everyone reaches this highest level.

(Kohlberg, 1983)

Children's morality will grow at different rates. While some young children will continue to make decisions based on punishments or self-interest, others will begin to base their actions on social approval.

Benjamin Bloom

Bloom's Taxonomy is a hierarchical model used to classify educational learning objectives into levels of complexity and specificity. The higher up the pyramid, the more complex the thinking skills. The skills are represented as verbs on the pyramid. When answering questions on the PLT regarding critical thinking, reference Bloom's Taxonomy. The figure above is a modified version of Bloom's Taxonomy. We have modified it to include other skills (verbs) you may see on the exam.

The skills (verbs) at the highest points of the pyramid are evaluate, analyze, create, and apply. When you are faced with a critical thinking problem on the test, visualize this pyramid, and look for answer choices that reflect the higher portions of the pyramid.

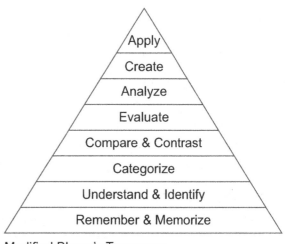

Modified Bloom's Taxonomy

Theories in the classroom

Because you will be required to identify which theorist influences different practices in the classroom, it is important to be able to identify how these theories present themselves in classroom activities.

Dewey in the classroom (schema)

- After a lesson about Naturalism in American literature, the class goes to an outdoor classroom to observe a particular aspect of their natural surroundings and then write a short story about their observations.

- As part of a seed germination unit, students plant seeds in clear containers, observe the plants at regular intervals, and note the changes they observe.

- Before reading about rocks, students collect and categorize different rocks.

Piaget in the classroom (cognitive learning theory)

- Provide students with pre-cut letters to form words.

- Allow opportunities for students to participate in age-appropriate experiments.

- Connect new concepts to previously learned concepts (prior knowledge or schema).

Vygotsky in the classroom (ZPD)

- Cooperative learning activities

- Scaffolded activities

- Peer and teacher support

- Gradual release (I do, we do, you do)

Bruner in the classroom (constructivist theory)

- Students are thinking aloud, forming ideas, and engaging in discussions. As they do this, they learn new things.

- Curriculum should be organized in a spiral manner so that the student continually builds upon what they have already learned.

Bandura in the classroom (social learning theory)

- Students regularly participate in routines for learning new skills, strategies, and concepts.

- Self-efficacy is promoted by giving students immediate and specific feedback for completed tasks, applied skills, and new learning.

Kohlberg in the classroom (moral development)

- Ask students to describe the motives behind a character's actions and consider a story from various perspectives.

- Promoting social awareness through community actions.

- Researching environmentalism and other activism movements.

Bloom in the classroom (critical thinking)

- The teacher guides students to answer a variety of comprehension questions with increasing level of complexity from recall to analysis and application.

- A teacher designs a science assessment on reptiles asking students to not only recall the names of reptiles and their features, but to also compare reptiles to amphibians.

Erikson in the classroom (social development)

- Cooperative learning is structured based on students' levels of socialization.

- Develop independence by assigning students roles in the classroom, such as paper collector, group administrator, white board washer, etc.

Example question

A 9th grade English teacher asks students to role-play a scene from an Ancient Roman gladiator event. Students have to work cooperatively to chose roles, represent different perspectives, and perform in front of classmates. For the role-play to go well, participants must collaborate or uphold the social contract of completing the role-play task. The teacher is implementing which of the following development theories?

   A. Cognitive learning theory (Piaget)

   B. Zone of Proximal Development (Vygotsky)

   C. Moral development (Kohlberg)

   D. Bloom's Taxonomy (Bloom)

Correct answer: C

While there is overlap with other theories, the primary purpose of the role-play task is for students to practice team-work. Morally, some students are still instinctively thinking about laws, rules, and social approval (stages 3 and 4). The teacher is trying to support their understanding of social contracts and working together for the common good (stage 5).

3. Learning theories

Teachers need to be able to apply learning theory into their practice and classroom. The following terms and concepts come from the most common theories currently implemented in education. You will see these theories presented in different ways on the PLT. You might be prompted to define a theory, compare theories, or evaluate theories in a scenario.

Metacognition

Metacognition is often referred to as, "thinking about your own thinking" (Flavell, 1979). Some examples of metacognition in the classroom include students planning how to complete an assignment, tracking their own learning process, or self-reflecting on how they learned a new skill. Students are taught metacognitive strategies such as questioning, visualizing, inferring, and making connections. Supporting students to identify and use these processes with fidelity supports comprehension and critical thinking. It also promotes students to take ownership of their academics.

Schema (Piaget)

Using schema (or prior knowledge) to increase comprehension of new concepts is a central theme of Jean Piaget's stages of cognitive development, as previously discussed. For students to comprehend complex concepts and text, they must have prior knowledge and understanding. If they do not, the learning is compromised. Therefore, teachers must provide opportunities to activate and build prior knowledge.

Examples of activating prior knowledge are:

- Students are discussing what they already know about rocks before reading a passage on different types of rocks.

- Students watch a short video about Native American culture before reading Native American poetry.

- Before starting a lesson on cells, students fill out a KWL[1] chart. The *K* in the KWL chart helps to activate background knowledge.

The following table is an example of a KWL chart.

	K	W	L
Question	What do I already know?	What do I want to learn?	What did I learn?
Example	Cells are small.	What do cells do?	Parts of the cell and how they interact to support life.

Quick Tip

Constructivism asserts that old knowledge is a building block for new knowledge. Many of the correct answers on the PLT reflect constructivism philosophy. Pay attention to the following:

- Teachers need to help students connect new material with their prior experiences.

- Piaget theorized that learners use schema (cognitive framework) to make sense of new experiences.

---

1 A KWL table, or KWL chart, is a graphic organizer designed to help build prior knowledge and guide learning. The letters KWL are an acronym for what students in the course of a lesson already know (K-prior knowledge), what they want to know (W), and what they ultimately learn (L).

Transfer

Transfer refers to the process of applying learned knowledge to a new context. For example, students learn to add two-digit numbers in a whole-group lesson. Then, the teacher asks them to complete problems independently. In this scenario, the teacher is having them transfer or apply their new knowledge.

Teachers can support transfer of knowledge by creating learning experiences where the learning environment for new tasks relates to the new knowledge. For example, a class of students is setting up a garden and needs to build a fence to keep animals out. They will need to transfer math concepts to measure the area, layout the design, and build the fence.

Self-efficacy

Self-efficacy is a student's belief in herself to accomplish a goal. Students with higher self-efficacy are confident, goal-oriented, and productive.

Self-regulation

Self-regulation is the ability to monitor your own thoughts, emotions, and actions. Developmentally, school-aged children have not mastered self-regulation but are refining this skill on varying growth curves. Many students need scaffolded support to build self-regulation competencies in various learning settings.

Zone of proximal development (Vygotsky)

On a learning curve, the ZPD is just beyond where students work independently. In the ZPD, a student can complete tasks and process new information with the support of a more knowledgeable learner. Helping someone move through the ZPD depends on 3 core aspects:

1. The presence of someone with knowledge and skills beyond that of the learner (i.e. teacher, tutor or peer).

2. Social interactions with a skillful person that allow the learner to observe and practice their skills.

3. Scaffolding, or supportive activities provided by the educator, or more competent peer, to support the student as he or she is led through the ZPD.

Classical and Operant Conditioning

Classical Conditioning

Passive: A student learns to associate a desired behavior with a specific signal or environmental cue.

Example: Using a special clap to signal clean-up time or transition to a new class.

Creating a condition to influence and direct behavior

Operant Conditioning

Active: A student volunteers a behavior based on an understanding of incentives.

Examples: A teacher provides a student with a reward (positive reinforcement) for keeping his work area clean.

Quick Tip

The theory of constructivism is present throughout the PLT. Constructivism is a holistic philosophy that supports the idea that learning and problem solving should reflect real-life contexts where the environment is very rich in information and there are no right answers (embedded knowledge). Learning should include authentic tasks. Keep this in mind when answering questions, especially scenario questions.

Example question

An 8th grade teacher is beginning a new geometry unit on triangles. She wants to teach them how triangle math is used in architecture and construction. According to ZPD theory, what is the best activity to prepare students for this new learning?

A. Give students a multiple-choice pretest with different units of measurement in the answers. Then review the correct answers as a class.

B. Ask one student to explain to the class why triangles are used to build sturdy structures.

C. Give students a hand out explaining triangles and structures to read independently. Praise them as they retell what they have read to the class.

D. Ask students to observe photos of structures and identify what makes them sturdy. Have them experiment by creating strong bridges with different types of shapes.

Correct answer: D

Teachers should emphasize connecting what students already know to new concepts. Accessing prior knowledge allows students to build on that knowledge. In this example, students are accessing prior knowledge through observations and experimentation. These activities will help them understand the purpose and application of the computation and concepts in triangle math.

4. Stages of human development

Domains of Human Development

Students progress through different stages of cognitive, physical, social, and moral domains. Each stage has a range of typical variances because not all children progress at the same pace. In addition, it is possible for children to demonstrate characteristics across more than one stage of development at the same time. It is important to understand each stage so you can identify when a student is far out of the expected age range, either above or below her peers. This might be an indicator of a larger developmental issue.

Cognitive development

- Thinking, reasoning, problem-solving, understanding.

- Recall Piaget's stages of cognitive development.

Social development

- Interpersonal, initiating play, interactions with peers.

- Recall Erikson's stages of social development.

Moral development

- Process of deciding what is right and wrong; the development of environmental factors influencing how one makes ethical decisions or observes right and wrong.

- Recall Kohlberg's stages of development.

- Kohlberg emphasized that while an individual will develop through the stages in order, the pace of development will vary between people.

Physical development

Theories of physical development focus on three main stages: early childhood, middle childhood, and adolescence. You need to understand the differences in these stages to address possible barriers in the classroom. For example, a student with poor fine motor skills may have difficulty writing. A student with delayed gross motor skills may need additional support to complete basic tasks like keeping their work area clean and moving around the classroom.

Early childhood (1-6 years)

- Refining skills like jumping, hopping, skipping, walking backwards, bike riding.

- Improving hand-eye coordination while drawing shapes and cutting.

Middle childhood (6-12 years)

- Slow, steady growth: 3-4 inches per year

- Use physical activities to develop gross and fine motor skills

Adolescent (12-18 years)

- Growth spurt: girls: 11-14 years, boys: 13-17 years

- Puberty: girls: 11-14 years, boys: 12-15 years

(Rycus J., 1998)

Understanding atypical variances

Match each of the following examples of atypical variances to the correct domain of human development.

1. A 12 year old (7th grade) student hesitates to begin any activity without teacher approval. This includes activities that the teacher allows students to do independently like organizing materials for the next class, leaving the class to go to the bathroom, or choosing a book to read independently. When asked about her hesitancy, she says she doesn't want to get in trouble for disobeying.

2. A 14 year old (9th grade) student is shorter and smaller than all his classmates and struggles to fit in during physical education games.

3. A 17 year old (12th grade) student asks, "Is this work okay?" He is looking for confirmation of his effort and success completing a task.

4. A 15 year old (10th grade) student uses trial and error to solve a math problem rather than using deductive reasoning to solve the problem.

   A. Moral development

   B. Cognitive development

   C. Physical development

   D. Social development

Correct answers:

1. **A. Moral development** – In this example, the 12 year old is still exhibiting behaviors in stage 1 of preconventional morality. She is mainly concerned with obeying the rule of authority. Most children at this age have moved to stages 3 and 4 and are concerned with school rules and socially acceptable behaviors.

2. **C. Physical development** – Most boys are going through puberty at this age and have had at least one growth spurt. Some students start puberty later and may be physically smaller than their peers.

3. **D. Social development** – This student is looking for outside approval rather than being confident in her own competency. Typically, a 17 year old student has moved out of the industry versus inferiority stage and into the learning identity versus identity diffusion stage.

4. **B. Cognitive development** – According to Piaget, students at this age are typically in the formal operational stage and able to apply abstract reasoning like deductive thinking to solve problems. Trial and error problem-solving is a behavior of the concrete operational stage.

5. How learning theory and human development impact instruction

As a teacher, you will consider aspects of learning theory along with developmental theory when designing, implementing, and differentiating instruction. For the PLT, be prepared to consider scenarios where you need to differentiate learning theory and developmental theory. At times, you will need to synthesize your understanding of both to identify the correct answers.

Relationship between learning theory and human development

Human development and learning theory can guide both learning expectations and the design of learning experiences. For example, developmentally, children are typically able to sit and actively listen to an adult talk to them for about as many minutes as their age. Learning theories emphasize the importance of introducing new material. Synthesizing these perspectives means a mini-lesson for 1st graders should be no more than 6-7 minutes long while a mini-lesson for 12th graders can be 17-18 minutes.

Another example is how we consider human development when asking children to engage in a discussion. Younger students are more ego-centric and need modeling and practice to learn to listen and respond to the ideas of others. Older students engage in the opinions and perspectives of their peers as well as fictional characters and historical role models.

How learning theory is impacted by human development

Human development theory provides insight into which instructional strategies will be most successful to reach a specific learning goal.

Example question

An 8th grade science teacher wants students to understand the purpose of microorganisms. Considering the developmental stages of 13 and 14 year old students, which is the best activity?

A. Assign an article for students to read in a small group and then summarize for the class.

B. Give a 60-minute presentation on the features of microorganisms.

C. Using a reference handout, have students analyze their lunch to identify good and bad mircoorganisms in and around their food.

D. Show students a photo of a rotting log and ask them to discuss in their small groups what they see.

Correct answer: C

While each of these activities may be engaging for a different age group of students, 13 and 14 year old students are not developmentally ready to listen to a 60-minute presentation. Answer choice C is correct because learning is visual. Students will use appropriate social, moral, and cognitive development skills to collaboratively analyze and discuss the role of microorganisms in food. Answer choices A and D are less engaging for students at this age than analyzing lunch food.

Learning theory to solve educational problems

Like developmental theory, learning theory provides insight into educational problems. For example, students unable to grasp a new concept may need a new instructional approach. A teacher can use social learning theory to consider how the learning behaviors are being modeled. The teacher may also want to use Bloom's Taxonomy to consider what type of cognitive thinking is required for the task to support the students processing.

Example question

A teacher is working on encouraging and cultivating critical thinking during her science block. The students are learning about cells. What would be the most effective way to increase creative thinking?

A. Fill out a worksheet by labeling parts of a cell.

B. Build a model of a cell and label it.

C. Write a comic strip about a cell and all the adventures it encounters.

D. Draw a picture of a cell and label its parts.

Correct answer: C

The highest level of engagement is critical thinking, which requires students to apply knowledge in a creative way. Writing a comic strip describing the adventures of a cell is applying the knowledge of cells in a creative way. Filling out a worksheet is never a good answer on the PLT. Answer choices B and D are essentially the same skill, labeling, which is a low cognitive skill.

Caution

When you see two answer choices that are the same idea worded differently, they are likely to be the wrong answer. Look for answers with key words that align with the question.

Human development to solve educational problems.

At times, learning is interrupted by typical and atypical variances in human development. For example, a 7-year old student who is cognitively unable to consistently apply logical reasoning may have trouble processing a typical two-step math problem in a 2nd grade classroom. Human develop theory is a tool to address and overcome these challenges.

B. Students as Diverse Learners

1. Variables that impact student learning

    - Gender

    - Culture

    - Socioeconomic status

    - Prior knowledge and experience

    - Motivation

    - Self-confidence, self-esteem

    - Cognitive development

    - Maturity

    - Language

2. Student exceptionalities

    - Cognitive

    - Auditory

    - Visual

    - Motor/physical

    - Speech/language

    - Behavioral

3. Major legislation governing students with exceptionalities

    - Americans with Disabilities Act (ADA)

    - Individuals with Disabilities Education Act (IDEA)

    - Section 504, Rehabilitation Act (504)

4. Traits, behaviors, and needs of intellectually gifted students

5. English language acquisition and English language learners (ELLs)

6. Accommodations for students with exceptionalities

1. Variables that impact student learning

On the PLT, you will identify different variables and how they impact student learning and performance. It is critical to think about these variables as generalizations. Every student is unique and should not be stereotyped based on preconceived notions of what informs their learning experience. While the variables discussed below may affect their learning experiences, they should have no impact on students' capabilities to learn or perform.

Gender

Gender refers to social, cultural, and relationship norms that characterize girls, boys, and transgendered people (World Health Organization, 2020). Research comparing the development and performance of each gender identifies contrasting trends in physical, cognitive, and social-emotional development of girls and boys. While these generalizations can be helpful for understanding behaviors, children who act outside these trends are not abnormal or cause for concern. In fact, differences within gender groups are more pronounced than between boys and girls. Students who contradict gender norms may need extra encouragement or reinforcement to affirm their confidence and performance in these areas.

Development Area	Trends
Physical	• Boys tend to be more physically active than girls which can cause them to be restless at times. • Girls tend to develop fine motor skills earlier than boys. • Boys tend to be more active and need more opportunities to move than girls.
Social	• Boys tend to play in large groups that may take up more physical space with physical games and sports activities. • Girls tend to spend time with smaller groups where they are more likely to disclose and discuss personal information. • The more visible games and conflicts of boys may overshadow or distract attention from the quieter interpersonal play and conflict of girls. • Boys are more likely to bully than girls.
Cognitive/ academic	• Girls tend to be more motivated to conform to rules and complete assignments. • Boys tend to perform better on visual-spatial tasks. • Girls tend to have stronger verbal skills and larger vocabularies.

(Seifert, 2009)

Culture

Culture is a shared language, set of values, beliefs, customs, traditions, and goals of a group of people defined by ethnicity, religion, and nationality. Culture is not static and continues to evolve. For example, Native American cultures differ by region, tribe, urban, and rural communities.

Understanding cultural differences is important to understanding your students and supporting their success. Culture differences will impact how a child interacts in a learning environment with their peers and teachers. Effective educators consider the specific cultural differences in their school community. The following are some examples of how culture can affect how children learn.

- **Use of dialect**. Students may use a different dialect of English. They may pronounce words differently or have different names for objects in the classrooms or actions they observe.

- **Answering questions.** In many cultures, asking questions is a sign of engagement in learning. However, in other cultures, asking questions is considered rude or implies the student does not trust the teacher or person offering the information.

- **Eye contact.** In some cultures, it is rude to make eye contact with anyone in an authority position while in others, it is rude not to. Consider that a child who is looking away when given a direction or asked a question may be showing respect to you as someone they admire and look up to.

Socioeconomic status

Diversity is not always about the language students speak or the customs in which they participate. Diversity also applies to students' socioeconomic circumstances. Some students will come to school without having breakfast. Some students will come to school without basic necessities. It is the role of the teacher to provide effective instruction for these students. Taking the time to consider all aspects of diversity in the classroom, including socioeconomic status, is essential in being an effective teacher.

Here are some circumstances to consider:

- Assigning homework that requires computer and Internet access is not being considerate of students' socioeconomic circumstances because some students do not have access to these tools at home.

- Communicating with parents via email may not be most effective because not all parents have access to the Internet at home.

- Statistically, students who come from families with higher levels of education, tend to perform better in school. Therefore, it is critical to support all students to become lifelong learners, so they can continue the cycle of student achievement.

Test Tip

When answering questions about cultural responsiveness in the classroom, be sure to select answer choices that reflect an ongoing approach to celebrating diversity. Celebrating Black History Month or Hispanic Heritage Month is beneficial to building a culturally responsive classroom. However, these happen one time per year. It's best to focus on everyday culturally responsive approaches, like continuously analyzing literature written by marginalized people or people from other cultures.

Prior knowledge and experience

Children come to school with a range of prior knowledge and experience. Culture, gender, and socioeconomic status are just some of the variables that impact prior knowledge and experience. Even children from the same family can have widely different perspectives and experiences before and during their elementary school years.

Example question

A high school teacher is beginning a unit on climate change. One student enthusiastically shares that he learned about disruptions to ecosystems and rising sea levels in middle school. How should she proceed with her unit?

- A. Skip the oceans and ecosystems because students will be bored.

- B. Find photos of the impacts of climate change and ask students to describe what they see and what they wonder. Use their background knowledge to build enthusiasm for the unit.

- C. Give students a pretest including diagrams of the impacts of climate change they will learn about to see what they already know.

- D. Ask the student to prepare and present what he knows about climate change to the class.

Correct answer: B

Answer choice B is the best answer because accessing prior knowledge will lay the ground work for learning new information and discovering new processes, natural and human causes, and solutions to climate change. Answer choice A can be eliminated because of the general, negative tone. Answer choices C and D are not good choices because a pretest could be more confusing than clarifying, and a student presentation is not appropriate.

Motivation

Motivation is the reason or purpose for an action. In a learning context, students demonstrate and develop intrinsic motivation, or internal motivation, when the learning feels purposeful or satisfactory. Individual motivation for various tasks will differ between students. Some motivation is related to a child's developmental level while other motivation is determined by prior learning or external factors. Extrinsic motivation is when a student wants to accomplish a task for the promise of a reward. While children's actions are motivated by different reasons, they may not always understand why or where the motivation comes from.

Low motivation

- Young students who struggle to read may not be motivated because they prefer someone to read to them.

- A student may struggle to complete a grammar worksheet because the content does not feel immediately relevant to their life.

High motivation

- A student works with sustained focus on her essay because she wants to win the annual school essay contest.

- Students cannot wait to go to science class because the clouds of purple smoke coming from the science classroom are enticing.

Self-confidence and self-esteem

Self-esteem is how students think of themselves and self-confidence is how students feel about a specific situation or task. Learning is primarily taking risks to try new skills, gain knowledge, and communicate in new ways. Students who lack confidence in themselves or their ability to succeed at specific activities will struggle to take the risks needed to learn.

Examples of self-confidences and self-esteem

High self-confidence: A student waves her hand wildly to answer the math problem because she is sure her answer is correct.	**High self-esteem**: A student does poorly on a math quiz and asks the teacher for feedback to better understand her mistakes. While math is challenging for her, she knows with hard work she can get better.
Low self-confidence: An ELL student does not want to read in English because he is afraid he will make a mistake speaking out loud in his second language.	**Low self-esteem**: A student acts out for attention on the playground because she is unsure others will befriend her.

Cognitive development

As discussed in the previous section, cognitive development happens on a continuum. However, not everyone develops social-emotional and learning processes at the same rate. For example, one student can read when she is 4 while two others begin reading at age 7 or 8. All three students grow up to be equally good at reading.

Maturity

Maturity generally describes a students' level of development across physical, social, moral, and cognitive domains. Social maturity describes how well students interact with peers, other children, and grown-ups in their lives. Cognitive maturity describes how they think. The brain continues to mature until people are in their twenties. Maturity is influenced by genetics and environment, so children mature at different rates. Maturity impacts how children perceive, comprehend, and communicate information and how efficiently a student can complete a learning task. The effect of maturity on capabilities may vary depending on the content and nature of the task. For example:

- A mature student will be engaged in a learning task and self-motivated to learn

- A student with social maturity may make friends or be comfortable not communicating with friends during learning times.

- Students in a 10th grade class may excel or struggle depending on their cognitive maturity, and ability to process abstract ideas.

- A student with physical maturity may have better hand to eye coordination or excel at sports.

- A student who is highly concerned with activist movements like environmentalism or is able to identify multiple perspectives on one issue.

Language

Language is what students use to communicate. Students come to school with a variety of language skills. Formal or academic English learned at school and used in professional settings is different from what most children experience in informal settings at home or in their community.

In addition, some children come to school speaking a different language from English with their family and in their communities. Some students have accelerated cognitive development because they are fluent in multiple languages.

Regardless of the causes, students with limited academic English may communicate well with their peers and in casual conversations but struggle to understand directions, participate in class discussions, read literature or informative text, or complete writing assignments well. They may need support to understand words, phrases, and themes primarily presented in academic settings.

Think about it!

One way teachers can support diversity in the classroom is by communicating effectively with parents. Because many families speak languages other than English, teachers must remember to send important information home in the native language. Also, not every student has access to the Internet or email. Therefore, providing a hard copy written in students' native languages is the most effective way to communicate upcoming events, classroom expectations, and other important information with families.

Example question

A middle school teacher sees two students playing outside of the bathroom when they need to be back in their classroom. She approaches the boys to redirect their behavior and remind them of the school expectations. One of the students refuses to make eye contact with her. What is the most likely reason the student is not doing what the teacher is asking?

A. The student is being disrespectful.

B. The student is looking down in deference to the teacher.

C. The student doesn't understand why the teacher is upset.

D. The student is not paying attention.

Test Tip

On the test, you will likely be given a scenario where you need to analyze one or more of the variables described in this section. Steer away from any answers that are critical of the student (A and D in the example). These questions are designed to test whether you can identify how variables like culture can impact student behavior and learning experience.

Answer: B

In many cultures, it is disrespectful for students to look an authority figure in the eye, especially when they have made a mistake. It is most likely that this student it trying to demonstrate remorse and respect for the teacher.

2. Student exceptionalities

The term exceptionalities in K–12 schooling refers to both disabilities and giftedness. The US Department of Education (2019) estimates that 13-14% of students have exceptionalities or an average of 2-3 in every classroom of 25 students. While teachers may play a role in identifying signs of exceptionalities, diagnosing these impairments and disabilities is the responsibility of medical professionals and the school's special education team. Every student with exceptionalities has unique characteristics, traits, and needs. Many students present more than one exceptionality. On the PLT, you will be asked to differentiate between exceptionalities as well as understand how they impact student learning.

Cognitive

Cognitive exceptionality are difficulties and delays with thinking processes including memory, perception, speech, and language. Here are some examples

- **Learning disabilities (LD).** An impairment that interferes with completing academic tasks. An LD may not interfere with all areas of learning or types learning activities. LDs are the most common form of exceptionality in a mainstream classroom.

  - **Attention deficit hyperactivity disorder (ADHD).** Difficulty sustaining attention and controlling impulses. Students with ADHD move, talk excessively, change from one activity to another, fidget, get distracted, talk out of turn, or become impatient easily. They may misplace, lose, or forget classroom supplies and materials. Some students with ADHD are likely to repeatedly and chronically exhibit some of these behaviors, even after interventions and redirection from the teacher.

  - **Dyslexia.** Reading disabilities that interfere with a student's ability to read with fluency and accuracy, decode words, and spell correctly.

  - **Dysgraphia.** Writing disabilities that interfere with processes controlling memory, hand movement, grammar, and vocabulary. There is usually a big difference between what a student can express orally and what they can share in writing.

  - **Dyscalculia.** Math disabilities that interfere with processing abstract concepts. Therefore, making computation, recognizing and using symbols and numbers, remembering facts, and sequencing are challenging. Students with dyscalculia tend to have more trouble remembering numbers and their properties than letters. These student have challenges recognizing patterns, keeping events in order, or playing strategy games.

- **Intellectual disability.** Students with intellectual disabilities are challenged to learn at the pace of their peers. They may struggle with reasoning, problem solving, communication, as well as social and practical skills. Like many disabilities, there is a large range of how intellectual disabilities present themselves and impact a person's everyday life.

Impact on student learning

- Trouble focusing on a learning task or whole group lesson.

- Over stimulated by peers and other parts of the classroom environment.

- Completes work in creative ways, not conforming to the parameters of the assignment.

- Frequently forgets expectations for classroom behaviors and assignments.

Speech and language

Students with a speech or language exceptionality might have a stutter, speech delays, trouble pronouncing sounds, or difficulty understanding a speaker. Students with a language disorder cannot use words to express themselves or struggle to understand speech.

- **Autism spectrum disorder.** This is a complicated disorder that can create cognitive, speech, language, sensory, and behavioral exceptionalities. Behaviors vary in students with ASD. Some have social interaction and communication challenges while others become extremely focused on specific repetitive behaviors. Some forms of ASD are called Asperger's syndrome. It is important to collaborate with parents, special education teachers, and other learning specialists who can assist students with ASD, so you can understand and implement appropriate accommodations.

Impact on student learning

- Students may not be able to communicate their needs or their learning.

- Oral directions may be confusing or forgotten, especially when there are multiple steps in a task.

Behavioral

Students with behavioral exceptionalities might not engage in appropriate relationships with their peers. They might have a general mood of unhappiness or depression. They might develop physical symptoms of fear about school or social situations. They might have an inability to learn about things that cannot be explained by intellectual, sensory, or health factors. Some examples of behavioral exceptionalities are anxiety, mood disorders, and oppositional defiance disorder.

Impact on student learning

- Difficulty expressing feelings.

- Accommodations needed for social periods during school like recess, lunch, and cooperative work.

- A variety of physical symptoms like anxiety, irritability, or excessive worrying.

- Defiant behavior demonstrated by social withdrawal or aggression.

Sensory

Sensory exceptionality happens when students are challenged by processing one or more of their senses. Along with the five senses, sight, taste, sound, touch, and smell, students can also be challenged by movement or an internal sense. Students with sensory exceptionalities can be sensory seeking or sensory sensitive.

Impact on student learning

- Difficulty sitting still.

- Has trouble holding a pencil well enough to form legible letters.

- Asks to switch activities often.

- Has meltdowns that disrupt class transitions or learning.

- May be uncomfortable with clothing, carpet or other textures and need accommodations.

Motor and physical

Motor and physical exceptionalities can include limited mobility of body parts, missing limbs, congenital diseases that impact physical movement, challenges with flexibility, brain injuries, paralysis, and spinal cord injuries. Like other disabilities, learning the specifics of some categories will help to contextualize questions and scenarios on the PLT.

- **Gross-motor** disabilities are when coordinating arms, legs, or other part of their body is difficult for students.

- **Fine-motor** disability is when students struggle with writing, even after continuous practice and accommodations are made.

- **Cerebral palsy, spina bifida, and muscular dystrophy** are more severe physical disabilities. They usually impact movement, but depending on their stage, students need different levels of accommodation for learning.

Impact on student learning

- Students may need adaptive technology that requires modification to the learning environment.

- Students may need accommodations for communicating with the teacher and their peers.

- Students may have special equipment or need extra time and accommodations to access resources in the classroom and travel around the school.

Visual

Vision impairments include limited field of vision, difficulty focusing, light sensitivity, color blindness, and legal blindness. While potentially helpful, corrective lenses do not solve these visual challenges.

Impact on student learning

- May not be able to read and visually understand their learning environment without assistive technology.

- May need special seating to participate in learning experiences.

- May need hands-on and audio experiences because visual tools and signals are challenging to see.

(Seifert, 2009)

Auditory

Auditory exceptionalities can be mild to severe. Severe auditory exceptionalities are typically identified and treated early, so children can participate in all learning. Mild to moderate hearing loss is often overlooked but impacts a student's everyday experience. Behaviors of undiagnosed hearing loss include repeated wrong answers to questions posed to the class, partial hearing of presentations and discussion, and trouble locating the source of the speaker. Because these signs can be so nuanced or come from other root issues, routine hearing checks are critical to identifying students who need support.

Impact on student learning

- Delayed literacy skills: phonological awareness, writing, oral comprehension, and speaking.

- Difficulty understanding verbal directions.

- May be prone to social isolation because communicating feels awkward.

- Teacher may need to wear a special microphone to assist with hearing.

(Seifert, 2009)

Example question

A student gets agitated and moves around the room in a clumsy way each time she hears a pencil being sharpened. The teacher notices that the child seems sensitive to other loud or irregular sounds as well. At other times, the student seems lost or unsure about who is speaking during a class discussion. What type of exceptionality is most likely challenging this student?

A. Cognitive

B. Visual

C. Auditory

D. Behavioral

Correct answer: C

In the first clue, the student is showing sensitivity to some sounds. This can be associated with auditory, cognitive, and behavioral exceptionalities. The key to getting this question correct is the second clue. Being unable to find the source of a sound is a clear sign of mild to moderate hearing loss.

3. Major legislation governing students with exceptionalities

Children with disabilities who need specially designed instruction and related services are called exceptional students. The special help they are given at school is special education services, although each state may have its own designation and name. The purpose of special education is to help each child with an exceptionality progress in school and prepare for life after school. Special education services include specially designed instruction to meet the unique needs of the child. Special education services may also include technology devices, therapy, special transportation, or other supports. There is no charge for special education services. A team of school personnel along with the parents and student make decisions about the child's needs and services. The following are the main laws relating to students with exceptionalities in education today. On the PLT, you will need to demonstrate your understanding of how these laws impact classroom practices.

Individuals with Disabilities Education Act 2004.

The Individuals with Disabilities Act (IDEA) is the main law that makes available a free appropriate public education to children with cognitive, social, and physical disabilities. It ensures special education and related services to those children. IDEA was first passed as law in 1975 but has been updated several times to be more inclusive. There are six main principles of IDEA that govern how states and public agencies provide early intervention, special education, and related services to more than 6.5 million eligible infants, toddlers, children, and youth with disabilities (U.S. Department of Education, 2015):

1. Free appropriate public education (FAPE).

2. Appropriate evaluation, assuring all children are appropriately assessed.

3. Least restrictive environments, educating students with disabilities with their non-disabled peers whenever possible.

4. Parent and student participation in decision making.

5. Individual education plan (IEP) development by interdisciplinary teams of specialists to ensure appropriate educational development.

6. Procedural safeguards to protect rights, ensure information is provided, and give way for dispute resolution.

The IDEA applies to students belonging to at least one of the 13 qualifying categories:

1. Autism
2. Deaf blindness
3. Deafness
4. Emotional disturbance
5. Hearing impairment
6. Intellectual disability
7. Multiple disability

8. Orthopedically impairment
9. Other health impaired
10. Specific learning disability
11. Speech or language impairment
12. Traumatic brain injury
13. Visually impaired including blindness

Individualized Education Program

Students with special needs are evaluated and provided an Individualized Education Program (IEP). An IEP is a written agreement outlining services the school will provide to help the student meet his or her educational needs. By law, the IEP is reviewed and revised every 12 months.

Accommodations

A student's IEP includes a list of accommodations to assist in making grade-level standards accessible to students with exceptionalities. Students are taught skills and knowledge specified in the standards in kindergarten through 12th grade. Students with significant cognitive disabilities may have modified learning goals written into their IEP.

IEP accommodations can include:

- Assistive technology
- Environmental adaptations
- Extra time for tests
- Quiet area to perform tasks

- Specialized instructional strategies
- Peer support
- Curricular adaptations or modifications
- Collaborative teaching

Goals

An IEP also includes goals that the student and the IEP team create together. Throughout the year, teachers and the IEP team work with the student to help him or her achieve long-term and short-term goals.

Least restrictive environment

According to the U.S. Department of Education, students must be placed in the least restrictive environment possible. Students with disabilities will only be removed from a regular classroom if the nature or severity of their disability interferes to such a degree that education, even with additional supports and services, cannot be satisfactorily achieved in a regular class.

Keeping children with special needs in general classrooms helps to maintain equality. A student with a disability or exceptionality should have the same opportunity to thrive in a regular classroom as any other student. It is only when the disability cannot be adequately accommodated for in the general classroom that the student should be placed in a separate classroom. Providing students education in the least restrictive environment is essential. Though the regular classroom is the first placement option for special education services to be considered, federal regulations and state laws also recognize that additional placement options may be necessary (U.S Department of Education 2015).

In the classroom:

- A list of modifications and accommodations that need to be made in the classroom in accordance to the student's IEP.

- Routine services from a special education teacher in the student's main classroom (push-in) or in another classroom (pull-out).

- The amount of intervention a student receives will depend on the details of their IEP and should not be altered unless directed by the IEP team.

Quick Tip

In the classroom, teachers can use accommodations for all students based on students' needs. However, a student taking a state standardized test can only receive accommodations, such as extra time and assistive technologies, if those accommodations are listed in the student's IEP. If a student does not have an IEP, the student cannot receive accommodations on state tests.

Section 504 of the Rehabilitation Act of 1973.

Section 504 was originally developed to protect students with a documented disability from discrimination by federally-funded programs and facilities. Like the IDEA, Section 504 regulations require a school district to provide a "free appropriate public education" (FAPE) to each qualified student with a disability who is in the school district's jurisdiction, regardless of the nature or severity of the disability. IEP plans under IDEA cover students who qualify for Special Education. Section 504 covers students who do not meet the criteria for special education but who still require some accommodations. Both ensure that students with disabilities have access to a free and appropriate public education.

In the classroom:

- Teachers need to be given access to the 504 plan of any student in their classroom.

- While parents are made aware of the classification as well as accommodations, parent consent is not required for a 504 plan to be written.

- By law, teachers are required to make daily accommodations, in accordance to the 504 plan, to the their learning environment and instruction.

- Documentation of measurable growth, unique to each student, is required as part of a 504 plan. Teachers collect data and record academic progress to contribute to this documentation.

Americans with Disabilities Act of 1990.

The Americans with Disabilities Act (ADA) is a civil rights law that prohibits discrimination based on disability that goes beyond the scope of Section 504. It provides similar protections against discrimination to Americans with disabilities as the Civil Rights Act of 1964 (U.S. Department of Education, 2019). In addition to the protections of Section 504, it is inclusive of all students with disabilities.

In the classroom: The ADA requires that a student receives the accommodations they need to engage in a school learning environment as their peers do. ADA impacts before and after school activities, transportation to and from school, the physical learning environment, instructional tools and necessary services. Here are some examples of how this looks in a school setting:

- Wheel chair ramps and an elevator making it possible for students to enter any classroom in the building.

- Technology support systems for students to read and communicate with teachers.

- Railings, special types of swings, and other modifications made to the playground so all children can play.

Due to a rising school population, the music class has been moved to a portable room outside the main school building. The only way to enter the portable is by walking up two stairs to a single doorway. Immediately, the principal recognizes that the school needs to build a ramp to the enter the classroom. Which law requires that the classroom be accessible to all current and future students?

A. ADA

B. Section 504

C. IDEA Act

D. Free and appropriate public education (FAPE)

Correct answer: A

ADA requires that students not only receive services and access to education, but that they are able to learn in the same environments as their peers. This is an expansion on the protections of Section 504. FAPE and IDEA are not as explicit as ADA about the physical environment where students learn. ADA usually has to do with the physical environment.

4. Traits, behaviors, and needs of intellectually gifted students

Like students with other exceptionalities, gifted students may need specialized instruction to reach their learning and performance capacity. Gifted students perform or are capable of performing at higher levels than their peers. Gifted students come from all social, economic, and cultural backgrounds. Special capabilities may include intellectual, creative, academic, leadership, and performance abilities. Like students with other exceptionalities, they are eligible for special services. More than one assessment is used to identify gifted students to take into consideration various strengths and avoid the bias of simple IQ tests. Below are lists of characteristics and consideration for gifted students. Every gifted student has a unique set of traits and will demonstrate their exceptionality in a different way.

Common traits:

- High achieving: early readers, accelerated acquisition of knowledge, and application of learning strategies.
- Advanced language and social skills.
- Divergent thinkers who communicate ideas well, orally and in writing.
- High self-efficacy and highly motivated to learn.

Common needs:

- Access to learning opportunities to realize their potential.
- Strong mentors and role-models to promote confidence and self-esteem in their talents; they may feel like an outlier or self-conscious of their differences from others.
- Attention to talents as well as areas of challenge; gifted students are not always gifted in all academic areas.
- Attention to IEP accommodations and other exceptionalities; It is common for gifted students to also have developmental delays and processing disorders that require accommodations and interventions.
- May need support and guidance to develop social-emotional skills.

(National Association for Gifted Children, 2019)

Example question

A gifted student performs well on tests and always has interesting contributions to class discussion but has trouble completing independent assignments. She is easily distracted and likes to talk with her classmates during work time. The teacher has tried to redirect the student and give verbal warnings, but her behaviors persist. What is the next step the teacher should take to improve the situation?

    A. Reprimand the student and have her complete assignments at recess.

    B. Let the student create her own assignments since she is gifted, and the work may be too simple for her.

    C. Send the student to the principal's office.

    D. Review the student's IEP to ensure all accommodations are being made and to address any additional exceptionalities.

Correct answer: D

Answer choices A and C are incorrect because they are both negative toward the student. Answer choice B is incorrect because gifted students are not responsible for teaching themselves. Answer choice D is the correct answer because gifted students frequently have other exceptionalities and need additional accommodations to perform at their potential.

Example question

A gifted student has successfully completed her algebra assignment with 45 minutes left in the period. Which additional learning task would be most appropriate to assign?

    A. Give her additional computation problems to solve with more numbers.

    B. Let her work ahead, and give her the next assignment planned for the group.

    C. Ask her to write her own algebra equations to address a real world problem.

    D. Ask her to help a classmate who is struggling.

Correct answer: C

Gifted students need challenges to realize their potential which typically involves using higher order thinking. Writing equations to solve real-world problems gives her the opportunity to apply principles of algebra. Answer choice A is wrong because she has already demonstrated that she has mastered the skills being practice in the lesson. Answer choice B is incorrect because she should not be expected to teach the new content to herself. While answer choice D may be ok sometimes, this should not be her role for the full 45 minutes. Furthermore, not all gifted students want to help others, and this should not be an expected routine for them.

5. English language acquisition and English language learners (ELLs)

Every teacher should be prepared to accommodate ELLs. As students learn a new language, they go through several stages. It is very important that teachers understand these stages when planning and delivering instruction because they impact the learning experience of the student. You will encounter questions on the PLT that reference these specific stages.

Stages of second language acquisition

1. **Pre-production.** The learner watches and listens in an attempt to absorb the language. Referred to as "the silent stage."

Students need to get to know classroom routines, names, places in the school, procedures, classmates, and the school community.

2. **Early production.** The learner starts to use some words but has not yet mastered forming sentences. Using pictures (just as in first language acquisition) is helpful in this stage.

   Provide simple sentence stems, photos, visuals, movement, and illustrated key vocabulary.

3. **Speech emergence.** The learner uses simple sentences that may or may not be correct. He or she begins to understand simple phrases in this stage.

   Begin pre-teaching important vocabulary for science, math, and social studies. Pre-teaching can be five minutes before the rest of the class arrives.

4. **Intermediate fluency.** The learner has a much better grasp on the language, begins to comprehend information taught in the second language, and speaks in longer sentences.

   Continue to support the student with pre-teaching the most important vocabulary. Help the student learn connective words like pronouns. Be prepared for words the student can read but does not know the meanings.

5. **Advanced fluency.** The learner can speak and understand the new language with little to no support. This is when students demonstrate cognitive language proficiency and can think and respond critically in the acquired language.

The following example is how this will be presented on the PLT.

Example question

What can a teacher do to help an ELL who has just entered the classroom and is in the pre-production stage of language acquisition?

   A. Require the student to start speaking English as soon as possible.

   B. Consistently change the student's peer group so she gets to know everyone.

   C. Provide the student with an English to Spanish dictionary for testing purposes.

   D. Honor the silent period and provide safe times to speak academic English.

Correct answer: D

Try to think what it would be like if you were in a new country and had to go to school where everyone speaks a language you do not know. You would want to sit quietly and absorb as much as you can before speaking. Teachers must honor this period and provide a safe place for students to try the new language. The other answer choices are negative in nature, so avoid those. Also, switching a new student's group can cause anxiety. Try to keep things simple and consistent for students who are in the pre-production stage of language acquisition.

Concepts related to English language acquisition

While students are going through these stages of language acquisition, they will engage in several processes where L1 (first language) and L2 (second language or language currently learning) merge and intermingle. Understanding these concepts will help you on the PLT.

Code switching. This is when an ELL switches back and forth between L1 and L2 when speaking or writing. For example, a student says, "*I am going a la playa tomorrow.*" The student uses elements of English and Spanish when speaking.

Acculturation. Acculturation is social, psychological, and cultural change that occurs when a student balances two cultures. It is the process of adjusting and adopting the new culture. (Cole, 2019).

Assimilation. This occurs when the original culture is wholly abandoned; the new culture adopted in its place.

Transfer. The replication of rules from L1 applied to L2. For example, grammar and even pronunciation will transfer from one language to another.

Caution

Avoid answer choices that promote an English only approach to teaching ELLs. Research supports the use of a bilingual approach. This means teachers allow students to use L1 and L2 when learning English. Teachers must also allow students to speak their native language when needed. It is helpful to think about all the learning happening in school besides language. For example, students who can discuss an idea in their first language typically can write about it more fluently in their second language. Just say no to English only practices on the PLT and in your classroom.

It is very important that you understand the stages of language acquisition and the processes students go through while becoming fluent in L2. The following example is how this may be presented on the PLT.

Example question

Jose has been in the United States for about a year. He is dressing more and more like his American friends. At home he is reluctant to speak Spanish with his parents because he is trying hard to be more like his peers. Jose is going through the process of:

    A. Acculturation

    B. Assimilation

    C. Code switching

    D. Transfer

Correct answer: B

Assimilation occurs when the student abandons the heritage culture and adopts the new culture. This can be very traumatic for families. Teachers must be aware and sensitive to this process many students go through. Earlier in this section, we discussed the impact of cultural differences on classroom practices.

6. Accommodations for students with exceptionalities

Accommodations do not change the expectations for learning. They are meant to create broader access to content and learning experiences so that children with exceptionalities can demonstrate knowledge like their peers. While all curriculum and instruction are built with student needs in mind, you will need to be aware of how to manage the learning experiences for children with exceptionalities. Some of these accommodations will come from IEPs while others will be up to you to implement. On the PLT, you will need to recognize that students with exceptionalities require particular accommodations and know how to adapt instruction, assessments, and communication to meet these needs.

Instructional accommodations

Presentation of content, student responses, timing, and setting are the main categories of instructional accommodation. Below are examples of each type of accommodation you will see on IEPs and implemented in classrooms.

Accommodation	Classroom Implementation
Presentation	• Pictures and word labels • Access to pre-written notes for presentations • Available in an audiobook or read-aloud • Photo, pictures and/or drawings • Visual reminders/cues to stay on task
Materials	• Large print text • Fidget toy • Adult assistance with reading • Worksheet cut into chunks • Work materials color coded or organized to support self-regulation and organization
Student responses	• Students should respond in ways they can convey the most information or share what they know • Whisper a response to a partner • Respond orally or in writing • Response with the support of technology • Alternative to assignment -- a visual, written, or oral presentation
Timing	• Frequent and short breaks from direct instruction, independent work, or cooperative learning • Changing the amount of time allocated for a learning task (project, assignment, or activity) • Changing the schedule for a task: specific time during the day, specific day of the week or quarter, etc.
Setting	• Seated with peers • Seated with a working buddy • Seated away from peers for fewer distractions • Working on the carpet • Working at a table high enough for a student to stand while writing • Working in a comfortable place - special chair, sofa, pillow, windowsill • Seated in a specialized flexible seating option – bean bag, create chair, roller, yoga ball

(National Center for Educational Outcomes, 2020)

Assessment accommodations

Standardized test accommodations will be written into students' IEPs. However, accommodations you make in your classroom for assessments will vary according to the type of assessment you are conducting. You need to be aware of the scope of accommodations and how they will differ depending on student needs. The table below provides examples of assessment accommodations students receive.

Assessment	Classroom Implementation
Presentation	• Repeated directions • Instructions and/or problems read aloud • Large print • Braille
Equipment and material	• A calculator • Book or paper to write answers on • Amplification equipment • Manipulatives • Specialized seating • Doodling paper
Student responses	• Mark answers in book rather than transfer to an answer sheet • Provide oral responses instead of written • Student points to the correct response
Timing/schedule	• Extended time • Frequent breaks • Early in the day or late in the day
Setting	• Use blinders on all sides of work area • Take the test in another room or at home • Low lighting, natural lighting, or halogen lighting

(National Center for Educational Outcomes, 2020)

Communication accommodations

Teachers must be aware of students' communication accommodations and ensure anyone who supports the students are also made aware of these accommodations. Communication accommodations range from simple to complex and can require assistive technology or support staff. Below are examples of communication accommodations.

- Assistive technology for hearing impaired and visually impaired students.

- Alternative visual cues, signals, and support material on the walls, at students' desks, or in their learning folder.

- Frequent communication and collaboration with parents, special education teacher, student therapists, and other stakeholders.

Quick Tip

You will need to know the difference between accommodations and modifications on this test.

Accommodations. Changes how the student learns the material.

Modifications. Changes what the student is taught or expected to learn.

For example, a student with a learning disability might need accommodations to take an assessment, but the skills being assessed remain the same for all students.

In contrast, a child with a cognitive delay might need a modified assessment to better understand the child's growth or learning needs.

Like all children, communicate with students who need accommodations with intention and integrity:

- Speak directly with confidence and use a normal tone of voice.

- Ask the student if he needs help and what kind of help he needs.

- Speak to students at eye level to demonstrate your interest and engagement with what they are saying.

Example question

A teacher is starting a science unit on the scientific method in his 9th grade classroom. He is concerned about how to teach the steps of the scientific method to his four early-emergent ELLs. He plans to teach the steps by modeling and then letting students work in groups to conduct a simple experiment building fast ramps for cars. What accommodations should he consider to support his ELL students' learning?

A. Translate all the steps to the student's first language using translating software.

B. Make flashcards with photos illustrating the key vocabulary for the ELL students to review before the class begins.

C. Ask students to draw the steps of the scientific method before joining a group to design a ramp.

D. Make the ELL students watch the other students do experiments but not participate until they can explain the steps and how to conduct an experiment in English.

Correct answer: B

Providing visual vocabulary cards to preview key words will be helpful for all students to remember the steps of the scientific method. This accommodation does not change the content or the learning expectations for the ELL students. Answer choices C and D are incorrect because having the students sit out of the experiment or do another activity will hinder their learning. The learning experience itself is the best learning tool the teacher has to improve both the ELL students' scientific knowledge and language acquisition. Answer choice A is wrong because taking time to read all the steps translated will detract from the oral language development and content learning gained from cooperative work with peers and participation in the learning experience.

Example question

A student with ADHD has specific accommodations for classroom instruction written into her IEP to help her stay focused. Which of the following is most likely not written in her IEP?

A. Frequent and short breaks from direct instruction, independent work or cooperative learning.

B. Keeping a fidget toy.

C. Simplified tasks that require lower order thinking.

D. Visual reminders/cues to stay on task.

Correct answer: C

ADHD is a learning disability that may keep a student from performing to their capacity. Accommodations are meant to give students access to content and learning experiences. Answer choices A, B, and D are all accommodations that change the learning experience but not the academic content. Modifications, like simplified learning activities, change the content and expectations for performance which is not necessary in this situation.

C. Student Motivation and Learning Environment

1. Foundational behavior theorists and their contributions to education

   - Thorndike
   - Watson
   - Maslow
   - Skinner
   - Erikson

2. The implications of foundational motivation theories in education

   - Self-determination
   - Attribution
   - Extrinsic/intrinsic motivation
   - Cognitive dissonance
   - Classic and operant conditioning
   - Positive and negative reinforcement

3. Strategies for classroom management

   - Classroom routines and procedures.
   - Accurate records maintenance.
   - Standards of conduct.
   - Classroom arrangement.
   - Promoting a positive learning environment.

4. Strategies for helping students develop self-motivation

   - Assigning valuable tasks
   - Specific and meaningful feedback
   - Students' inclusion in making instructional decisions
   - Reducing emphasis on grades

1. Foundational behavior theorists and their contributions to education

Motivational theory has roots in behavioral, cognitive, and constructivist traditions. Behavioral theorist study observable behaviors and what seems to motivate them. In general, they believe that behaviors are learned through one's interactions with the environment. Theorists argue that these factors can be manipulated and positive and negative consequences can be used to promote or deter individual behaviors. Applied to the classroom, this means that teachers can directly affect how students interact and respond to learning opportunities.

In this section, you will read about the foundational theories of five scientists from the 20th century. Highly effective teachers can relate what they do in their classroom to science. For the PLT, you need to know the foundational behavioral scientists and how their research and theories influence common classroom practices.

Edward Thorndike

Thorndike was one of the earliest behaviorists. He is best known for his connectionism theory that outlines three main learning laws emphasizing rewards, repetition, and signs of readiness (Thorndike, 1932).

Law of effect. Thorndike argued that people will repeat a behavior when they receive positive reinforcement and be deterred from a behavior with negative reinforcement. His theory is different from negative consequences and punishment. Punishment or extinction is used when negative and positive reinforcement fail to reach the desired outcome.

- **In the classroom.** When a student is praised for reading for 30 minutes every day, he is more likely to continue this behavior. The teacher can **positively reinforce** this behavior with a rewarding such as allowing the student to choose which book he will read next. When a student does not read for 30 minutes every day, he does not get to choose his next book. This is an example of **negative reinforcement**. A punishment (sometimes called extinction) should be used only when positive reinforcement does not achieve the desired outcome.

Law of readiness. A student needs to be ready to learn something for instruction to be effective. This means that children need adequate rest, exercise, and physical ability before a learning goal can be met.

- **In the classroom.** A student who comes to school overtired or without eating breakfast may not be able to learn from the negative and positive consequences.

Law of exercise: The more often a reward is associated with a specific behavior, the more likely it is to become a habit. Conversely, fewer associations will lead to fewer repetitions.

- **In the classroom.** The teacher uses positive and negative rewards to reinforce productive reading behaviors. This will lead to a better chance of 30-minute reading to become a daily habit for her students.

John Watson

John Watson said that human behavior can also be explained by classical conditioning. Watson observed that humans can be conditioned to associate tastes, noises, positive feelings, and negative feelings with cues from their environment. He is famous for the "Little Albert" experiment where he conditioned a baby to be fearful of a white rat by associating it with a loud noise. The graphic below shows the process of the "Little Albert" experiment.

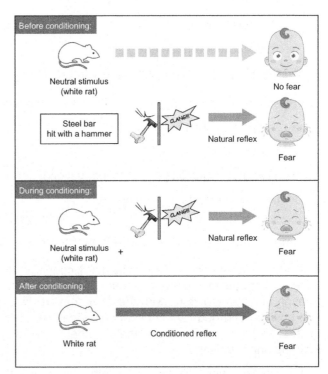

- **Watson in the classroom.** Conditioning can be used in a classroom to encourage students to find predictability in their environment and feel comfortable and safe to learn.

    - Using a hand or bell to signal class transitions such as time to line up, clean up, or take out learning materials and transition to a new learning task.

    - Students can be conditioned to associate calm feelings with behaviors that might otherwise be anxiety producing like participating in a class discussion or working on reading new words.

Abraham Maslow

Maslow is widely known for the hierarchy of needs (as shown). Maslow asserted that people are motivated by 5 basic factors: physiological, safety, love, esteem, and self-actualization. According to Maslow, when a lower need is met, the next need on the hierarchy becomes the focus of attention. If students are lacking a lower need, they cannot be motivated by one of the other needs. For example, if a student does not have basic needs like food or shelter, the student will not be motivated by esteem. Food and water are fundamental to all the other needs. Maslow started his career as a behaviorist but shifted into humanist psychology when he presented his hierarchy of needs.

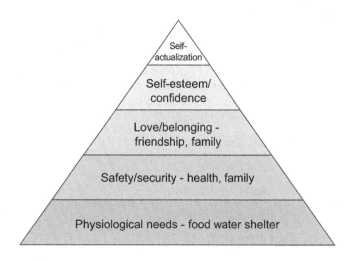

- **Maslow in the classroom**

    - Meeting students' needs before moving on to high-level assignments/activities.

    - Considering students' situations at home before assigning work.

B.F. Skinner

Skinner's operant conditioning theory is based upon the idea that learning is a function of change in overt behavior. Changes in behavior are the result of an individual's response to events (stimuli) that occur in the environment. A reinforcer is anything that strengthens the desired response. It could be verbal praise, a good grade, or a feeling of increased accomplishment or satisfaction. External rewards and motivations are often associated with Skinner's learning theory.

- **Skinner in the classroom**

    - Positive reinforcement; increasing positive behaviors through incentives (token economy) or positive feedback.

    - Negative reinforcement; increasing positive behaviors through the removal of an undesired stimulus (a toy).

    - Like Thorndike, reinforcement of positive behavior is preferred to punishment.

Erik Erikson

Earlier, Erikson's psychosocial stages of development were discussed in the context of social development. He argues that people go through eight stages in life during which their development is directed by external factors. In the first four stages, Erikson argues that development is determined by how a person is treated and the environment they inhabit. After that, he argues that a person's development is mostly impacted by a person's choices or how they react to external factors.

- **Erikson in the classroom**

    - Provide opportunities for students to participate more regularly in creating, building, modeling, and learning.

    - Encourage students to develop a sense of pride for their accomplishments and capabilities.

    - Give students responsibilities to develop ownership and independence.

A new teacher wants to increase his students' participation in class discussions. He decides to help students build their confidence, so they want to share their ideas out loud. To do that, he knows they need to feel safe and accepted in the classroom. He begins each day making sure all his students have had breakfast and are feeling well. Before starting academic tasks, he asks the class questions and encourages them to share their personal experiences. Which theorist is the teacher implementing into his instructional techniques?

A. B.F. Skinner.

B. Erik Erikson.

C. Abraham Maslow.

D. Edward Thorndike.

Correct answer: C

The teacher is using informal class discussions to promote self-esteem and prepare students for academic discussions. He is also making sure the students' basic needs of eating breakfast and feeling well are met. These techniques align with Maslow's hierarchy of needs.

2. The implications of foundational motivation theories in education

Behaviorist theory influences how teachers create motivational learning environments, engaging learning experiences, and manage classroom behaviors. In this section we will explore terms and concepts of motivational theories that you may see on the PLT. On the exam, you will relate a learning or scenario to a concept or theory, or conversely, apply a theory to a classroom management, learning, or an instructional situation.

Motivation theory

The best teachers motivate students by designing and delivering engaging and relevant instruction. In this section we will explore terms and concepts of motivational theories that you will see on the PLT. Increasing students' motivation to learn is a common theme on the PLT. These types of test questions will be presented as scenarios, and you will be expected to choose the most effective approach. The best teachers motivate all students—high-achieving, low achieving, culturally diverse, and economically diverse students. A good teacher has more than one motivational strategy happening at once and is ready add more motivational tools to their instruction and learning environment when needed.

Attribution

Attributions are the factors someone believes causes their behavior. This means students are motivated to attempt and complete a task because of their confidence in their ability to be successful. For example, "I can do well because I always do well when I study." Conversely, a student might think, "I can't do well because the teacher makes all the tests too hard." Attribution theory is useful for understanding the reactions and behaviors of students in a classroom as well as what you can do to influence and improve a student's approach to learning. Attribution theory has three guiding principles:

1. **Locus.** Attributions are on a continuum from internal to external. External is an event, person, or environment that contributes to your success. Internal is something you did yourself.

2. **Stability.** Attributions can vary from stable (difficult to change) to unstable (easy to change). For example, in science class, a student does poorly on the quiz because she was feeling ill. Feeling ill is an unstable attribution because it is easy to change while knowledge of test content is stable attribution because it can only be changed with hard work and dedication.

3. **Controllability.** Perception of an attribution can range from highly controllable like practicing a new skill to uncontrollable like the weather.

(Weiner, 1976)

Attributions and student motivation

- Successful students tend to believe they do well because they are intelligent (stable attribute), work hard (controllable attribute), and can be divergent thinkers (internal attribute).

- Attributions can challenge success when students believe their success was because of "luck" or a teacher's kindness (external attributes).

- Perceptions about controllability can impact motivation. Students are more likely to be successful if they believe they can control attributes that will bring success such as: being to class on time, knowing the subject matter, or being able to speak in front of a group.

- In general, teachers should encourage internal and stable attribution to facilitate students' belief in their own abilities and resilience.

Self-determination

Self-determination is to make decisions for yourself and control your own future. Students with strong self-determination are motivated by opportunities to collaborate on instructional design, set goals for themselves, and navigate obstacles to succeed. The application of self-determination theory is best understood through intrinsic motivation.

Intrinsic motivation

Intrinsic motivation is behavior driven by internal rewards rather than external rewards. According to self-determination theory, intrinsic motivation is driven by three things: autonomy, relatedness, and competence.

- **Autonomy**. This has to do with students' independence and self-governance. Allowing students to decide how and what they learn helps to increase autonomy and increase motivation. Students should be permitted to self-select books and work on things that interest them.

- **Relatedness.** Students must see the value in what they are learning as it pertains to their everyday lives. The best teachers make learning relatable and applicable to the real world.

- **Competence.** Students must feel they are equipped to meet your expectations. It is important to challenge students while also providing them with activities based on readiness levels and ability.

Extrinsic motivation

Extrinsic motivation refers to behavior that is driven by external rewards. Providing students with a party if they reach their reading goal or allowing students extra playtime because they cleaned up the classroom are examples of extrinsic motivation. Grades can also be considered extrinsic rewards. Extrinsic motivation is often unsustainable because once the reward is removed, the student is no longer motivated to achieve. The following example shows the way this might be presented on the test.

Example question

A student scores consistently in the top percentile of the class on tests and quizzes. However, the student rarely attempts to finish classwork and homework. What can the teacher do to help motivate this student to put effort towards classwork and homework?

- A. Allow the student time to go to the library provided he finishes his classwork and homework.

- B. Send detailed weekly reports home to his parents so they can encourage him to finish homework.

- C. Document how many times he finishes his homework and reward him when he reaches 3 days in a row.

- D. Conference with the student and determine activities that will challenge the student while also allowing him to show mastery of the standards.

Correct answer: D

Because the student scores well on the tests and quizzes, we can assume the student has mastered the concepts and standards but is unmotivated to compete the classwork and assignments. In this case, we want to be on the lookout for an answer choice where the teacher and the student find a solution by increasing intrinsic motivation for the student. Allowing the student to choose activities increases autonomy, a component of intrinsic motivation. Answer choices A, B and C all highlight extrinsic rewards. While extrinsic rewards work in the short term, they will not be sustainable over time.

Caution

Avoid answer choices that highlight extrinsic rewards. In the real-world, teachers use extrinsic rewards—pizza parties for meeting reading goals, extra time on the computer after students finish their work, candy for getting questions correct, etc. However, on the PLT, look for the answers that promote intrinsic rather than extrinsic rewards.

Cognitive dissonance

As a learning theory, cognitive dissonance is when a new belief or understanding is outside of someone's schema or what someone knows. The belief or understanding can conflict or be opposite of one's attitudes and ideas. For example, a young child who has always lived where it is warm and sunny in the winter sees a video about winter being covered in snow and cold. The student may feel conflict or cognitive dissonance because her schema is being challenged. She has to broaden her schema to accept that this experience is possible. Students experiencing cognitive dissonance may feel uncomfortable and want to resolve the conflict. Piaget argued that cognitive dissonance is a powerful instructional tool for teachers to sharpen students' cognitive processes which are integral to knowledge development. Cognitive processes are refined when students contextualize new knowledge and synthesize information as schema (Piaget, 1975).

- **Cognitive dissonance and student motivation in the classroom**

  - Challenging students' own ideas about their ability to learn; supporting students to do something they have never tried or failed at before.

  - When students believe one thing and they learn something new to contradict that belief. For example, how could life be easier without electricity, cars, and electronics?

  - Encouraging hypotheses, data collection, and experiments to explore student inquiry. The conclusions cause cognitive dissonance because they reveal information that shifts students' schema.

Classic and operant conditioning

Classical conditioning (Watson) is when a person is conditioned to associate a cue with a desired behavior. For example, a teacher uses a raised hand to signal to the class that she wants their attention.

Operant conditioning (Skinner) is when a person is taught a desired behavior using specific rewards and consequences. For example, when a teacher gives students more choice time for staying on task but takes away choice time when they do not stay on task. Operant conditioning has various forms of implementation depending on what phase of learning students are in.

- **Continuous reinforcement.** A student receives a reward each time they complete the behavior. This is most effective when a new behavior is being taught. The behavior is strongly connected to receiving the designated reward.

- **Partial (intermittent) reinforcement.** Partial reinforcement is used when a new behavior is becoming routine and reinforcement is only used as a reminder. This is most effective for sustaining a behavior over time. A student receives a reward some of the time on one of four partial reinforcement schedules:

- **Fixed-ratio schedule.** Reward presented after a set number of occurrences.
- **Variable-ratio schedule.** Reward presented after an unspecified number of occurrences.
- **Fixed interval schedule.** Reward presented after set intervals of time.
- **Variable interval schedule.** Reward presented intermittently.

Positive and negative reinforcement

Positive and negative reinforcements are used to condition students to routines, procedures, and learning opportunities. Below is a comparison of the two types of reinforcements and examples of how they can be used in the classroom.

- Can be used to effectively change student behavior.
- Intended to increase the likelihood of a desired behavior.
- Can be intentionally used to condition a desired behavior in the classroom.
- Need repetitions and consistent implementation to be effective.
- Has to happen immediately when a negative behavior should be stopped.

	Positive reinforcement: *something is added*	Negative reinforcement: *something is taken away*
Classroom Management	Offering positive feedback for desired behaviors, "thank you for raising a hand, Jose," "you are doing a nice job putting your books back where you found them, Ayla."	Taking away a toy that students are playing with during class. Even if you give it back at the end of the school day, you have begun to condition students to believe the behavior was unacceptable. Taking the toy away stopped the play (distracting behavior).
Instruction	After students complete a writing assignment, teacher shares 1-2 strong examples with the class. She offers detailed feedback to all students to let them know what they have done well.	If students successfully complete a specific learning activity in class, they will not have homework. In this case, you are taking away homework to reinforce the on-task and focused behavior.
Learning	The teacher asks for students to individually answer a question on their whiteboards and hold them up for her to see. She winks at each student with the right answer reinforcing the learning and the behavior.	A teacher sets up math centers every day. She gives a set of "must do" centers and "can do" centers to every student. She lets students know that as they master the skill being practiced in their "must do" center they can take it off their daily list, leaving more time for "can do" or choice centers.

A teacher is setting up her independent reading and writing routines at the beginning of the year so that students can work independently and she can pull small groups to work with her. Which of the following types of motivation techniques should be used first when trying to condition students to actively participate in a daily literacy routine?

 A. External motivation

 B. Positive reinforcement

 C. Punishment

 D. Extinction

Correct answer: B

Teachers should always begin with positive reinforcement techniques. Answer choice A, external motivation, is positive reinforcement. However, it draws the students' attention away from learning to earning a prize. Answer choices C and D mean almost the same thing, so they can be ruled out.

3. Strategies for classroom management

Classroom management includes following routines, keeping records, setting expectations, managing space, and promoting a positive learning environment. Effective teachers organize time and resources in a way that maximizes instructional time and minimizes disruptions. This is not easy; it takes lots of trial and error. On the PLT, you will have to select the most appropriate and effective ways to manage the classroom.

Classroom routines and procedures

Classroom routines and procedures are critical to creating a safe and productive learning environment. Routines and procedures are established at the beginning of the school year and provide space and time to focus on learning. The teacher should introduce the routines and reinforce them throughout the year. Students will need time to practice the routines and procedures. This process of introducing, reinforcing, and practicing routines and procedures will minimize infractions.

Having procedures in place for gathering materials for an assignment, getting into groups, and participating in activities helps the teacher spend less time on managing students and more time on instruction. A classroom with well-defined, well-communicated, and well-executed procedures means students know the expectations and lose very little, if any, instructional time from transitions and interruptions.

Test Tip

Routines and procedures are important for every classroom. Look for answer choices that outline practicing routines and procedures consistently in the classroom.

Effective procedures and classroom management

One of the main points to remember when answering questions about procedures and classroom management on the PLT is that teachers should spend the majority of their time on instruction and academics and very little time on managing the processes and procedures happening in the classroom. When classroom procedures are not well thought out, tasks, such as returning graded papers, handing out materials, and transitioning to groups, take two to three times longer than they should, causing a loss of valuable instructional time. You can establish effective classroom procedures and routines in a number of ways.

- **Involve students.** When setting expectations and procedures for the classroom, it is effective to involve students in the process. For example, at the beginning of the year, have a classroom discussion to establish rules such as be on time, be respectful of others, and be engaged in classroom activities. When students are involved in the planning process, they are more likely to reach those expectations.

- **Clearly communicate routines and procedures**. Students thrive when they receive clear directions and expectations for a particular task. Remove all ambiguity from the procedures process. Show students an explicit step-by-step process for completing tasks or moving through procedures. It is helpful to post these routines and processes where students can see them. You can also use icons, photos, or illustrations of students following each step.

- **Practice, practice, practice**. Effective teachers have procedures for classroom activities such as entering the classroom, storing materials, starting and ending cooperative group work, and moving through transitions. Students and teachers must practice procedures together over and over again until they become automatic. When procedures are in place and practiced regularly, the focus can be on academics and not on management.

- **Observe another teacher.** Taking the time to watch another teacher who has experience in successful classroom management is a way to gain helpful insights and tactics. Never be afraid to spend your planning period observing other teachers.

Time management

Effective time management means that you prioritize learning when planning and delivering instruction. It is important that you plan ahead and anticipate barriers. Inevitably, something will come up like a fire drill or students needing to spend more time on a concept for understanding. This can disrupt the learning schedule. However, good planning and effective time management will allow you to be flexible when interruptions occur while still prioritizing learning. Keep in mind a few things regarding time management.

- Plan ahead using the state standards.

- Prepare materials before class begins.

- Decide how much time it will take to distribute materials and give instructions.

- Plan a set amount of time to introduce the lesson.

- Decide on the most efficient and effective instructional method for the skills you are teaching.

- Anticipate students' readiness levels.

- Provide adequate time for students to practice the skill(s) taught while being monitored.

- Build in formative assessments and checks along the way.

- Allow time at the end to wrap-up the lesson; closure and debriefing are necessary elements to learning.

- Decide how to move forward by evaluating the data collected during the learning.

Maintaining accurate records

Accurate record keeping allows teachers to make informed decisions about additions and changes to their instruction. The records teachers keep in a classroom are essential for measuring progress, as well as identifying challenges and strengths in instruction. Maintaining accurate records requires consistency, organization, and immediacy. While teachers need to collect a broad range of data, it is important to only collect what can be used to improve learning. Too much data can be distracting, overwhelming, and more likely to have mistakes. For the PLT, you will need to know the main categories and types of data a teacher needs in the classroom.

Types of records to maintain in a classroom

Summative Assessment	Formative Instructional and Assessment	Assignment Management	Classroom Management	Attendance
• Tests • Quizzes • Culminating tasks • Project based learning presentations	• Writing tasks • Rubrics • Conferring notes • Observations / anecdotal data • Group work • Running records	• Complete • Incomplete • Late • Missing	• Patterns and changes of student behavior • Student exceptionalities • Behavior management plans	• Tardies • Absences

Standards of conduct

Standards of conduct are different from expectations because they are often established by the school, district, or state and apply to all students in your classroom and in the school. Standards of conduct, sometimes referred to as the code of conduct, specify behavior that is accepted or prohibited in the school. They also incorporate a plan for consequences and communication. The standard of conduct generally states the behavior expected to be demonstrated by the student. You can typically find the student standards of conduct on your state's department of education website. You can also refer to the district's standards of conduct, or ask your school leadership staff for a copy.

Positive behavior support

Sometimes students need individualized instruction to learn or reinforce standards of conduct. Positive behavior support (PBS) is a set of research-based strategies used to prevent and reduce problem behaviors by teaching students new skills and changing their environment.

Student behavior should be approached the same way student learning is approached: teachers must observe behavior, collect data on that behavior, and then devise a plan of action. Sending students to detention does not fix a behavior problem. Learning about the behavior and differentiating the approach to the behavior is most effective.

On the PLT, you will be required to determine the best approach to increasing students' positive behaviors and reducing their negative behaviors.

- **Observe the behavior first.** Before a teacher can prescribe a consequence or solution, the behavior must first be observed.
- **Involve the student in creating a plan.** Allowing students to set behavior goals and devise a plan on how to attain them helps students take ownership of the process.
- **Use behavior contracts.** In the behavior contract, help the student outline a goal. Let the student be part of the creation of the contract. Revisit the contract to celebrate gains and to make new goals.

Classroom space

Classrooms come in all shapes and sizes. How you design this space informs how successfully students can use it. The first thing to consider when determining the layout of your classroom space is safety. Consult with your school's safety plan and any applicable student IEPs to ensure the configuration of your classroom meets these standards. Effective use of classroom space also encourages learning, collaboration, movement, group work, and quiet time. Successful classroom spaces decrease the likelihood of disruptive behavior, provide structure and predictability, increase student engagement, and positively impact student performance (Poole, 2020). Here are some tips to plan your classroom space.

- Create pathways for navigation around the room to access materials.

- Encourage and support collaboration, cooperation, and mentorship.

- Create spaces to enhance your instructional methods: consider separate places where whole group, small group, and individual work will happen.

- Find ways to minimize distractions. If your classroom is adjacent to the playground, consider putting quiet learning areas away from the windows.

- Have a central meeting area.

- Have a purpose for all classroom floor and wall space.

- Keep wall postings functional, active, and engaging. Classroom walls should reflect what students are learning in class. For example, hang student work, references, recent mini-lesson, and learning strategies.

Group dynamics

Effectively managing group dynamics means that you can lead students in their learning and still manage behaviors and disruptions that inevitably happen in class. When answering questions on the PLT about managing group dynamics, look for answer choices with a method that is the least disruptive to learning.

For example, during whole-group instruction, two students start to socialize, and it becomes disruptive. Rather than breaking the instruction to reprimand the students, the teacher walks over to the students and stands close by while he continues to explain the lesson. Using techniques like proximity control to reduce the negative behavior is more effective than yelling across the room for the students to stop talking.

Proximity Control. Proximity control is when a teacher stands in close proximity to disruptive students. This strategy allows the teacher to continue teaching without interrupting the learning to address the behavior. Usually the close proximity of the teacher encourages students to stop the negative behavior.

Quick Tip

Anything that sounds negative or punitive is usually not the correct answer on this test. It is important to choose answers that align with the positive behavior support model. Sending students out of the room, calling home to complain about student behavior, and having the principal speak to students who are misbehaving are not the correct answers on the test.

Promoting a positive learning environment

A positive learning environment aligns to a constructivist philosophy of education. A positive learning environment includes the following characteristics.

- **Encouraging innovation**. Encouraging students to discover new things and find new solutions helps students to develop a more global way of thinking and increases their ability to think critically. Global thinking often improves student engagement because students can make connections between what is being learned at school and how it applies to the world around them. Project-based learning, service-learning, and activities that encourage active engagement in solving authentic problems are all examples of encouraging innovation.

- **Fostering a climate of openness**. Students need a safe place to learn as they try, fail, and reengage. Teachers must encourage students to see the learning environment as a place where they can express themselves in their learning without fear of criticism.

- **Fostering a climate of inquiry**. Inquiry-based learning is experiential. Students should be encouraged to ask questions and make hypotheses and inferences.

- **Fostering a climate of equity**. Teachers must always provide students with equal opportunities for learning. That means teachers should accommodate students based on their individual needs, provide supports for struggling students, and support diversity (cultural, economic, and academic) in the classroom.

- **Support for all students**. Teachers must engage all students: high-achievers, low-achievers, students from different cultural and socioeconomic backgrounds, and students with disabilities or exceptionalities.

Example question

A new teacher is spending a lot of time on redirecting inappropriate behavior, transitioning to activities, and cleaning up after activities. She has both the classroom expectations and the steps for moving through transitions and cleaning up posted on the wall. However, students are often unfocused, and the classroom is very chaotic. What would be the best approach the teacher can take in this situation?

A. Call home to students' parents and ask them to intervene.

B. Ask the principal to come in and speak with the students.

C. Revisit classroom procedures as a class and practice them before doing any more activities.

D. Ask a peer teacher to observe the situation and offer support in this area.

Correct answer: C

In this situation, the teacher and students have procedures in place. However, they are not using them properly. Therefore, the best decision is to stop all activities to review class expectations and practice the procedures. It may seem counterintuitive to interrupt class time. However, teaching students to follow these expectations with clarity, consistency, and practice will eventually allow academic learning to be effective. Calling home and asking the principal are not effective classroom management tactics when answering questions on the PLT. Asking a peer teacher can be a good strategy, but revisiting the plan and practicing the procedures should come first.

Caution

Pay attention to practices that are usually the *incorrect* answers on the test. For example, sending students out of the room or calling in a resource teacher to instruct struggling learners is usually not the best practice. Never outsource instruction or interventions. You, the teacher, know what's best for your students because you have evaluated the data to make decisions. Therefore, eliminate those bad answers immediately when you see them on the test.

4. Strategies for helping students develop self-motivation

Strategies to encourage students to be self-motivated rely heavily on behaviorist and humanist philosophies of learning.

The stages of development outlined by Erickson provide a framework for understanding how teachers can influence students' self-motivation. According to Erikson's stages of development, students need reinforcement and encouragement of feelings of pride and self-assurance. Maslow's hierarchy of needs demonstrates that students can attain self-motivation after their basic needs are met. Self-motivation is cultivated when students feel loved and cared for and have a sense of belonging. In both perspectives, teachers have tremendous power to impact a students' development of self-motivation. This section outlines five highly effective strategies for building self-motivation.

Assigning valuable tasks

Tasks that promote self-motivation feel meaningful to the learner. While the value of a task for promoting self-motivation is dependent on the learner, they have some characteristics in common.

Characteristics of Self-Motivation

Characteristic	Example
Learners are synthesizing and applying newly acquired skills.	• A high school class making signs for a bake sale to raise money for a charitable group.
Learners are exploring tasks that feel significant.	• Inquiry-based, project-based, thematic or experiential learning tasks. • Students design and propose new playground equipment to be more inclusive of the student body. They may also lead fundraising and community education.
Tasks reveal a students' high self-efficacy.	• A task that students feel confident they will do well at, even if they are not sure yet whether they like doing the task. • Tasks are close to the ZPD and within what the students can accomplish independently. • Tasks that follow gradual release method; "I do, we do, you do."
Tasks feel connective, purposeful, and interesting to the learner.	• Engaging cooperative learning tasks and discussions of controversial themes and topics. • Self-portrait and autobiography.
Tasks feel time and effort efficient.	• Students can image themselves working through a task. • A project with a deadline or clear end date. • Beginning, middle and end of a task are predictable.

Provide frequent positive feedback

Positive feedback is one of the simplest and most effective motivators. When you are teaching students classroom rules and expectations, positive reinforcement is one of the strongest strategies you can use to affect behaviors. Positive feedback lets students know they are meeting your expectations. When done publicly, it also creates a situation where the behavior becomes a model for others. Students should receive proportionally more positive feedback than negative feedback every day to nurture and maintain their strong self-esteem.

The following table provides examples and techniques of positive feedback.

Positive Feedback to Promote Self-Motivation

Feedback	Example	When is this method effective?
To an entire class	"Excellent work getting started in the lab. Everyone came in and got their stations set up in under two minutes."	This method is effective for reinforcing whole group routines, procedures, and expectations.
A private comment.	"I really appreciate how you helped Zoe finish the experiment when you were done."	• When a student has struggled to consistently follow procedures and you catch them doing something well. • When the praise is only relevant to the immediate actions of one student. In the example, the praise was specific to the one student who helped her classmate in the moment.
Written response to a student	"Today you were a great leader during our science fair. You modeled excellent behavior when the class started to get distracted. You also asked insightful questions that kept the class engaged."	• When you want the student to share the praise with their family. • When praise is in relation to procedures being followed.
Specific to an observed behavior being observed by one or more students	"I really like how many different perspectives I see in your essays."	To reinforce behaviors you want to see all students practice and use on a routine basis.
A public comment praising a student or group of students	"Look how well-organized team 3 is keeping its lab station. This helps to maintain the integrity and safety of the experiment."	When you want a student or group of students to serve as a model for the rest of the class.

Student-centered instructional decisions

Students should always be at the center of instructional planning, design, implementation, and assessment. When students are involved in the instructional process, they are more likely to be successful in their learning achievement. Students will take ownership of their academics and feel more confident in their capabilities when they are part of the design.

Students can be involved in making decisions about their own individual instruction and decisions that impact the whole class. The list below provides examples of how to involve students in instructional decisions.

- Setting their instructional and behavioral goals.
- Creating classroom expectations.
- Choosing which learning materials and methods they will use for a lesson.

- Designing their own rubric to assess their work.

- Choosing discussion topics for whole-group learning.

- Choosing research topics and information they are interested in learning more about.

De-emphasizing grades

De-emphasizing grades can develop students' self-motivation and self-esteem because it means putting more emphasis on growth and other measures of learning. Grades can be an effective motivator for some students. However, emphasizing grades can have negative consequences for two reasons:

1. They are abstract and limited indicators of growth and success.

2. They are essentially extrinsic rewards for learning. Relying on grades as motivators detracts from intrinsic motivation. If the grades are removed, the student might not be as motivated to learn. De-emphasizing grades means focusing on intrinsic rewards and internal motivation.

De-emphasizing grades shifts the focus to motivational strategies that are highly effective such as:

- Immediate, detailed, and constructive feedback from teachers to students.

- Increased metacognitive work; students self-reflect on what was learned and how they learned it rather than on meeting the teacher's expectations.

- More opportunities to celebrate growth and provide instruction in students' ZPD.

Example question

An at-risk student has started showing a decline in achievement within the last month. The student excels in activities like cooperative learning and labs but falls behind on writing assignments. Which of the following would be the most appropriate way to assist this student?

    A. Encourage the student to engage in all activities, not just the ones they like most.

    B. Call the student's parents and ask that they implement writing activities at home for practice.

    C. Conference with the student and plan for writing activities that will motivate the student.

    D. Continue with the lessons as is because the student needs to learn to work hard.

Correct answer: C

Because the student excels in cooperative learning and labs but falls behind in writing assignments, you can assume motivation is the issue here. Therefore, involving the student in the decision-making process by building a plan for writing assignments that interest him is the best option.

This page intentionally left blank.

Content Category I – Practice Questions and Answer Explanations

1. Ms. Bines is a science teacher and is well-liked among her students because she is smart, has high expectations for all students, and treats students with respect. Students admire her and emulate her behavior. Which of the following foundational theories aligns with this school scenario?

   A. Kohlberg – 3 Levels of Morality

   B. Piaget – Stages of Cognitive development

   C. Bandura – Social Learning Theory

   D. Bloom – Taxonomy of Educational Objectives

2. A science teacher is beginning a lesson on heredity and genetics. She knows the vocabulary and content will be challenging for students. Which of the following would be an appropriate sequence in helping students understand these concepts?

   A. First, students work in groups to read the textbook. Then students participate in a whole group activity and share out. Finally, students read silently and independently.

   B. First students complete a small reading assignment to start the lesson. Then students get into groups to discuss the reading. Then students share out in a whole group activity.

   C. First, the teacher facilitates small group interventions. Then students work with partners to read the text. Then students work independently on answer questions at the end of the reading.

   D. First the teacher facilitates whole-group instruction to discuss main concepts of genetics and heredity. Then students work through an activity in small groups or in pairs. Then students work independently to generate follow-up questions.

3. Mr. Rodriguez is a teacher who focuses on helping his students use knowledge in one area and apply it in other areas. For example, when he teaches math, he will often connect it to the science lesson he is teaching. Mr. Rodriguez is supporting:

   A. Transfer

   B. Self-Efficacy

   C. Self-Determination

   D. Zone of Proximal Development

4. Mr. Scales is working with students on a short essay for a social science unit. What would be the most effective way to ensure he is meeting the needs of every student while also paying attention to learning preferences?

   A. Mr. Scales presents students with a list of main topics and allows students to choose their own topic from that list.

   B. Mr. Scales allows students to work in groups and divide up the tasks of project among group members.

   C. Mr. Scales pulls up the calendar on the SMART board and allows students to decide the deadline for the project.

   D. Mr. Scales reviews the objectives and allows students to show mastery in a variety of ways: essay, presentation, webpage, or podcast.

5. Which of the following would be the most significant advantage to 1-1 writing conferences between each student and the teacher?

    A. The teacher can give students an anchor activity as a challenge.

    B. The teacher can target specific skills struggling learners need.

    C. It provides the teacher with norm-referenced data to compare students.

    D. It provides the teacher with extra time with each student.

6. Ms. Jensen has two students with exceptionalities in her English class. What is the most important thing Ms. Jensen can do to help these students?

    A. Read the students' IEPs and help students achieve their goals outlined in the IEP.

    B. Request a 504 for each student so they get extra time on tests.

    C. Let the students work in groups on a regular basis.

    D. Stay in contact with the students' parents and offer assistance when needed.

7. Which of the following outlines Piaget's stage of cognitive development if students are able to have a class debate on a new school-wide rule in the lunchroom?

    A. Sensorimotor

    B. Concrete operational

    C. Pre-operational

    D. Formal operational

8. An ELL who is a fluent speaker of conversational English is having trouble with some concepts in the science article students are reading in class. What would be the most effective thing for the teacher to do.

    A. Request the student be placed in an ESL class to support the student's understanding of science concepts.

    B. Ask that a paraprofessional be placed in the class to translate for the student.

    C. Use scaffolding techniques to support the student when needed.

    D. Pair the student with another ELL student and have them work together on activities.

9. During play time, Zara likes to organize items into groups by characteristics like shape, size, and color. What is most likely Zara's preferred learning style?

    A. Kinesthetic

    B. Audio

    C. Visual

    D. Logical-mathematical

10. Which of the following would be considered intrinsic motivation?

    A. A student feels accomplished after finishing a complex task.

    B. A student feels accomplished after a teacher gives the student praise.

    C. A student feels supported when he works in groups with other students.

    D. A student feels disappointed when she does not win a prize for best essay.

Number	Answer	Explanation
1.	C	Bandura is known for his social learning theory on modeled behaviors or observational learning. The theory outlines how students learn from what they observe and that teachers can be proactive about how they demonstrate and promote behaviors.
2.	D	Answer D outlines the gradual release model or the *I do, we do, you do* model. In this scenario, the teacher starts with explicit whole group instruction (I do). Then the students work together in cooperative groups (we do). Finally, students work independently to finish up (you do). This is the most appropriate sequence because it is the only one that starts with a whole-group instruction to introduce the new topic.
3.	A	Transfer refers to the process of applying skills or concepts a student has learned to a new context or environment. It is a very important skill teachers should help students develop.
4.	D	Paying attention to learning preferences means letting students show mastery in ways that suit them. Auditory learners may want to make a podcast. Read/write learners may decide to write the essay. Visual learners may decide to make a poster or presentation. Either way, answer D is the best choice. It is the skill or knowledge the students need to acquire. How students show that knowledge can be flexible.
5.	B	Targeting specific skills for each student is a good practice for this exam and in the real-life classroom. Out of all the other answer choices, focusing on the individual needs of struggling learners is most effective.
6.	A	The most important thing educators can do for their students with exceptionalities is to read their Individual Education Plan (IEP) and follow all accommodations in the plan. The goals in the plan should guide the teacher when making instructional decisions for these students.
7.	D	Debating current events involves critical thinking. Abstract thinking such as logic, deductive reasoning, comparison, and classification are demonstrated by the individual in the formal operational stage.
8.	C	Not only is scaffolding on the good word list, it is also the most effective practice listed. Requesting the student be remitted to an ESL class is not appropriate here. Asking for a paraprofessional is unnecessary because it is the teachers' job to scaffold and support this student in the classroom. Finally, pairing students based on their language is not effective here.
9.	D	Logical-mathematical thinkers tend to prefer patterning and classification activities. They like working with numbers and later on, thinking through and solving logic puzzles.
10.	A	Intrinsic motivation is the act of doing something without any obvious external rewards. Feeling good because you finished something is intrinsic. Praise and prizes are external rewards. Feeling supported is not appropriate here.

This page intentionally left blank.

CONTENT CATEGORY

II

Instructional Practices

This page intentionally left blank.

A. Planning Instruction

1. Standards-based planning and instruction
2. Predominant educational theories, specifically constructivism
3. Scope and sequence of instructional planning
4. Measurable learning objectives
5. Planning enrichment and remediation
6. The role of resources and materials in supporting student learning

1. Standards-based planning and instruction

Standards drive all curriculum and instruction. In this first section, we will look at the theory behind standards-based education, resources, and what they mean on a national, state, and district level. We will also discuss how standards guide instructional planning.

Theoretical basis of standards-based education

Standards-based education is focused on what students should know and be able to do. This means that assessments, instruction, and planning are all focused on facilitating students' ability to learn, practice, and then demonstrate knowledge and mastery of skills outlined in common standards. In comparison, up until the late 1990s, education was primarily focused on what was being taught and how it was presented in the classroom. Comparing standards-based education to traditional education is helpful for understanding its characteristics.

Standards-Based Education vs. Traditional Education

Traditional Education	Both	Standards-Based Education
Curriculum, school calendar, and ideas about what students need to be taught drive instructional planning.	Organized with scope and sequence.	Standards drive instructional planning. Planning considers what needs to be done for students to demonstrate knowledge and skills. More emphasis on developing complex cognitive thinking skills than in the past.
Curriculum, text, routines, and school traditions for learning drive instruction. Whole-class instruction is the primary means of sharing information.	Textbooks and curriculum guides are used as tools for instruction and learning.	Learning goals drive instruction. Small-group and one-on-one instruction used to remediate, enrich, and support all students to acquire new knowledge and practice skills.

Traditional Education	Both	Standards-Based Education
Evaluation based on relative comparison to other students. Final grade decided by averaged assessment scores and learning over time. Participation, effort, and completion of tasks plays into evaluation and grades. Grades calculated based on percent score. Narrative usually reflects students' participation and effort to learn.	Assessments can be in the form of rubrics, tests, quizzes, performance assessments, projects, and anecdotal observations.	Evaluation based on whether students' performance indicates understanding of content and mastery of skills. Final grade decided by mastery or growth measured in assessments and learning over time. Student report cards usually have scores assigned to standards indicating growth and mastery. 1-100 percent scores not used. Narrative descriptions of student growth and evidence of mastery.

Glossary of Education Reform, 2017

Example question

Which of the following statements are true for standards-based education? Select all that apply.

A. All lessons should begin with direct instruction.

B. Grades are based on effort, participation, and mastery of content and skills.

C. Instruction should emphasize developing complex cognitive thinking skills.

D. Final grade decided by mastery or growth measured in assessments and learning over time, not the average score of relevant schoolwork.

E. Small-group and one-on-one instruction are used to remediate, enrich, and support all students to acquire new knowledge and practice skills.

Correct answer: C, D, and E

Answer choice A is incorrect. While some lessons will begin with direct instruction, this is not a formula for all learning or an emphasis of standards-based instruction. Answer choice B is also incorrect because student assessment is based on whether they have demonstrated mastery of the standard. Demonstrating mastery can be done through discussions, culminating tasks, projects, and other learning products. Effort and participation are often discussed in the narrative report but do not influence assessment of mastery.

Accessing district, state, and national standards and frameworks

Nationally, we have Common Core State Standards (CCSS) to provide a critical base for what all students should know and be able to do at each grade level. These standards are vertically aligned to build knowledge and skills on each school year. They were created by teams of expert teachers and educators from around the country. The section below describes standards at each level of education.

- **National.** CCSS were developed as a national set of standards to reference what children should know and be able to do. They are organized into two groups, English language arts (ELA) and math. Technology, science, and social studies are addressed within the ELA standards.

  For example, in high school and college, there is a large emphasis on informational text. Therefore, ELA standards from kindergarten through 12th grade emphasize teaching students to navigate and read informational text such as lab reports and primary historical documents.

All but 8 states have adopted some version of CCSS. You can find the CCSS and each states' adopted version of the CCSS at www.corestandards.org.

- **State.** Every state has adopted their own standards-based framework for curriculum and instruction. While social studies and science are unique to each state, many states are adopting a version of Next Generation of Science Standards (NGSS). You can find NGSS at: https://www.nextgenscience.org/.

  Some states are more closely aligned to the CCSS than others. Besides the CCSS website, you can find a comprehensive list of state standards on your state's department of education website.

- **District.** School districts implement the state standards using a unique set of learning objectives, curriculums, scope, and sequencing. Teachers are expected to provide instruction that align to the district's goals and objectives to ensure all students can meet the state standards. District goals and objectives are typically revisited and revised every year.

  You will need to become familiar with district documents and expectations for how to provide instruction and learning in your school and classroom. This will include grading and reporting systems, curriculum guides, and expectations for interdisciplinary collaboration.

Using standards and frameworks in instructional planning

Standards will drive all planning, instruction, and assessment. You will need to know how to access these standards to plan, implement, and assess student learning. This includes the following:

- How to build and use scope and sequences.
- How to plan learning goals and lesson objectives.
- When and how to remediate and add enrichment opportunities.

Backwards design. Backwards design is very effective for organizing skills and content for planning units and individual lessons that align to the state standards. The key to backwards design is to start with the state standards and work backwards to create assessments before specific lesson goals and instructional activities.

Alignment is critical. Start with the standards, plan the assessments, monitor the students' progress at key intervals, and adjust short-term objectives accordingly. The steps to backwards design are as follows:

1. Identify the state adopted standards for the concepts you are teaching. Be sure you are following the scope and sequence outlined by the state standards. The goal is student mastery of the standard(s).

2. Choose what assessments you will use to determine if the students mastered the standard(s).

3. Plan the lesson and activities.

4. Monitor progress as students move through the unit, lesson, or activity.

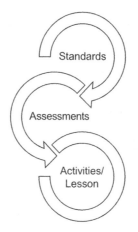

- Start with the state adopted standards. That is the end goal–to have the students master the standard(s).

- Determine how you will know the students mastered the standard and what assessments you will use to measure success.

- Decide what lessons and activities you will have students engage in to work toward standards mastery.

Spiral curriculum. Spiral curriculum is the process of revisiting topics and building deeper understanding each time the topic is encountered. While general knowledge is often taught by exploring a topic in depth, skills such as decoding and comprehension, writing in different genres, and solving math problems are best taught by revisiting the core concepts. Teachers can use backward design to develop a range of units and learning tasks including a spiral curriculum.

Example question

Which of the following describes how to use standards to inform instruction?

A. Teach students what they need to know to perform well on standardized test.

B. Use district adopted curriculum to ensure all standards are being taught and assessed.

C. Use standards to build learning objectives and assessments that inform instructional strategies and learning experiences.

D. Teach students the standards so they can self-assess their progress.

Correct answer: C

Answer choice C outlines the steps of backwards design. Answer choice A is a common misunderstanding. Standardized tests are not a part of standard-based education. Standardized tests are a general assessment used to report baseline competency and to measure and compare learning from different schools and districts. Answer choice B is incorrect because standards are not the same thing as curriculum. Answer choice D is wrong because students should not be taught to recite or learn standards out of context.

2. Predominant educational theories, specifically constructivism

Cognitivism

Cognitivism emphasizes mental processes like memory, languages, thinking, knowing, and problem-solving. Along with constructivism, cognitivism is a leading theory behind education models for building curriculum and leading instruction. Cognitivism became a strong part of educational psychology in the 1940s and 1950s. Cognitive theorists believed that learning was a more nuanced process and could not be explained only by observable behaviors as claimed by behaviorists. We discussed some themes of cognitivism like schema and Zone of Proximal Development, in Content Category I when exploring Piaget and Vygotsky's theories of learning.

Schema. Schema is a general idea about something. As discussed in detail in Content Category I, schema is a central theme of cognitivism because it is the basis for how a student receives and incorporates new knowledge and skills. Children become aware of their cognitive abilities and can even identify schema at a very young age before formal schooling.

Information processing. Information processing is an ideology describing how we sense, perceive, and take-in information. It describes how various types of information are stored in short- and long-term memory. New information is easier to remember when it connects to what we already know or have experienced. For the PLT, you need to know the 4 memory types associated with information processing theory:

1. Sensory register

2. Short-term memory

3. Declarative

4. Procedural memory

These four types will be discussed in detail in following sections.

Mapping. Mapping is making a visual representation of an idea or concept. It may be an image or information organized into a graphic organizer to illustrate connection or relationships such as cause and effect, beginning, middle and end, or big ideas and details. Comparisons can be mapped to show similarities and differences. The graphic shown is an example of mapping the cause of fire.

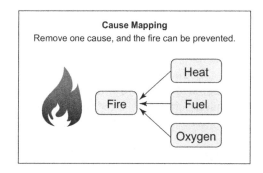

Cause Mapping
Remove one cause, and the fire can be prevented.

Social learning theory. Social learning theory (SLT) is discussed in detail in Content Category I. SLT emphasizes explicitly modeling and performing learning behaviors and procedures for students.

Modeling. This is the theory behind "I do (model), we do (students recall, teachers guide and encourage), you do (students practice independently, teacher observes). The idea is to achieve the following:

1. Hold students' attention while modeling.

2. Facilitate students' memory.

3. Students can then practice and replicate behaviors.

4. Students have the confidence and motivation to do it on their own.

Vicarious learning. Like modeling, vicarious learning is what a student learns from observing. Unlike modeling, vicarious learning is an indirect observation of their teachers and peers at school as well as from family, friends, and their community. Vicarious learning is in contrast to modeling or what is learned from direct instructions and carefully planned out learning experiences.

For example, a student sees classmates redirected by a teacher for talking together and then decides not to talk to her friend because she does not want to be reprimanded. Another example is when a student realizes he needs to begin listening to the teacher because everyone else is silently looking at the teacher.

Reciprocal determinism. Reciprocal determinism means behavior is influenced by a student's environment, but also the student's behavior itself.

For example, a timid student might not want to read. The students' behavior influences how a teacher confronts and works to support the student. The teacher might give her more one-to-one attention than other students. Her shy behavior impacted her learning experience because she received more attention from the teacher.

Children are not all the same person being molded by the forces around them. Students' actions (informed by their thoughts, feelings, ethics, and perceptions) also play a role in shaping the environment where they learn and perform.

Example question

A teacher is instructing on a written and verbal communication unit. Which of the following would be most effective?

A. The teacher lays out the criteria for effective written and verbal communication.

B. The teacher models effective written and verbal communication with students.

C. The teacher rewards students who display appropriate and effective written and verbal communication

D. The teacher encourages parents to work on these skills at home.

Correct answer: B

Modeling is the most effective way to encourage students to communicate. Teachers should first lead by example when they expect their students to use certain techniques in communication. Answer choice A, the teacher lays out the criteria, is not as effective as modeling the behavior. Students do what the teacher does more than they do what the teacher says. Remember, using external rewards, as in answer choice C, is usually not the correct answer on the exam. Finally, answer choice D is incorrect because it is the teacher's job, not the parents' job, to help students with these skills.

Constructivism

The basic premise of constructivism is that students seek answers and make connections to prior knowledge. Constructivism asserts that learners arrive to school, a lesson, a learning task, or goal with different perspectives based on what they already know and how the learning relates to their previous experiences. This means that a students' social, cultural, economic, and values impacts how and what they learn from a given lesson or task.

Constructivism also asserts that learning is cumulative; new information is built upon prior knowledge and experience. The implication of constructivism for teachers is that they must help students make those connections between new material presented and their prior experiences.

Learning as experience. Constructivism emphasizes the student experience. What they are doing makes all the difference in how they construct knowledge and contextualize a learning task. Learning as experience generally means to go deep with one skill or piece of knowledge rather than asking students to listen to the teacher or read a lot of text to cover a large amount of content.

For example, a teacher may present a math problem with the steps to an incorrect answer to begin a discussion with the class. The idea is for the class to co-construct knowledge by identifying the problem and reworking each step to find and explain the correct solution. Another example is taking a class on a field trip to the grocery store to learn how to compare prices or understand sales tax.

Problem-based learning. Constructivist theory promotes learning and problem solving that reflect real-life contexts where the environment is very rich in information and there are no right answers (embedded knowledge). Learning should include authentic tasks.

For example, a class could be presented with the problem of no libraries in walking distance to their community. Together, they may decide to address the problem by finding more ways to circulate books throughout their community.

One solution could be building Little Lending Libraries at laundry mats or at a nearby park. To implement this plan, they have to organize funds, building materials, allocate time, and find opportunities to educate community members of the lending rules. They will also need permission from the various locations for installing the mini libraries. All of this will require math, reading, and persuasive writing as well as other learning.

Zone of proximal development (ZPD). ZPD is Vygotsky's theory of learning discussed in Content Category I. Students need to be challenged with content and learning experiences that both connect to what they already know and understand but are not overwhelming and frustrating. This is the time and place when instruction is the most effective because it is just beyond what a student can do independently. ZPD is a students' instructional level. Identifying students' ZPD is especially useful when planning small-group and one-on-one instruction. There may be multiple questions on the PLT regarding ZPD.

Example question

During a class discussion on the transitive property in algebra, 9th grade students' responses demonstrate an understanding of the concept. Which two answer choices are most likely NOT in the students' ZPD?

    A. Applying the concept to a new scenario in a discussion with their partner.

    B. Using an example to explain the concept in writing.

    C. Solving complex functions with exponents.

    D. Solving a simple algebraic problem with one variable.

Correct answer: C and D

Answer choice C is moving on to a new and complex skill which is unrelated to current learning. Answer choice D is a simpler skill that the student is likely to already do independently. Neither answer choice is in the ZPD where guidance, modeling, or coaching would support their learning.

Scaffolding. Just like scaffolding used in construction to support workers as they construct buildings, instructional scaffolds are temporary supports teachers use to assist students in accomplishing complex tasks students could not typically achieve on their own. Once students build their skills and are able to work through activities on their own, the scaffolding is gradually removed, and the responsibility of learning shifts from the instructor to the student (Northern Illinois University Faculty Development and Instructional Design, n.d).

Scaffolding converges themes from social learning theory (SLT), cognitivism, and constructivism. One of the most common scaffolding techniques is the gradual release method—**I do, we do, you do**—as described above in SLT.

Teachers scaffold everyday while planning and implementing lessons. Other examples of scaffolding include:

- Mini lessons
- Using visual aids
- Chunking information
- Activating prior knowledge
- Checking for understanding while students practice in small groups and alone
- Front-loading or pre-teaching important vocabulary

Inquiry/discovery learning. Inquiry learning is when students are encouraged to share their own curiosity about a topic by asking questions and sharing ideas. In turn, students participate in the planning and process of learning rather than simply collecting information provided by their teacher.

Inquiry learning is highly motivating and engaging. It can be as simple as asking students to record questions while reading a new text or planning a unit based on students' questions about why the sky is blue. The inquiry process involves generating questions, researching for answers, sharing discoveries, and reflecting on the learning.

Behaviorism

Behaviorism is a useful tool for promoting learning routines. You need to understand how to apply behaviorism theories to instructional planning for the PLT. Here, you will read examples of how each strategy applies to instruction. For definitions and origins of these strategies, refer to Content Category 1.

Conditioning. Learning routines like "bring your white board and dry erase marker and sit in your designated carpet space to begin math," create internal signals and readiness for students to be prepared for instruction. These routines are created and maintained primarily using classical and operant conditioning.

Intrinsic rewards. Intrinsic rewards are internal feelings of gratification for doing a good job. These are long lasting motivators for students. Teachers should establish an environment for students to gain intrinsic rewards. Examples include:

- Celebrating learning with a poetry café for families and school community members to attend and hear students perform their original writing.

- Incorporating opportunities for positive feedback into lesson plans by scheduling one-on-one conferring, small-group instruction, and sharing 1-2 examples from the class at the end of the period.

Extrinsic rewards. Extrinsic rewards are external, tangible prizes that have short-term motivating effects. Extrinsic rewards should be avoided as a method for rewarding academic success such as acknowledging understanding, selecting correct answers, completing work, or achieving high scores. Extrinsic rewards are outcomes rather than behaviors and they can alter students' self-image, inadvertently replace intrinsic motivators, and become unsustainable.

Reinforcement (operant conditioning). These examples are meant to illustrate each type of reinforcement and punishment. They are not equally effective. You need to know these terms because on the PLT, you may need to identify what is happening in a scenario.

Caution

Extrinsic rewards (i.e., pizza parties, no homework, and extra free time) are typically not in the correct answer choices on this test. Effective teachers support **intrinsic rewards** (i.e., positive feedback, student-led discussions, and self-selecting books) to motivate students.

- Positive reinforcement (encourage by adding): add extra recess when the class cleans up their learning materials in record time.

- Negative reinforcement (encourage by taking away): take way restrictions for what books students can choose during independent reading.

- Positive punishment (discourage by adding): requiring students to practice transitioning from whole-group to small-group learning until it is done efficiently (adding practice); talking to a child about classroom expectations one-on-one when they make a mistake (adding confrontation).

- Negative punishment (discourage by taking away): taking away the option to work with a partner when students are off-task.

(Akerman C., 2020)

Example question

A teacher has projected an essay in the front of the class. The students watch as she goes through the essay, deleting fragments and revising sentences. The teacher is using what technique with her students?

   A. Reciprocal determinism

   B. Cooperative learning

   C. Modeling

   D. Writing workshop

Correct answer: C

The teacher is showing students how to do something, and the students are watching. This is modeling. Cooperative learning is when students work in groups. Reciprocal teaching is when students facilitate the class. Finally, a writing workshop is when students write and edit their work in cooperative writing groups.

3. Scope and sequence of instructional planning

The PLT will assess your ability to effectively plan and design lessons. The scope, sequence, and activities in the lesson should be paced so that they are coherent. Not only do you have to present the material, you have to organize it in a way that maximizes learning.

Scope (breadth and depth). Scope refers to the content to be covered and the depth at which it will be taught. For example, the CCSS are known for having fewer, more targeted standards than standards used by schools in the past. The focus is on depth of content rather than the amount of content students need to know and what they need to be able to do (visualize a bucket full of knowledge and skills).

Sequence (order). Sequence is order. Content is organized so that skills and knowledge build on itself throughout a unit, school year, and across grade levels. The progression of content is dependent on student developmental readiness. For example, students practice and review addition and subtraction before learning the basics for multiplication and division.

CCSS as well as curriculum adopted by school districts are used to build scope and sequences. Here is an example of scope that is sequenced for planning instruction.

Scope: Overview of content for Revolutionary War unit determined by state standards.	Sequence: The order that these concepts and knowledge will be taught.
• The perspectives of women, enslaved people, rebels, and loyalists of the time • Primary documents: Declaration of Independence, Federalist Papers, Constitution, etc. • The Founding Fathers • The events leading up to the Revolutionary War	1. The events leading up to the Revolutionary War 2. Declaration of Independence 3. The perspectives of women, enslaved people, rebels, and loyalists of the time 4. Arguments for and against the revolution 5. The Founding Fathers 6. Primary document: Federalist papers and Constitution

Scope and sequence in standards of learning

CCSS and other adopted standards are organized so that they build on themselves from kindergarten to 12th grade. They also represent the scope of what students need to learn and be able to do by the end of each grade level. Two terms used to describe the organization of standards are **vertical** (k-12 sequence) and **horizontal** (scope). Teachers work in professional learning communities (PLCs) within schools or districts to plan and revise their scope and sequence of instruction to align with their CCSS (what students need to know and be able to do).

Vertical alignment. Vertical alignment occurs when lessons and activities in the classroom support one grade level to the next. The CCSS are vertically aligned—every skill in each standard supports one grade level to the next.

For example, the skills outlined in the CCSS for 1st grade math are designed to help students prepare for what they will need in 2nd grade math, 3rd grade math, and so on. While the standards are designed to be vertically aligned, it is the responsibility of the educator to ensure students are receiving lessons that are vertically aligned.

Vertical Alignment

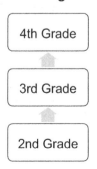

Educators can vertically align their lessons by:

- Collaborating with other teachers in PLCs.
- Paying close attention to the standards that come before and after the year being taught.
- Attending professional development that focuses on standards alignment.

Horizontal alignment. Horizontal alignment occurs when lessons are aligned to other academic disciplines and content areas.

For example, 9th grade social studies teachers plan with the 9th grade English teachers to design a common lesson focusing on the Civil Rights Movement. This lesson will fulfill social studies standards in U.S. history and English language arts standards in reading and writing. This relationship between the two content areas to focus on common content, goals, and standards is horizontal alignment.

Horizontal Alignment

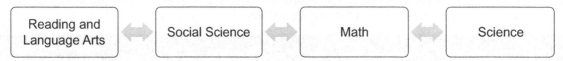

Effective educators can be sure lessons are horizontally aligned by:

- Collaborating with other teachers in PLCs.
- Researching other content areas that relate to the content being taught.
- Looking for connections where curriculum can support other content areas.

Scope and sequence in curriculum planning

When you prepare for an entire school year, new unit, or the coming week of study, you have to think through the scope and sequence of what students need to know and be able to do, This includes what instruction needs to be done to get them there. For example, when starting a new unit on persuasive writing, you need to use or create a scope and sequence of skills to be taught. The scope and sequence need to have:

1. Start and end time.
2. Explanation of how standards will be taught (goals and learning objectives).
3. Formative and summative assessments of the skills and knowledge students need to know and be able to do.

As mentioned before, backwards design is an ideal method for moving from standards to learning objectives. The scope and sequence will keep your planning organized and efficient.

4. Measurable learning objectives

Learning objectives are clear statements of what students will know and be able to do. They can define long-term (unit or semester) or short term (day or weekly lesson) intentions. Selecting content depends on:

1. Available curriculum resources: Has your school or district adopted curriculum resources with content aligned to your state's standards?
2. Unit and lesson objectives: there is an art to picking what will be most engaging and resonate best with your students, there are also some big ideas to keep in mind: objectives need to be measurable and content needs to align with standards outlined in your scope and sequence.

Measurable objectives

Objectives detail what a student will be able to do by the end of the learning activity. Objectives should be measurable because teachers have to determine if the objectives of learning were met before moving on to new content.

Effective teachers don't just write the learning objective on the board; they communicate the objective to the students and use the objective to guide instruction and learning throughout the lesson. Effective teachers regularly check in with students to communicate learning objectives.

Objectives contain three main components.

1. The skill or behavior to be performed.

2. The conditions under which the students will perform the skill or behavior.

3. The criteria used to measure the objective.

Think about it!

Teachers write objectives on the board before the lesson, so students understand what skills and behaviors are expected at the end of the lesson.

Here is an example of a well-written objective that is aligned to the state standards for a 6th grade life science class:

At the completion of Unit 3 – Cell Functions, students will apply their knowledge of cell structures and functions by writing an expository essay and scoring at least a 3 out of 4 based on the assigned rubric.

Notice that the objective above contains all 3 components:

1. The skill or behavior performed – students will apply their knowledge.

2. The conditions under which the students will perform the skill or behavior – writing an expository essay.

3. The criteria used to measure the objective – scoring a 3 out of 4 based on the rubric.

To make learning objectives measurable and observable, use verbs to refer to the learning domain.

- The **cognitive domain** pertains to how students think about thinking.

- The **affective domain** pertains to students' attitudes, values, and beliefs.

- The **psychomotor domain** pertains to students' physical movements.

Test Tip

On the PLT, you will need to identify one or more domains implied by a learning objective. To select the right answers, read the verbs and visualize what the student is being asked to do. A learning objective can fit into more than one domain.

Learning domains

Cognitive domain. These are the thinking processes most often used to write learning objectives. Bloom's taxonomy provides a framework for the types of thinking required to meet a learning objective. Using Bloom's taxonomy, you can infer from each verb the level and complexity of thinking the task will require.

Look at the pyramid of Bloom's Taxonomy again to consider the varying levels and types of thinking that should be integrated into learning objectives.

Bloom's Taxonomy Stage	Verbs	Examples
Remembering	Define, duplicate, draw, list, recall	Students will list the five most common vertebrate classes of animals.
Understanding and identify	Describe, discuss, identify	Students will describe the defining features of mammals.
Categorize	Classify, organize, categorize, adhere, alter, arrange	Students will classify animals into five groups based on their habitat as well as physical and adaptive features.
Compare and contrast	Compare, contrast	Students will find similarities and differences between animals from two of the five common vertebrate classes.
Analyzing	Analyze, examine	Students will diagram an animal life cycle.
Evaluating	Argue, decide, critique	Students will argue whether or not wild animals make good pets.
Creating	Construct, create, compose assemble	Students will create and explain their own animal and construct a habitat it is adapted to.
Applying	Apply, change, choose, demonstrate, interpret	Students will demonstrate how animal features help them to survive in their habitat. Students will describe the potential impact of climate change on an animal's habitat.

Bloom and his colleagues also created taxonomies for affective and psychomotor domains. While Bloom's Taxonomy focuses on cognitive processes, the progression from simple reflection to integrated learning is evident in the progression of thinking in all three learning domains.

Affective domain. This area of learning relates to the values, attitudes, and a student's personal connections to learning. You will notice an overlap in verbs from the cognitive domain because many objectives require learning in more than one domain.

For the PLT, you will need to identify whether objectives fall into the affective domain. Study the characteristics of the affective domain objectives below.

Affective Domain Levels	Verbs	Examples
Receiving (attentive, listening)	Acknowledge, choose, attend, hear, give	Students will listen to a story read aloud.
Responding (participation through oral response or activity)	Answer, contribute, clarify	Students will answer questions about a text.

Affective Domain Levels	Verbs	Examples
Valuing (judging or discriminating)	Argue, challenge, compete, persuade	Students will discuss the reasons for choosing their favorite character from a book.
Organization	Build, arrange, combine, compare, contrast	Students will choose 3 learning centers to explore information from the text.
Characterization	Act, display, influence, practice	Students will roleplay a scene from the text.

Psychomotor domain. This domain refers to physical movement and coordination. Connecting psychomotor skills to physical education is straight forward. However, the psychomotor domain is used across disciplines.

Examples of psychomotor domain include:

- Learning to print and write letters and numbers.
- Using manipulatives to explore math concepts.
- Playing an instrument.
- Creating art or drawing a world map.
- Setting up a microscope in science.
- Building stamina in writing.

Like the affective domain, you will need to identify objectives from the psychomotor domain detailed in the table below.

Psychomotor Domain Levels	Verbs	Examples
Imitation and manipulation	Follow, copy, trace, grasp, bend	Students will hold the pencil correctly to form letters and numbers as modeled by their teacher. Student can imitate the motion of throwing a ball underhand.
Precision	Demonstrate, show, control	Students will write letters and numbers independently. Students will kick a ball into the goal from 30 feet away.
Articulation	Construct, create, solve, adapt, modify, build, revise	Students can form legible letters and numbers on paper without lines. Student confidently creates a self-portrait.
Naturalization	Perform, operate, perfect	Student can prepare a slide of cells and examine it under a microscope. Student effortlessly dribbles, passes, and catches a basketball adjusting to the needs of the team.

Example question

Select the domain(s) associated with each learning objectives.

Learning Objective	Cognitive	Affective	Psychomotor
Students will discuss the causes of the Civil War.	A	B	C
Students will read and write whole numbers up to 1,000.	D	E	F
Students will create a replica of their favorite part of the book.	G	H	I

Correct answer: A, D, F, H, I

A. Discussing the causes of the Civil War demands higher order thinking skills or complex cognition to integrate pieces of information.

D, F. Students have to recall the numbers and letters which is a cognitive skill. They also have to write them which is a psychomotor skill.

H, I. Students will use fine motor skills to create their replica. Discerning their favorite moment is a judgment and part of the affective domain.

When answering questions like this on the PLT, look for answers to eliminate. For example, in #2, writing numbers and letters involves no judgment and eliminates affective domain while in #1 a class discussion will not include gross or fine motor skills and therefore eliminates the psychomotor domain.

Observable behavior

Assessing and monitoring student progress is essential for successful teaching. This is done by collecting formative data or data that informs instruction. Here are three ways you might see this on the PLT.

Anecdotal notes. These are detailed notes you take while observing specific student learning behaviors. The notes provide valuable data the teacher can use to make decisions in the classroom. For example, a teacher takes anecdotal notes when observing a student as he identifies the title and author of a book. Observation should be specific to the learning objectives which should also align to a standard.

Checklists. Another way to observe students in action is with checklists. A checklist will have a list of the skills and knowledge the students are expected to demonstrate during the lesson. For example:

1. Can identify and use collective nouns

2. Can identify and use irregular plural nouns

3. Can use reflexive pronouns

4. Can identify and use adjectives and adverbs

Particularly for younger students, checklists and anecdotal notes are an effective way to collect data on their learning to identify mastery and areas of need.

Running record for reading. Running records are commonly used in elementary schools to record observations of students reading. They are done one-on-one and use symbols to identify the types of mistakes (miscues and self-corrections) students might make while reading aloud. Teachers also ask a variety of comprehension questions. Running records usually take less time than a comprehensive, quarterly reading assessment.

Example question

A student has finished her independent reading book and reflection notes. She wants to choose a new book. Her most recent classroom assessment from 3 weeks ago implies she should choose the same level book. However, the teacher has notes from small-group learning suggesting that the student is reading with almost 100% accuracy at this level and demonstrating strong comprehension. What should the teacher do to support the selection of the student's next book?

    A. Let her choose whatever book she wants.

    B. Conduct a running record to gather data and reassess her independent reading level.

    C. Have her write more about the book she just read.

    D. Ask her to pick a book from a different genre.

Correct answer: B

First, notice the good words in B: *data, reassess, independent reading level*. During a reading lesson or reading workshop, students should be reading books at their independent or instructional level. It is common for students, especially young ones, to make progress before summative reading assessments are implemented. In this case, the teacher should do a rapid running record to assess fluency and comprehension to inform changes in what the student chooses to read.

Measurable outcomes

It is important for teachers to establish learning objectives in a way so that they can measure outcomes. This can be measured using qualitative and quantitative data. Teachers must have a way to measure progress toward desired outcomes. This begins with establishing goals and documenting results.

Goals. Goals are broad statements that focus on what learners will know at the end of the year or the end of a course. Students should have the opportunity to set short- and long-term goals for themselves and progress monitor over time to determine when they meet those goals. Goals should be recorded in data folders or journals where students can reference their goals on a regular basis.

Quick Tip

Qualitative data – descriptive and conceptual (like notes and observations).

Quantitative – can be counted (like test scores and words per minute).

When drafting goals, it is helpful for students and teachers to use the SMART method. SMART stands for **S**pecific, **M**easurable, **A**chievable, **R**elevant, and **T**imely.

- **Specific.** The goal must contain a statement that details specifically what the student will accomplish.
- **Measurable.** There must be a way to measure progress towards the goal—using assessment data.
- **Achievable.** The goal must be within the scope of abilities for the student.
- **Relevant.** The goal must be relevant to what the student is doing in school/life.
- **Timely.** The goal must be completed within a targeted time frame.

Examples of SMART goals:

- By the end of the quarter, Patricia will increase written language skills by using proper spelling and punctuation in 4 out of 5 trials with 80% accuracy as measured by formative assessments.
- By the end of the semester, Jocelyn will increase her fluency from 93 words per min to 125 words per minute as measured by informal fluency reads.

You need to know the difference between long-term and short-term goals. Long-term goals typically happen over the course of a semester, and short-term goals typically happen within a unit, month, or grading period. You will also need to know how to apply goals to the instructional planning process.

Data folders. Students use data folders to track their progress by recording their achievements. Teachers and students reference data folders throughout the year to progress monitor, set new goals, and conduct student-led conferences. This is an example of teachers and students using data together to make decisions.

Portfolios. A student portfolio is a compilation of academic work and other forms of educational evidence assembled for the purpose of:

- Evaluating coursework quality, learning progress, and academic achievement.
- Determining whether students have met learning standards or other academic requirements for courses, grade-level promotion, and graduation.
- Helping students reflect on their academic goals and progress as learners.
- Creating a lasting archive of academic work products, accomplishments, and other documentation.

Compiling, reviewing, and evaluating student work over a period of time can provide an authentic picture of what students have learned and are able to do (The Glossary of Education Reform, 2016).

Progress monitoring. Teachers and students progress monitor by continuously looking at data, both qualitative and quantitative, to measure academic improvement. Teachers progress monitor by using ongoing formative assessments to measure students' skills throughout the learning process.

Example question

The teacher writes on her board:

- *Students will identify parts of a sentence: subject and predicate.*
- *Students will understand the difference between fragments and complete sentences.*

These are examples of:

    A. Standards

    B. Objectives

    C. Rules

    D. Rubrics

Correct answer: B

Objectives are the skills and behaviors students exhibit after a lesson. Objectives are often written using Bloom's verbs. In this case, the objectives are using the verbs *identify* and *understand*.

5. Planning enrichment and remediation

The term *high expectations for all students* is prevalent in education today. It means effective teachers challenge all students, regardless of students' abilities, learning preferences, readiness levels, or achievement scores.

The goal that all students learn the state standards remains the same, regardless of skill level. However, teachers should scaffold material and make accommodations as needed to help students master the standards and reach expectations. Furthermore, consistent tracking of learning will uncover areas where students are ready for enrichment or to learn beyond the defined expectations.

Enrichment keeps learning in motion and student growth continuous. Because of the diverse learning needs of students, many states and districts require that enrichment and remediation curriculum be integrated into unit and daily lesson plans.

Think about it!

Scenarios on the PLT (and in real life) dealing with remediation and enrichment may include dependence on educators outside of the classroom. If identified in students' IEPs, both remediation and enrichment may require support from specialists in the school. Therefore, it is important to continuously collaborate with these specialists to share your learning goals and curriculum trajectory.

Remediation

Remediation is necessary when students need more practice or alternative presentation of content to accomplish learning goals. You may identify students who need remediation immediately after a mini lesson because their initial responses are not proficient or during guided learning because their attempts to practice do not demonstrate understanding.

In your lesson plans, include time to review and practice with individuals and small groups using manipulatives, added visuals, other learning tools, and additional guided practice.

Examples of remediation

- Include learning centers that students can rotate to for practice and reviewing essential skills.

- If a special education teacher is working with one student in the class, sometimes he or she may want a group to work with to encourage learning and to present a skill or idea in a new way.

- Work one-on-one or in a small group with students who need to relearn to review content.

- Assign "prework" such as learning essential vocabulary for upcoming concepts.

Enrichment

Enrichment is especially important for motivated and gifted students but can be highly motivating and meaningful to all students in a class. Hands-on learning, discussions, and field trips are opportunities for whole-class enrichment. Identifying students for specific types of enrichment can come from formative and summative assessments that happen on a routine basis or in the moment.

You may have one or two students or at times, a majority of the students, who grasp new concepts quickly and need additional challenges. However, accelerated learning is not the same as completing a task quickly. Student work needs to be assessed before it is clear whether remediation, additional practice, or enrichment is needed.

Caution

When answering a question about enrichment or acceleration, **AVOID** the following:

1. Asking a student to help a peer who needs remediation.

2. Moving on to the next lesson.

3. Asking students to complete worksheets practicing different skills.

Examples of enrichment

- **Guided reading, writing, and math groups.** Students who achieve high scores on their reading placement tests need to read and learn to comprehend material at their instructional level. Their instructional level might be beyond the learning expectations described in unit or lesson standards. Small-group work is an excellent opportunity to enrich reading, writing, and math instruction.

- **Higher order thinking.** The best way to routinely integrate enrichment into lesson plans is to find ways to engage higher order thinking. For example, if the learning goal is for students to understand slope-intercept, students who reach this goal can explain y-intercept in real-world scenarios.

- **Whole-class enrichment.** Examples of whole-class enrichment are field trips, experiential learning such as planting and maintaining a garden, and reading once a month with older or younger learning buddies.

Curriculum guides, PLCs, and district learning resources are good places to find direction and resources for remediation and enrichment tasks.

Test Tip

Be sure to look at the answer choices and determine which ones contain *good words* about using data to make decisions and prescribing specific and targeted interventions. Often, you will not have to interpret the data in the graph. You will need to find only one answer choice that contains good words.

Example question

Directions: use the graph to answer the question that follows.

Given the data, what should be the teacher's next step regarding this student?

A. Continue with current reading instruction by using the district-mandated materials with fidelity because the student showed an increase from December to February.

B. Provide the student with extra independent reading practice at home in order to increase reading skills such as comprehension and vocabulary acquisition.

C. Conference with the parents and assist them in implementing an at-home practice program.

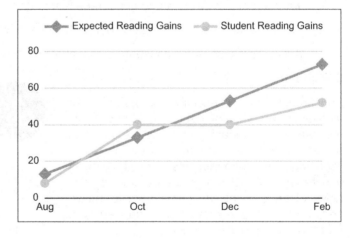

D. Provide the student with reading interventions during the school day to target his specific literacy issues.

Correct answer: D

Notice that answer choice D has all of the good words—interventions, target—associated with using data to meet the needs of every student.

6. The role of resources and materials in supporting student learning

The PLT emphasizes standards alignment. Therefore, when choosing resources like textbooks, activities, and ancillary materials to implement curriculum, be sure to base your decisions on the criteria associated with standards such as measurable objectives, student learning needs, and student performance levels.

To really understand what resources and materials are effective to meet learning goals, identify what learning domains, cognitive processes, knowledge, and skills students will be introduced to, practice, and master while completing the task. If the materials and resources selected do not enhance this process, find something else that does. Reflect on the lesson to decide if the materials and resources served their purpose. If a resource caused disruptions or did not support the intended outcomes, again, find something else.

Think about it!

Resist the urge to used flashy new resources only because they are available. This can waste learning time and distract from learning goals. For example, it can be tempting to ask students to research topics using a Google search because the devices are available. However, this may not be the most effective way to gather the information or practice the skill the students need to meet objectives associated with standards.

Resources to support student learning

Integrating learning resources can be powerful for motivating learners, presenting clear instruction, and engaging different learning styles. Here is a list of resources with examples of how they may be used in a classroom.

- **Computers, the Internet, and other electronic resources**

  - Researching topics of interest such as animals of China, New Year's celebrations across the world, a favorite author.

  - Remedial software programs to support number fluency and phonics.

  - Planning, rehearsing, writing and revising on a shared drive

  - Collaborating on a class blog

  - Virtual field trips

Be mindful of how much time students are watching and using electronics. The American Academy of Pediatrics has strong recommendations for limiting screen time because it inhibits different types of developmental growth. On the PLT, the use of electronics will always be purposeful and complimentary to other learning.

- **Library collection (books, magazines, pamphlets, reference works)**

  - Books, magazines and other library materials give students an opportunity to explore and engage in new topics.

  - Search for thematic vocabulary.

  - Use mentor text to model writing strategies.

  - Encourage students to draw from a variety of sources when researching a topic and not rely on Google searches.

- **Videos, DVDs**

  - Show ideas from social studies and science lessons.

  - Prepare English language learners for a new topic or new text by previewing the story or theme with a video.

  - Use musical tunes to help students with rote memory like learning multiplication tables, and principles of science.

- **Artifacts, models, manipulatives**

  - Show a model of a large building or human construction to support student's understanding of the complexity of its form and function.

  - Use counters, unifix cubes, base ten blocks, fraction pieces, and place-value charts, etc. to model and guide learning of math topics. This helps to bridge students' understanding of abstract equations, theories, and concepts.

  - Use period art to introduce, give context and bring a narrative or new perspective to historical periods and events.

- **Guest speakers and community members**

  - Use community experts and guest speakers to enrich and motivate student learning.

  - Ask a meteorologist to talk about weather. Other professionals who can share and model their work may be entrepreneurs, scientists, construction workers, engineers, election volunteers, or conservationists.

  - Community members can present and describe their work.

  - Guest speakers can role play, read stories, and provide new perspective on class themes and topics of study.

Interdisciplinary units

Teachers must integrate subjects when they are planning lessons. For example, language arts and social studies or math and science will often be integrated. Ideally, lessons should have a math, reading, social studies, and science component. Integrating arts is also important. Thematic and interdisciplinary units are beneficial because they:

- Provide students with opportunities to connect the skills and knowledge, and more importantly, apply what they have learned.

- Increase engagement and achievement because students learn information as it connects to other meaningful real-life situations.

- Maximize instructional time.

- Allow for deeper exploration of a topic (quality over quantity).

- Facilitate the use of culturally relevant texts.

- Focus on student-centered approach that encourages students to take ownership of their learning.

Thematic instruction

Thematic instruction is a type of interdisciplinary study based on a common topic. The basic idea behind a thematic unit is to use a topic like autumn, community, ancient Greek culture, or inventions of the 20th century to create content that includes interdisciplinary learning tasks. Academic vocabulary, writing, reading, math, and science can all be centered on a theme.

Sometimes teachers create a bubble map or curriculum web to brainstorm and connect instruction across disciplines. Look at the 7th grade unit below. This unit was developed using CCSS. Consider how science, writing, reading, and math learning objectives have been integrated into one focused learning theme.

Astronomy Unit (7th Grade)

Objectives

- Students understand size, composition, and surface features of planets.
- Students can develop a model representing the Earth, moon, and sun and describe the Earth's rotation and revolution.
- Students can describe lunar phases, eclipses, and seasons.
- Students can compare and contrast characteristics of objects in the solar system.
- Students understand how to use and interpret data to determine scale properties of objects in the solar system.

Essential questions

- How do contributions from scientists of the past affect our understanding of the solar system today?
- How can data from telescopes help to determine scale properties of objects in the solar system?
- How can a model be used to describe the cyclic patterns of the seasons, eclipses, and lunar phases?
- How does the distance from the sun affect a planet's physical features?

Misconceptions

- Seasons are caused by the weather.
- The sun and moon don't move; only the Earth moves.
- The sun and moon move; the Earth doesn't move.
- The moon generates light.
- There are other stars in our solar system besides the sun.
- The solar system and the galaxy are the same thing.

Vocabulary

Tier II: Astronomy, horizon, rotation, revolution, gravity, velocity, trajectory

Tier III: Apogee, celestial body, chromosphere, constellation, parallax, refracting telescope, reflecting telescope, zenith

Culminating activity

Students will design and redesign their solar system models to understand scale. Using unit vocabulary, students will describe solar and lunar eclipses, seasons, and lunar phases.

Thematic units

To design a thematic unit, continue to use the backward design method discussed earlier and begin with the standards that will drive what students need to know and be able to do. Project-based learning, culminating tasks, and interactive assessments align well with thematic learning however more traditional assessments can be integrated as well. Here is a flow chart with the development of a thematic unit in a classroom.

Theme: Unusual animals

Timing. Themes can be broad enough to cover an entire school year or as short as 2 weeks. Generally, thematic units are about 4 weeks. This is enough time to introduce new material and for students to demonstrate new knowledge and skills.

Topics. Align topics to standards and student interest.

1. Organize standards to guide the selection of a topic. You want a topic that is broad enough to incorporate standards from a variety of disciplines.

2. Choose a topic that is age appropriate and engaging for your group of students. It can be problem-based, related to a question that sparked great discussion, or a theme that is likely to be appealing to students year after year such as the rainforest.

Designing integrated learning activities

When designing integrated learning activities, focus on knowledge and skills students need to know and be able to do. Think about how skills from one discipline can be applied to another. For example, using primary documents to explore historical topics in social studies and applying close reading strategies learned in language arts. In this case, students can simultaneously be learning strategies to dissect text from primary sources in ELA while also learning about a historic period in social studies.

Planning guide. Use a planning guide offered by your school or district developed in your PLC. It will help keep content, activities, and attention to various essential knowledge and skills organized. Here is an example of potential activities for unit on unusual animals. Notice the correlation of learning activities to multiple disciplines and learning domains:

Learning Activity	Interdisciplinary Objectives	Learning Domains
Why do zebras have stripes? Identify adaptive features seen across species and habitats. Explore the origins of animal features that make them unusual.	**ELA:** Learning features of non-fiction text. Reading, note taking, synthesizing from a variety of sources. Researching science and social studies. **Science:** Identifying adaptive features and physical attributes of animals. Contrasting animal habitats.	Cognitive domain
Create a model of the animal, label its features, and build its habitat including life sustaining features.	**Art**: Identifying materials and building a model. **Science:** Labeling animal and habitat features. **ELA:** Explaining the features.	Cognitive, affective, and psychomotor domain
Measure and compare the wingspan of unusual birds. Use tape to mark out wing spans on the floor. Find the bird whose wingspan is closest to your own. Plan and construct a set of bird wings, replicating their aerodynamic features.	**Math:** Measuring and comparing. **Art:** Planning and constructing a set of aerodynamic wings **Science**: Understanding the impact of wingspan and meaning of aerodynamic.	Cognitive, affective, and psychomotor domain

Selecting resources. Make resources purposeful. Regardless of what resources you have available, the ones you select to use must support the essential learning of the unit.

For example, let students help decorate the classroom like a rainforest instead of doing it yourself. While decorating, have them identify what plants and animals they are making and explain their interdependence. In a unit on inventions use a variety of props including a display of artifacts, posters, and watch short videos of inspiring inventors to engage discussion, careful observation, and inferencing.

Finally, be selective. A virtual field trip might not be necessary if the class can visit a real animal sanctuary or observe unusual animals in the wild.

Designing assessments. Assessment should reflect learning related to standards. When possible, use rubrics, integrate self-assessment, and give students opportunities to revise their work. At times, students go beyond the standards in their learning during thematic units. However, assessments need to be directed at learning goals shared by everyone.

Interdisciplinary instruction. When teachers design interdisciplinary activities, they are combining two or more academic disciplines into one activity. This technique is effective in:

1. Making the routine practice of skills like reading and writing more engaging and purposeful.

2. Promoting real-world applications of subject matter because it integrates learning by drawing knowledge from several content areas.

Using interdisciplinary activities helps students to transfer their knowledge and become flexible thinkers. This technique also promotes critical thinking.

The following are example questions of how this might look on the PLT.

Example question

Which of the following would be the most effective way to help students relate their learning in one class to other disciplines?

    A. In English class, students write essays about science and math.

    B. In chemistry class, students use algebra to balance chemical equations.

    C. In social studies class, students listen to a guest speaker.

    D. In PE class, students work together on their fitness goals.

Correct Answer: B

In answer choice B, students are applying skills across content areas, which is interdisciplinary. Answer choices C and D have nothing to do with other content areas or disciplines. Answer choice A mentions other disciplines, but this is not an application of science and math in English class. Answer choice B is best because students are using a skill from one content area to accomplish a task in another content area.

Example question

Ms. Jensen is an English teacher trying to increase student motivation for reading informational text. Which of the following would be most effective?

    A. Reward students with extra computer time once they finish all of the required reading.

    B. Allow students to choose from current news stories that cover a variety of content areas.

    C. Send a letter home informing parents that students must read more informational text.

    D. Have the reading coach talk to the students about the importance of reading informational text.

Correct answer: B

Answer choice B encompasses two things: allowing students to choose text based on interest and relating text from different content areas to the real world (current events). External rewards, as in answer choice A, are not the best way to motivate students. Sending a letter home to parents or asking the reading coach to talk to students, as in answer choices C and D will not motivate students to want to read informational text.

Components of interdisciplinary units

Interdisciplinary units can be found in curriculum guides. To make them fit the interests of your students, meet the learning goals you have planned, and incorporate the resources you have available, they need to be planned at the school and classroom level. The process depends on the following:

1. Collaboration with team members.

2. Generating potential topics.

3. Developing a framework to integrate learning goals and learning disciplines.

4. Designing and planning how instruction will work in each discipline.

5. Creating integrated assessments so students can demonstrate their learning.

Collaborating with instructional partners is critical to the success of this process because of the diverse specialties and instructional roles each stakeholder contributes.

Instructional planning partners

As you move into the implementation stage of a thematic unit, consider the resources you have within your classroom and school building to support your instruction and student learning. People in different roles will support and enhance teaching and learning in various ways.

- **Special education teachers** and **gifted and talented teachers.** Support teachers can enrich students in and out of the classroom as part of instructional planning, implementation, and assessments. While they are assigned to help specific students in accordance to their IEP plans, support teachers benefit from understanding the larger goals and scope and sequence of the class. Ideally, classroom teachers meet with their support teachers on a routine basis to stay updated on their recommendations for modifications. In addition, support teachers can stay abreast with upcoming learning goals and tasks. They need to know what the teacher's instructional plan is so that they can make suggestions and design their interventions to support student learning.

- **Library media specialists.** Many schools have a media specialist who can support instruction and learning by finding relevant text in the library. The library specialist can also compile and support students to navigate online research sites. Some media specialists are licensed library scientists. In other cases, they are paraprofessionals assisting with organization and distribution. It is important to learn what the position details at your school.

- **IEP team members.** The IEP team assembles at least once a year to create, update, and revise IEPs for every student who is eligible for special services. During these meetings, the group will assess whether students have met IEP goals, need new IEP goals, or need to continue with the same goals with added scaffolding and modification from classroom and special education teachers. Teachers need to keep notes on the learning of students with IEPs so that informed changes and updates can be made during these meetings.

- **Paraprofessionals (or para educators).** The role of the paraprofessional is to support instruction and learning by working with students. They can meet with small groups, provide guidance during independent learning, and support whole-group learning. Paraprofessionals support learning by modeling. They often give gentle reminders to students who may be distracted or are still learning to self-regulate. The teacher should also provide paraprofessionals with specific instructions for evaluating small-group instruction or assessments. Paraprofessionals are not responsible for planning instruction or reflecting on student learning.

Roles in collaborative activities

When collaborating to design thematic, interdisciplinary units, all contributors have a specialty. Sharing responsibilities for planning includes deciding who will lead each learning task and be responsible for creating and evaluating assessments. It is also an opportunity to learn from others. On the PLT, look for answers with key words like *collaboration, interdisciplinary, and integration.* Collaboration is different than relying on partnerships to take over teaching.

Example question

A teacher is planning a culminating task for an upcoming unit on the space exploration and the solar system. She has integrated writing, reading, and math skills and knowledge into the culminating task and wants to make the appropriate accommodations and modifications for her IEP students. Who should she meet with to review the assessment?

A. The para educator who assists in her classroom

B. IEP team

C. Media specialist

D. Special education teacher

Correct answer: D

She needs to meet with the special education teacher to review accommodations outlined in the IEP and seek advice about modifications. The para educator may help to implement accommodations but is not involved in planning. The IEP team does not deal with day-to-day implementation of the IEP. The media specialist is most helpful for recommending and providing material resources.

This page intentionally left blank.

B. Instructional Strategies

1. Students' cognitive processes associated with learning

2. Types of instructional models and strategies

3. Promoting complex thinking

4. Strategies to support student learning

5. Promoting students' development of self-regulatory skills

6. Grouping techniques and cooperative learning

7. Strategies for achieving instructional objectives

8. Progress monitoring and adjusting instruction

9. Reflecting upon, analyzing, and evaluating instructional practice

10. Types of memory and their implications for learning and teaching

    • Short term

    • Long term

11. The role of teachable moments in the classroom

1. Students' cognitive processes associated with learning

Recall that cognitive processes are how students acquire knowledge and process information and can be described in the stages of Bloom's taxonomy. Just as Bloom's taxonomy is useful for learning objectives, it is useful for planning learning activities.

Critical thinking. This is multi-step, high-level thinking. Students are stretching in their thinking to analyze, evaluate, interpret, and synthesize information to reach a conclusion or make a judgment.

Creative thinking. This requires students to create something by applying their skills. When students apply their skills, they are operating at a high cognitive level.

Reflective thinking. Students look back on and reflect upon their learning process to promote abstract thinking and to encourage the application of learning strategies to new situations.

Questioning. Asking students questions at key points in the lesson is important because it keeps students engaged, develops critical thinking, and allows the teacher to check for understanding at various levels. Questions should go beyond simple recall questions (yes/no questions or low-level questions). Asking students to develop their own open-ended questions about a text or lesson is also a strategy to develop higher order thinking.

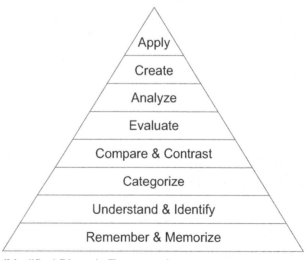

(Modified Bloom's Taxonomy)

Inductive and deductive reasoning. These are upper level cognitive processes used to improve students understanding of a concept or property. Look at the example in the table below. To decide the rule that changes the input number to the output number, students need to use *deductive reasoning*. Deductive reasoning can be used to figure out word patterns and other relationships across the curriculum.

In	Out
28	43
45	60
112	127

Inductive reasoning is the same process in reverse. If a teacher told a student, "My rule is to add 15," the student would need to show examples of numbers in the In and Out box that increase by 15.

Problem-solving. This can employ a number of cognitive processes. Typically, students are presented with a problem specific to the subject being studied. Then they have to follow a series of steps to find solutions and identify the best one. Problem-solving has many uses such as contemplating social issues, finding solutions to math problems, and making predictions while reading.

Planning. This is the analytical process of decision making and sequencing to create a plan to complete a task. It is an executive function that can be developed through explicit instruction followed by practice, feedback, and self-reflection.

Memory. Memory is essential to learning. Learning experiences influence the types of memory students use to engage with content as well as how they store new knowledge and practice new skills.

Recall. This is the process of remembering details related to a memory. For example, when a teacher asks students to solve a long division problem, students must recall the steps for long division.

Test Tip

On the PLT, you will see questions that ask about higher order thinking. Tasks that require students to evaluate, analyze, create, and apply are higher order thinking. A trick to identifying objectives and tasks with higher order thinking on the PLT is to consider student answers in the scenario. If student responses can be different or inconsistent and still be correct, the objective is likely higher order thinking.

Example question

A class of students is learning about Ancient Greek civilization. The class is asked to debate whether it was better to be a Spartan or an Athenian. To argue their claim in this discussion, students will primarily use which type of thinking?

A. Memorization

B. Compare and contrast

C. Deductive reasoning

D. Planning

Correct answer: C

To persuade the audience, students need clear reasoning to demonstrate why one side is better than the other using logical thinking. While they will need to plan their argument to cite evidence, and may want to compare and contrast elements of life in both cities, deductive and inductive reasoning are critical to being persuasive in a debate. Memorizing facts is not a sophisticated enough level of thinking for this assignment.

2. Types of instructional models and strategies

For the PLT, you will need to understand and identify different instructional models in practice. We combined sections 2 and 3, the features and strategies for different instructional methods, because they are closely related.

The following tables provide detailed descriptions of the characteristics and implementation strategies of various instructional models. Good teachers understand the following models for instruction and strategies to implement them.

Direct instruction

Direct instruction is straight-forward and sequential instruction delivered to students from the teacher. It is useful for introducing and explaining important knowledge and concepts. The following are examples of direct instruction used in K-6 classrooms.

Direct Instructional Strategies	Purpose	Example
Explicit teaching	Breaking down a topic into smaller parts and teaching them individually. The purpose is to simplify and clarify.	Teaching students to recognize and use suffixes like -s, -es, -ed, -ing by reciting and writing a list of words and categorizing them.
Drill and practice	Repetition of a specific set of facts. The intention is memorization.	Call and response practice of spelling words, phonemes, word patterns, math facts, or steps in a process.
Lecture	Speaking to students on a topic, typically using power point presentations, dry erase or chalk board, or other visuals as props.	Introducing a social studies topic such as events leading to the Civil Rights Movement.
Demonstrations	Showing students a process, concept, or idea.	Demonstrating a science experiment. Modeling learning behaviors such as revising a piece of writing using a document camera.
Guides for reading, listening, viewing	Often referred to as graphic organizers, they are used for reading, listening, or viewing new material. The guides typically include previewing vocabulary, summarizing main ideas, and questioning to check for comprehension.	A guide for viewing a video being shown on photosynthesis. A "cause and effect in narrative writing" guide used by students as they listen to an episode of a mystery podcast.

Indirect instruction

This comes from constructivism or the idea that students derive and construct their own meaning from experiences. As an instructional practice, it means teachers are responsible for creating an environment for meaningful learning experiences to happen. Indirect instruction is considered a student-driven instructional model.

Indirect Instructional Strategies	Purpose	Examples
Problem solving	Inclusive of many higher order thinking strategies including creative, critical, and analytical thinking. Allows students to apply learning by identifying problems and various solutions.	Math word problems. Finding the problem in a story and suggesting several possible solutions before reading to the end. Peer-resolution groups or playground representatives; students who are designated to help their peers to resolve disagreements and disputes.
Inquiry	Students explore, ask and seek answers to why and how things happen.	Using KWL charts and *Think, See, Wonder* routines. Asking and pursuing answers to phenomena of the natural world. Exploring numerical concepts or find the most efficient method for solving problems.
Case studies	Case studies are a type of problem-based learning. Researching or finding insight into a topic by looking deeply at one case or situation. Students can watch a short video or read a text to learn and find context about a case.	Reviewing global issues like schooling for girls or child labor. Tackling community questions like, *How can we start a student government for our school? Or What do we need to create a class garden?*
Concept mapping	A graphic display of information on a topic to contextualize and connect concepts. They are especially useful for visual learners.	Reviewing lecture notes. Contextualizing research from various sources. Summarizing a process or relationships between ideas such as food chains or life cycles.
Reading for meaning	Strategies for making sense of complex text. Prompts students to preview, search for significant information while reading and reflect after reading.	Analyze: • Math word problems • Charts, graphs • Article or short story

Indirect Instructional Strategies	Purpose	Examples
Cloze procedures	Assessing comprehension or understanding by supplying most of a paragraph or sentence and asking students to complete the rest.	Using verbs, nouns, or other parts of speech. Recalling the details of a short story or reading.

Independent instruction

These are learning opportunities directed by students. Students are seeking out specific knowledge and developing self-regulation skills. The teacher's role is having appropriate time and materials prepared and classroom structures in place for on-task work. Like indirect-instruction, independent instruction is considered student-driven instructional models.

Independent Instructional Strategies	Purpose	Examples
Learning contracts	A voluntary agreement, usually in writing, between a student(s) and teacher about what tasks will be completed and by what time.	"I will" statements for: completing work, staying on task, contributing to group projects, and being prepared with comments for class discussions.
Research projects	To explore and present information about a chosen topic of interest	Student choses a topic within a class theme of study.
Computer mediated instruction	Any instruction and learning that involves computers or technology.	Complete a Webquest. Write a story in a shared document. Watch informational videos. Use a QR code to locate research materials.
Learning centers	Short and contained learning tasks that students can manage by themselves and in small groups. Learning centers may be thematic or differentiated to meet student learning preferences and needs.	During a reading workshop, a class is set up for students to rotate in small groups to 1) read independently, 2) listen to reading, 3) solve phonic pattern puzzles, and 4) read with the teacher.
Distance learning	Virtual or online learning can be synchronous or asynchronous. Students may be listening and learning with the teacher in real time or have a list of tasks to complete on their own time accompanied by explanations or video instructions.	A student cannot come to school because they have an autoimmune disorder.

Experiential and virtual instruction

Experiential learning is learning by doing. This means learning tasks where students are actively engaged socially, physically, and mentally in the learning taking place. They often include going on field trips, acting out scenarios, and creating projects. This is also a student-centered instructional model.

Experiential and Virtual Instructional Strategies	Purpose	When you might use it
Field trips	Experiencing and connecting to content in a new way. Providing a shared experience for the class to reflect and process classroom learning.	A trip to the zoo before beginning (or after) a unit on animals and their habitats. Virtual field trips are a good substitute for real field trips when resources and time are unavailable.
Experiments	Developing, implementing, and understanding the process for proving claims and hypothesis. Students use problem-solving, inductive reasoning, and higher-order thinking in the process of setting up and conducting experiments.	Building ramps that make cars go faster and farther. Consider what happens when combining different substances.
Simulations	A situation where an environment is designed for students to experience a scenario or setting. The idea is for them to interact and glean meaning from the experience.	Oregon Trail is a stimulus game entailing the hardships and realities of exploring the landscape and natural resources of the northwest in the early 20th century. Setting up an event, time, or place for students to have an experience. Pretending to be planets orbiting the sun.
Role play	Pretending to be characters in a story, time, place, or event to better appreciate specific feelings, perspective, and experience.	Acting out a scene from a novel. Role playing an event from U.S. history. Children having a disagreement on the playground with positive and negative outcomes.
Games	Games help students understand concepts, practice them, and engage with classmates. They can be cooperative and competitive.	Whole group math games practicing percentages, statistics, and probability. Scavenger hunts Small group concept review games such as identifying famous battles on a map.
Observations	Observing the learning behaviors of another person or class. Recall social learning theory and the significance of modeling. These observations are self-motivated and initiated.	Watching a builder construct a house. Observing animals on a farm or navigating in the wild.

Interactive instruction

Interactive instruction is learning by interacting with other people. This includes student-to-student, student-to-teacher, and teacher-to-student interaction. Instruction is student-centered with social interaction as the key component.

Interactive Instructional Strategies	Purpose	Examples
Brainstorming	Collect many ideas at once, engage students in a new topic, or begin an inquiry.	KWL charts. Asking students to think of types of transportation or names of reptiles.
Cooperative learning groups	Students work on a project or task together.	Book clubs. Experimenting with building materials to make a sturdy bridge.
Interviews	To hear an expert opinion or new perspective.	Gathering information for an essay on community or an autobiography Conducting surveys to collect and analyze data.
Discussions	Discussions are a way of co-constructing knowledge with students, checking for understanding, gauging student interest, and diving deeper into a topic. Useful across the curriculum.	Discussing why a math problem is wrong and how to fix it. Discussing cause-effect in a novel. Discussing engaging topics such as how to help stray animals.
Peer practice	To discuss a text, students work in small groups, alternating role of teacher and students. They cycle through the tasks of predicting, questioning, clarifying, and summarizing in any order.	Guided reading groups. Reading a text to prepare for a science activity. Learning new content on a social studies topic.
Debates	These are discussions with at least two clear sides to an issue. They are used like discussions but also entail preparation to defend and address counter arguments to strong argument.	They can be used to improve comprehension of a text, understand multiple perspectives to an issue, or prepare for argumentative essay writing.

Example question

Which of the following is an example of indirect teaching?

A. Peer practice

B. Experiment

C. Reading guide

D. Cloze procedure

Correct answer: D

Remember, indirect instruction is where the teacher provides an environment for students to drive their own instruction. Answer choices A and B are student-driven instructional strategies; however, they are considered interactive and experiential and allow for more student direction than indirect instruction. Answer choice C is direct instruction because students are following a predetermined set of thinking tasks as they read.

3. Promoting complex thinking

Complex cognitive processes

In the classroom, learning tasks require various types of cognitive processing or ways of thinking. While cognitive processes include basic memory, recall, understanding, and identifying, complex cognitive processes represent the higher levels of thinking in Bloom's Taxonomy. We have discussed many of them, including **transfer, problem solving**, **metacognition,** and **critical thinking** earlier in this text. Concept learning is another cognitive process used to create meaningful learning tasks.

Think about it!

All cognitive processes need to be explicitly taught. For example, students will know how and when to use metacognition once they can identify it, see it modeled, and practiced many times. Like reading, students need guidance through these steps, or the thinking process will not be developed to its capacity.

Concept learning is both creating categories for objects and classifying objects into categories to improve, identify, and understand their relationships.

For example, a student uses a spreadsheet to record weather data to determine which regions are best for certain types of agriculture. The "good regions" will depend on the relationships between the variables (weather) and the ideal conditions for each type of crop. It is a complex cognitive process because it must be constructed through knowledge and analysis; it is not a simple memorization process.

Instructional activities for complex cognitive processes

On the PLT you will see patterns of questions that require you to identify activities and methods that will increase students' complex cognitive processes. These questions are embedded in every competency on the exam.

While memorizing facts, dates, and events is part of learning, memorization is considered a low cognitive skill. Although low cognitive skills are sometimes necessary to teach, teachers should strive for students to think critically by analyzing, evaluating, applying and creating. A lesson full of low cognitive skills with little or no higher order thinking is not considered highly effective.

Designing classroom activities to develop complex cognitive processes is intended to move students from concrete and sequential thinking to more abstract and complex thoughts and understanding. While complex cognitive processes need to be explicitly taught through direct instruction and modeling, subsequent practice is best facilitated through student-centered instruction (interactive, experiential, and indirect).

Quick Tip

Remember, when answering questions regarding complex cognitive processes, visualize Bloom's Taxonomy. Complex cognitive processes are applicable in all aspects of teaching and is embedded in questions from every competency on the PLT. Be sure to go back and reference the modified version of Bloom's Taxonomy in this book.

The following are some examples of techniques that develop students' complex cognitive processes or higher-order thinking skills. For the PLT, you will have to identify scenarios that support higher-order thinking skills. It is important that you have the ability to adapt the examples below when answering PLT questions. Notice the verbs in each example. The verbs indicate if the activity requires higher-order skills.

- Students **compare and contrast leaves** from different deciduous trees.
- Students **sequence** the stages of the water cycle.
- Students **generalize** the differences and similarities between weather in Africa and South America.
- Students **synthesize** their research on Ancient Greek civilizations to discuss the roots of modern democracy.
- Students **summarize** the main themes of the novel.
- Students collaborate to **make decisions** about their playground equipment proposal.
- Students **categorize** statements as fact or opinion in news articles.
- Students **detect bias** in a text by exploring what facts have been omitted and what words create a negative impression.
- Students **infer** how the setting impacted the characters choices and use this evidence to **predict** how the story will be resolved.
- Students **generate questions** to be answered in a science experiment.
- Students **analyze** the structure of two pieces of text and **determine** how the structure impacts meaning.
- Students **discuss** historical events and **evaluate** how those events impacted future events.
- Students **create** an at-home exercise plan based on what they learned about life-long fitness.
- Students **apply** their knowledge of chemical reactions as they **perform** a baking soda science lab.
- Students **create** an equation, then **graph** the equation to **make a prediction**.

Complex cognitive thinking processes for all ages

Good teachers use complex cognitive thinking processes (or higher order thinking) with all ages of students. Developmentally appropriate activities develop complex cognitive processes in all students. Regardless of age, learning style, disability, or English language proficiency, students can learn cognitive thinking processes with good support.

Example question

A 7th grade math teacher is preparing a unit on the slope-intercept form of an equation. Which of the following activities would be most appropriate if the teacher wants the students to engage in critical thinking?

A. Several word problems assigned for homework.

B. Choice board activity that requires explanations and application of slope-intercept form equations.

C. Write and memorize the parts of an equation in slope-intercept form.

D. Direct instruction lesson on how to graph equations in slope-intercept form with guided practice.

Correct answer: B

Although word problems may require the use of critical thinking skills, there is no guarantee that this is true for all word problems or that students won't just guess at the answers. Therefore, we can eliminate choice A. Memorizing is not a critical thinking skill, and the teacher providing all the instruction does not necessarily require critical thinking. The best answer choice for this question is B because students get to choose from activities where they are writing about or applying their knowledge of equations in slope-intercept form. Both these activities require higher order thinking skills.

Example question

A student sorts sentences in a paragraph as opinions or fact categories. She justifies her organization to a partner. What complex cognitive process is NOT being used to complete this task?

A. Generalizing

B. Categorizing

C. Distinguishing fact from opinion

D. Analyzing

Correct answer: A.

To complete this task, the student needs to analyze each sentence and then categorize them to distinguish fact and opinion. The students are not generalizing, or making inferences from only a few facts, but analyzing and organizing details.

Example question

A student says, "I think he will run away because he doesn't want to be hurt by the big dragon spitting fire everywhere." In this statement, the student is demonstrating which complex cognitive thinking process:

A. Summarizing

B. Distinguishing bias

C. Inferring

D. Decision making

Correct answer: C

The student is inferring that the character is afraid of the big dragon, especially because it is breathing fire. While all answer choices are higher order thinking, in the example, the student is not summarizing, making decisions, or distinguishing the character's bias.

4. Strategies to support student learning

The current educational philosophy is that every student can learn at a high level. However, supporting all students to understand content and use complex cognitive thinking strategies means reflecting on formative assessments and using a variety of instructional strategies. Teachers need to use strategies in their planning and everyday instruction. We have already discussed scaffolding and modeling as effective instructional strategies to support all learners. Be ready to use differentiated instruction, guided practice, development of self-regulation skills, and coaching on a regular basis as well.

Modeling

As discussed in Bandura's social learning theory (SLT), modeling is demonstrating and purposefully showing students how to complete a task, engage in a discussion, or use academic vocabulary.

When to use this strategy:

- Introducing and reviewing protocols and procedures.
- Demonstrating how centers, independent reading, or other facilitated, but not directed, learning will work.
- Showing students a learning behavior such as revising a paper, checking a math problem for accuracy, or using metacognition while reading.

Developing self-regulation skills

Teaching students to make informed decisions about their actions and behaviors is critical to academic success. Students need support to routinely identify their feelings, understand their choices of action, and reinforce positive self-regulation behaviors. They can be taught through games, explicit instruction, and with support items like a recentering corner, discussion scenarios, mindfulness and brain breaks, and reading and discussing mentor text.

When to use this strategy:

- On a daily basis, students are practicing self-regulation throughout the school day. Keep in mind that these are learned behaviors and not innate.
- When the whole class or just one student is struggling with self-regulation, adults can be quick to punish. However, this is an opportunity for learning through instruction.
- Routine teacher support and intervention reaffirms student development and supports conscious on-going practice.
- Integrate explicit instruction, games, modeling, and discussing as needed for whole group and small groups.
- Differentiate and scaffold for students who struggle with organization, staying on task, communicating in cooperative groups, and engaging in other learning activities.

Coaching

Coaching is a type of guided instruction. The teacher is not telling students how to go about a learning task, the teacher is simply listening, paraphrasing, and offering feedback to their process.

For example, a teacher is working with a small group to apply concepts of trigonometry. She posts a problem with a mistake in it and asks students if it is answered correctly. The students begin to discuss what they see. The teacher coaches them by letting them work through their misconceptions through peer questioning and building arguments with strong evidence. The teacher does not evaluate the content they discussed. The teacher only intervenes to make sure everyone is talking and to keep the conversation on task.

When to use this strategy:

- To support students reading a text at their instructional level.
- When students are conducting a science experiment by following directions in a book.
- Any time a student is working in their zone of proximal development.

Guided practice

This is a critical phase for all learners. It comes between explicit instruction and independent practice and learning. It is a time when teachers can specialize how they promote self-regulating behavior, differentiate instruction, offer feedback, scaffold learning, and encourage confidence. This is when teachers closely observe students and give constant feedback to support their understanding and confidence in their new knowledge and skill.

Creating guided practice routines:

- **Whole group.** After a mini lesson, teach students to stop and jot down ideas, turn and talk to a partner, rehearse their writing or steps in their learning task so that you, the teacher, can monitor their comprehension.

- **Small group.** In a guided reading group, students can read aloud at their own pace while teachers listen to one student at a time. Students also retell what they have read, share predictions, inferences, and analysis. Guided practice in small groups is useful to review and reinforce math and writing concepts as well.

Think about it!

Higher-order thinking needs to be scaffolded like other knowledge and skills. When prompting students to practice a skill, be more specific at first. For example, in the beginning of the year ask, "What do you predict Atticus will do after learning he would face 12 dragons instead of one?" Later in the year you can ask, "What do you predict will happen next?"

- **One-on-one.** When students are working independently, teachers can guide instruction to individual students. Prepare students to share their writing, ask questions, and/or continue working while teachers are observing their learning behaviors and understanding of the learning content.

Confer with students

As students begin to work independently, listen to what they say in their *think, pair, and share,* and read what they write when jotting down ideas. Ask questions to extend their thinking. Take time to reteach or refer to visual guides with a student or a small group when they need additional assistance. Take notes on who will need further scaffolding and support once the class moves to independent work.

As you observe and confer with students, note good examples of learning behaviors and strong answers. Share these out with the whole group before moving on to independent practice. This reaffirms students who are ready to work independently and gives one more model to all students.

(Reading Recovery, 2019)

Differentiating instruction

Differentiating instruction is a theme throughout the PLT. As a classroom teacher, it is important to acknowledge that not every student can learn at a high level at the same pace or with the same ease. This is where strategies to differentiate come in. It is important that the standards and expectations remain rigorous for every student in the classroom, regardless of their achievement levels. However, teachers can use differentiation in the form of accommodations and scaffolding to help struggling learners reach the standard or expectation for the lesson.

Teachers can use screening, diagnostic, or current state and district assessments to identify the patterns of development among their students. Teachers can then decide how to differentiate the lesson to make sure all students' needs are being met. Teachers can differentiate the lesson in a variety of ways.

- **Differentiated content**. This is the *what* of the lesson.
- **Differentiated process**. This is the *how* of the lesson.
- **Differentiated product**. This is the *result* of the lesson.

The following is an example scenario of differentiated instruction.

Element	Scenario
Differentiated content	Based on leveled groups, students will analyze poems at varying difficulty levels. This can be done through selecting various types of text at varying levels to accommodate learners. This can also be done by presenting content in various forms—written, video, interactive, physical—to support students' learning preferences.
Differentiated process	After a short, whole-group lesson on metaphors, students will split into small groups. The struggling students will first work in the teacher-led station to identify what is being compared in the metaphors that the teacher has highlighted in a poem at their level. They will then practice what they have learned with different poems at their level. The students who are on grade level will identify and interpret the metaphors in the set of poems they are given. They will visit the teacher-led center to check understanding and work on a slightly more difficult poem with teacher support. The students who exceed grade-level expectations will explain the effects of the author's use of the metaphors in the set of poems they are given. They will meet with the teacher to discuss their analyses and explore how the effects would be different had the author used literal terms instead.
Differentiated product	To demonstrate mastery at the end of a reading unit, students choose from the following performance-based activities: • Write a persuasive essay • Design a brochure • Record a podcast • Build a presentation

Given the data below, what instructional adjustments would be most appropriate?

Math Proficiency for Whole Class:

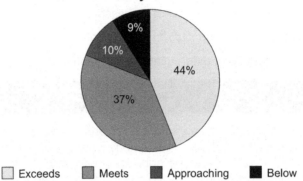

☐ Exceeds   ▨ Meets   ▨ Approaching   ■ Below

A. Deliver a short, whole-group lesson on a targeted math standard, then have students rotate through differentiated math centers while providing appropriate intervention and enrichment at a teacher-led center.

B. Group the students who are approaching and meet grade-level expectations with those who exceed expectations for peer tutoring while providing the students who are struggling with intensive interventions.

C. Send the students who are below grade-level expectations out of the classroom for intensive interventions while delivering whole-group instruction at grade level for the remaining students.

D. Tailor whole-group instruction to meet the needs of those students who meet or exceed grade-level expectations while calling in a resource teacher to work with the other students during the literacy block.

Correct answer: A

Notice all the good words in this answer choice A: *math standard, differentiated, appropriate intervention.* Also, because there are a variety of levels in this class, providing students the opportunity to work as a whole and then break out into differentiated math centers is most appropriate.

Example question

Which of the following is not a strategy for supporting student learning?

A. Meeting with guided reading groups.

B. Sharing inferences about the text while reading aloud to the class.

C. Chunking the steps in long division using an acronym.

D. Promising students free time after completing a task with 100% accuracy.

Correct answer: D

Answer choice A is an example of guided practice, answer choice B is an example of modeling, and answer choice C is scaffolding. These are all strategies for supporting student learning. Answer choice D is problematic because the teacher has offered no real support for understanding the task, only an extrinsic reward. No motivator will work if the students do not understand the content.

5. Promoting students' development of self-regulatory skills

Self-regulation skills can take a long time for students to master. Intentionally teaching and practicing these skills will support students' growth and development.

Supporting student self-regulatory skills

- **Setting goals.** Students set goals to have concrete ideas about progress as well as to be able to celebrate when progress is made. Goals should be specific enough so that students can reach them and understand their significance. Goals should relate to content learning. Goals can be made for independent work time. For example, a teacher ends her writing conferences with her students by setting a new goal to self-monitor their writing. This might include a goal such as, "I will add more dialogue to my narrative." This goal is revisited and discussed the next time they meet.

- **Managing time.** Support time management by giving students warnings before transitions between independent and group work, creating goals and deadlines for large writing projects during one-to-one conferring, and helping them build stamina as readers and writers. Using a classroom timer and graphing whole group time on task behaviors support students individually as well as underscore the significance of time management for all students.

- **Organizing information.** Be intentional about modeling organization of learning classroom and personal materials. Give students graphic organizers and other strategies for categorizing and connecting their learning from various experiences and explicit instruction. Model how to organize information and use successful student work as examples. The process of using organizational tools such as two-column note taking, the writing process, math procedures, and reading response logs need to be taught explicitly to students. Teachers need to provide time throughout the school year to practice how to organize information and how to use these valuable tools.

- **Monitoring progress.** Students can monitor their own progress through routine self-assessments, building personal portfolios, and graphing their own assessment data. Progress monitoring can also be checklists for independent learning tasks, and for literacy or math centers. Progress monitoring is aligned with metacognitive and reflective thinking as well as personal goal setting.

- **Reflecting on outcomes.** When students reflect on their outcomes, they are reengaging in the learning. They have to consider whether their learning process and product aligns with the expectations. Typically, this review is done with a rubric or checklist. Students do this through metacognition, analysis of expectations, goal setting, reviewing rubric scores, and considering their learning behaviors. Reflection can happen in whole group, small group, and individualized settings. It needs to be taught explicitly with modeling and reviewed with a focus on reflection.

- **Establishing a productive work environment.** All students can reflect on what they need to work efficiently. They can monitor the state of their work environment by considering how to best arrange and manage materials, organize their time, and when available, choosing where and how to sit. Teachers can model these behaviors, and prompt students to review their own choices with checklists and whole-class routines.

Group configurations for learning

Different group configurations are useful for engaging students in different types and stages in the learning process. Here are some of the most common configurations and what you might see on the PLT.

Group Configuration	Teacher Role	Student Role
Whole-class Students are all together sitting at desk, tables, or on the carpet with a central focus. **Small-group** Students are sitting together working in groups of 3-6. They may be led/facilitated by the students or their teacher. Small groups may reflect learning needs or be formed heterogeneously.	• Leading discussion. • Explaining protocols. • Modeling learning behaviors. • Giving explicit instruction. • Facilitating guided practice.	• Actively listening and responding to teacher and peers. • Asking clarifying questions. • Using higher order thinking and complex cognitive processes. • Demonstrating understanding. • Practicing new skills. • Contextualizing new learning and background knowledge.
Independent learning Students work alone in a separated work area.	• Creating sustainable structure. • Facilitating stamina. • Supporting learning and providing feedback when necessary.	• Engaging in inquiry and investigation. • Practicing skills. • Memorizing facts. • Composing writing. • Reading and thinking independently about the text. • Creating ideas, plans learning, hypothesizing.
One-on-one One student sits with a teacher. Sessions are usually 3-10 minutes long while other students work independently or in small groups.	• Conferring with a student. • Helping a student transition from rehearsing their writing to composing on paper. • Reading or listening to sections of writing and guiding revisions. • Conducting a running record. • Processing a math problem or concept for clarity and understanding of a student's thinking process. • Reviewing concepts and skills. • Assessing for understanding.	• Metacognitive thinking. • Communicating goals, questions, understanding of concepts and skills. • Sharing work on a task. • Engaging in learning. • Demonstrating understanding. • Asking questions. • Reviewing and setting new learning goals.

Group Configuration	Teacher Role	Student Role
Pair/share Usually happens during whole group or small group guided instruction. Students are adjacent to their pair and turn to face them when talking or listening.	• Observing and guiding learning.	• Sitting close to their partner. • Actively listening and responding to partner's contributions (paraphrasing, adding on, questioning). • Responding to teacher-initiated questioning.

Example Problem

A 9th grade student is struggling with identifying claims and supportive reasoning in a persuasive essay. The student prefers to work with others rather than on her own. What can the teacher do to promote learning for this student?

    A. Send the student home with additional homework to practice reading nonfiction text.

    B. Pair the student with an academic buddy with strong comprehension skills.

    C. Conduct explicit whole group instruction on identifying claims and reasoning in a nonfiction text.

    D. Reward the student with extra social time if she completes her work independently.

Correct Answer: B

Because the student prefers to work with others, pairing her with an academic buddy who is strong in the areas she is weak is most effective here. Answers A and C do nothing to promote learning specifically for this student. Answer D is incorrect because it promotes external rewards.

6. Grouping techniques and cooperative learning

Cooperative learning

Cooperative learning is an instructional strategy that focuses on students working together to achieve a common goal. This process uses mixed ability groups to increase all members' understanding of a subject.

It is important to remember, anytime you implement cooperative learning, all students must be accountable for their learning. Cooperative learning is not just group work where one student does all the work and the others sit back and put their names at the top of the paper. Effective cooperative learning requires all students to participate and add to the learning experience. Examples include the following:

- **Literature circles.** These are small group, in-depth discussions using a piece of literature or text. This activity is driven by student inquiry and reflection.

- **Socratic seminar (Socratic method).** This is a formal discussion, based on a text, in which the leader asks open-ended questions. Within the context of the discussion, students listen closely to the comments of others, thinking critically and articulate their critical responses to others. Students learn to work cooperatively and to question intelligently and civilly. Socratic Seminars can be small group or include the whole class.

- **Small group or partners.** This is an interactive activity where students work collaboratively during the learning process.

When students construct knowledge together, they are learning collaboratively. This can happen in partners and in small groups. Students need guidance or time to create group rules for productive teamwork. Group problem-solving, creating, and planning involves paraphrasing and adding on to ideas, defending claims, listening and responding to others, synthesizing and considering others' perspectives, and/or compromising for a better process and product.

The challenge of collaborative learning is picking the right tasks and teaching students the norms and routines of productive group work. When grouping students for cooperative learning, small groups, or remediation/enrichment groups, teachers can use homogenous or heterogenous grouping.

- **Homogeneous groups.** Everyone in the group has been identified as having the same learning need or are all at the proficiency level. For example, a group of all level 3 readers. Homogenous groups should be used to address specific needs such as reading fluency and comprehension skills. These groups should change regularly, always target a specific learning objective, and be reflective of the most recent assessments. ***Maintaining the same homogenous group for a long time can impact student self-esteem and be counterproductive.***

Caution

Using homogeneous grouping is typically NOT the correct answer on this exam. Groups should be heterogenous and reflect the different learning levels and interests of the class.

- **Heterogeneous groups.** Groups are formed so that there is a variety of learning levels and student interests. For example, grouping students by a reading strategy such as making inferences about character choices in a text rather than reading scores will provide more diversity among the group members. Heterogeneous grouping should be used most classroom activities.

- **Multi-age grouping.** Some learning philosophies such as Montessori, regularly rely on multi-age grouping to provide on-going opportunities for modeling, mentoring, and perspective taking. Research has shown many benefits to social-emotional, academic and language development for students in multi-age settings (Stone, 2019). For example, individual differences in development tend to be emphasized more than age level expectations which can support student growth without stigmatism. The disadvantage to this kind of grouping is rearranging and rewriting curriculum because Common Core Standards are aligned to single grade level classes as well as keeping up with individualized instruction and assessment.

- **Grouping by gender.** Grouping students by gender is a traditional way to quickly divide the class into equal parts that are typically heterogeneous. ***Unfortunately, there are disadvantages to grouping students by gender.***

    1. More than ever, some students are considering or already identifying as non-binary or gender neutral,

    2. Research shows students generally learn better in mixed gendered groups (Puntambekar, 2013),

    3. Grouping students by gender may reinforce gender stereotypes.

A teacher is designing a lesson on planning techniques for expository writing. She will model planning and rehearsing the organization of their writing out loud. Next, she wants students to work in small groups to plan and rehearse their own writing. What kind of grouping would be most effective for this learning task?

    A. Homogenous groups

    B. Gender based groups

    C. Heterogenous groups

    D. Collaborative learning groups

Correct answer: C

Students should be grouped heterogeneously for this task because it is a short opportunity for them to share their planning with peers. Answer choice A is wrong because this is not a leveled skill associated with assessment scores but a routine part of the writing process that everyone works through. Answer choice D is wrong because students are not writing a story together. They are only providing feedback for individual projects. Answer choice B is incorrect because it is no more effective and more complicated than simply creating heterogenous groups.

7. Strategies for achieving instructional objectives

Lesson planning requires careful alignment to instructional objectives in conjunction with engaging and meaningful learning activities. Once you know what students need to know and be able to do, select the best instructional strategies along with a sequence for using them, to support student learning. Here is a sample lesson plan with an emphasis on the instructional strategies. The plan includes the following:

1. Typical time frame for each step of a lesson.

2. Questions and considerations for each step in the process.

3. Sample instructional strategies.

Think about why these instructional strategies, and the order they are used, are effective. On the PLT, you will need to be able to identify what is an effective or ineffective instructional strategy.

Lesson Plan Stage	Questions and Considerations	Sample Instructional Strategies
Identify learning goals and write corresponding learning objectives	Keep informing standards and the number of learning objectives to a minimum. 1-2 learning objectives is enough, even for a lesson that lasts 2-5 days.	Students will explore the strengths of various magnets. Students will classify items according to their ability to be attracted by a magnet. Students will compare and describe their classification groups.
Connect to background knowledge (5 minutes)	Assess background knowledge: How much do students know about the content? Is this a reading strategy they have practiced all year or a science property they are learning for the first time?	**Whole group:** Show students two objects and ask them to predict what will happen if they are placed near magnets. **Pair/share:** Students share their predictions and reasoning with their partners.

Lesson Plan Stage	Questions and Considerations	Sample Instructional Strategies
Introduce new content (10 minutes)	Selecting instructional strategies that match the learning goals. Consider the interests and needs of the class. Focus on the thinking skills students will need to practice or demonstrate after the lesson. When breaking students into small groups, plan ahead of time how groups will be formed.	**Constructivist learning:** Share some of the answers overheard between partners (or have student share out). **Demonstrate:** Show what happens when the objects are placed in front of a magnet. **Explicit instruction:** Introduce *repel* and *attract* as vocabulary to describe the observed phenomena. Write them on the board. Use them while modeling. Emphasize them when describing magnetism. **Assess:** Use thumbs up/down and let 1-2 students rephase instructions for learning activity before students break into small groups.
Facilitate guided and independent practice (20-30 minutes)	Keep it simple. Rely on learning routines already in place such as independent work or center work while the teacher facilitates group work or reviews and differentiates for one group at a time small group. It is common that more than one strategy is necessary for students to fully comprehend the content.	**Small group:** Students work through a variety of objects predicting whether they will be magnetic or not and then testing them on a real magnet. **Independent:** Students classify their predictions and compare it to their tests. **Guide:** Review by modeling for students who need support.
Formative assessment	Guiding and facilitating independent practice require observation and attention to student behaviors. There is no written component to this lesson, so the assessment has to be done through presentation and discussion.	**Assessment:** Use a checklist and record anecdotal notes. • Did students classify objects? • Can they explain their findings in full sentences using key vocabulary?
Reflect and close (5 -7 minutes)	Always find a way to end the lesson where students reflect on their learning. This provides one more opportunity to assess their learning.	**Whole-group:** Student groups share their classified groups and describe the attributes of objects in each group. **Whole-class discussion:** Is there a pattern between objects in different groups? What is the same and different between groups? Are there any objects you would have classified differently and why? **Assessment:** Continue checklist and anecdotal note taking.

8. Progress monitoring and adjusting instruction

Monitoring is the process of keeping track of what students are learning with the intent of giving feedback and **adjusting** or making decisions about instruction.

Monitoring and adjusting instruction are:

- Changes, additions, and omissions to content and instructional strategies before, during, and after a lesson or learning period.

- A reflection of student understanding, engagement, and learning preferences.

- Informed by on-going formative assessment.

Strategies for monitoring instruction

Before and after a lesson:

- Review student responses, anecdotal notes, checklists, and student writing. Decide what needs to be reviewed, reinforced, and practiced by the whole class, small groups, and individual students.

During a lesson:

- Begin by connecting lesson to previous learning. Quiz the class on vocabulary, ask them to guess a concept by its description, have them draw a picture to organize notes from the previous lesson.

- Use white boards for students to work out math problems or word patterns and show their work discretely when they are finished.

- Ask students to self-assess their understanding by raising 1, 2, or 3 fingers or indicate red (completely lost), yellow (confused), or green (understand).

- Other strategies to use during the lesson include, teacher observations of stop and jot work, entry/exit tickets, oral responses to teacher questioning, and student questions and self-reflection.

Strategies for adjusting instruction

- **Be flexible.** Making adjustments from written lesson plans may feel risky at first. However, it is essential to making instruction effective. If students are not catching on, slow down, review, repeat, or try a new instructional strategy.

- **Adjust the pace.** Sometimes learning tasks are broken down so well a lesson moves too slowly for a class or in reverse, delivery of instruction goes too fast.

- **Differentiate.** If only a small group of students need extra support, differentiate for that group while other students work on their own. If one or two students need support, work with them individually, move their seating, provide more visual aids, and/or ask another student to explain big ideas in another way.

- **Adjust throughout the lesson.** During whole-group, small-group, and independent work time, monitor and adjust how you communicate with students and how they engage with the content.

A high school art teacher roams the classroom observing students mixing and making new colors. She realizes most students are struggling to choose the correct amount of color to mix. What should she do?

   A. Stop her lesson plan and adjust instruction to reteach how to portion colors to make new ones. Let students work in groups instead of alone to remind one another of the procedure.

   B. Feel confident that students will eventually remember how to portion the colors.

   C. Make a poster illustrating the rules of proportions for students to refer to.

   D. Ask students to self-assess their own understanding of mixing colors to make new ones with a thumbs up/down.

Correct answer: A

Notice the key words: adjust and reteach. The teacher needs to adjust because she will likely be unsuccessful with new skills without this basic knowledge. Answer choice B will likely not work because she has already observed multiple students making mistakes and not self-correcting. Answer choice C, making a poster, will take time and does not guarantee student understanding. Answer choice D is not helpful because she has already assessed that most students do not recall critical information.

9. Reflecting upon, analyzing, and evaluating instructional practice

Analyzing and evaluating the impact of instructional strategies improves:

1. Teacher innovation and problem-solving.

2. Student engagement and performance.

3. Teacher-student relationships.

Having a systematic way to reflect on your teaching practices reduces the possibility of being overly critical or careless. Keeping notes, journaling, reviewing video clips of your classroom, asking for student feedback, and inviting a peer to observe and offer feedback are all ways to improve instruction through systematic self-analysis and evaluation.

Example question

A teacher plans an engaging lesson on citing evidence to support inferencing while reading. She enthusiastically presents new material, gives students an opportunity to practice, and is available to answers questions and clarify the assignment. At the end of the lesson, the students' work suggests they do not understand how to make informed inferences. What should the teacher do next?

   A. Assign homework to continue practicing the same skills.

   B. Tell students they will need to repeat the lesson until they can demonstrate understanding.

   C. Move on to the next topic of study.

   D. Reflect on each stage of the lesson and consider how to readdress the content so that students can grasp the concept.

Correct answer: D

The teacher needs to understand why students are not understanding the concept. To do this, she needs to walk through each part of the lesson and decide what to do next. Answer choices A and B are incorrect because the teacher is not taking ownership for informing student learning. Repetition of something that did not work is unlikely to change in outcome. Answer choice C is incorrect because students need to demonstrate understanding before moving on.

10. Types of memory and their implications for learning and teaching

Memory is a significant part of the learning process. We know that learning styles, interests, and motivation impact memory. For the PLT, you need to be able to identify each type of memory described below and think about how it impacts classroom learning.

Types of memory and student learning

- **Sensory register** is how we recognize information and decide when and if it is worth our attention. It is how we interpret a word or concept. In the classroom, this is when a student becomes engaged in learning. The student decides if information is relevant and attainable.

  - **Connect:** When beginning a lesson, consciously connect to past learning and take time to access student's background knowledge.

- **Short-term memory or working memory** is information we are currently aware of and is where all knowledge is first held.

  - **Chunk it:** Teachers can plan to organize information into chunks to support short-term memory. For example, PEMDAS (parenthesis, exponents, multiplication, division, addition, and subtraction) is an abbreviation for the steps of solving a multi-step math equation. Teaching this acronym chunks information to support students' short-term memory of the problem-solving procedure.

  - **Rehearse:** Practicing and repeating information will help support short-term memory. For example, before writing an essay, students can rehearse and organize their ideas by explaining them to a partner.

- **Long-term memory** is the lasting retention of information over a period of time.

  - **Declarative memory** is memory of facts, events, procedures, general knowledge, and data. For example, the events of the Revolutionary War, names of states, memories from travel or events, and data that supports an argument or claim. It is called declarative memory because it is conscious memory.

    o **Episodic memory** is a type of declarative memory specific to personal memory of events, people, places and experiences. For example, memories of the first time you lost a tooth or performed in the choir, the last time you had ice cream, when you met your best friend, or what happened at recess.

    o **Semantic memory** is memory of information you have learned but did not experience yourself. For example, a timeline of when dinosaurs were alive and went extinct, the first President, or events of the Great Depression.

  - **Procedural memory** is your unconscious memory of how to do things like ride a bike, wash dishes, or drive to work. In school, students develop procedural memory for skills like reading, writing complete sentences, and thinking about numbers.

The following graphic shows how information moves through different types of memory from the sensory register to short-term memory and long-term memory. If the information is noteworthy and not ignored, it is captured in short-term memory. When that information is rehearsed and not forgotten, it can be retained in long-term memory for a long period of time.

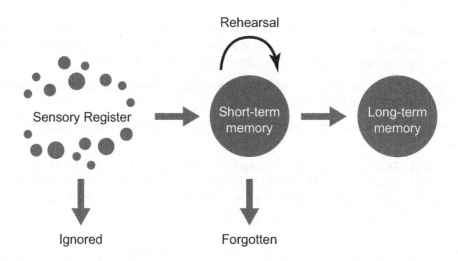

Example question

A science teacher asks students to explain the steps of tying their shoes so that someone with no experience could do it. The activity will prepare them for writing lab reports with many details. What type of memory is the teacher asking them to use to complete this assignment?

A. Episodic memory

B. Procedural memory

C. Sensory register

D. Short term memory

Correct answer: B

Students are being asked to describe a routine they complete every day. Routines are procedural memory because it is implicit and not always conscious.

11. The role of teachable moments in the classroom

A teachable moment is an unplanned event when students are able to engage in content in meaningful and memorable ways. It can take skill and experience to notice teachable moments as well as capitalize on them with appropriate teaching strategies.

Teachable moments

- Can happen at any moment in the school day: in the classroom, on the playground, in the lunchroom, during drop-off or pick-up.

- Are motivated by student questions, behaviors, writing and/or drawings. These cues demonstrate interest and engagement in a topic or theme.

The teacher's role is to recognize the moment and use appropriate pedagogy to teach or reinforce learning.

Examples of teachable moments

- Students look distracted and worried. The teacher says, "Let's try working this math problem another way."

- A class is working through a thematic unit on life cycles. A student brings in the shell of a cicada bug she found on the way to school. As other students come into the classroom, the teacher uses the specimen to look at the whole cicada life cycle and relate it to other insect life cycles.

- To help a struggling student understand cause and effect in narrative writing, a teacher reviews the concept with examples from his favorite book series, *Diary of a Wimpy Kid*.

Using teachable moments

While spontaneous, teachable moments enhance lessons and learning. They can relate to past, current, and future themes and topics. They can enhance a lesson, improve engagement, and build confidence with learning a task or skill. However, teachable moments are not tangential to core learning and do not replace learning goals and objectives.

Example question

In class, students are learning the difference between weather and climate. A few events happened in the class that sparked student interest and engagement. Which of the following events is an example of a teachable moment to reinforce the lesson on climate and weather?

- A. Watching a video on the impacts of sea levels and ocean temperatures on wildlife.
- B. Researching the local weather forecasts for the next week.
- C. Discussing a student's story about 30 days of above 110 degrees where her grandma lives in Arizona.
- D. Looking at a diagram of wind patterns across the Atlantic Ocean.

Correct answer: C

While the other examples may be engaging visual, audio, and experiential examples of weather and climate, the students' story is unexpected and sparked discussion among students. A, B, and D are planned instructional props introduced by the teacher.

Quick Tip

Get to know the terms in the Instructional Strategies section. You may have learned some of these instructional strategies as an education student but used different terms to describe them.

This page intentionally left blank.

C. Questioning Techniques

1. Components of effective questioning
2. Questioning techniques
3. Strategies for supporting students in articulating their ideas
4. Instructional methods that promote higher-order thinking skills
5. Promoting a safe environment for discussion

1. Components of effective questioning

Asking students questions at key points in the lesson is important because it keeps students engaged, develops critical thinking, and allows the teacher to check for understanding at various levels. Questions should go beyond simple recall questions (yes/no questions or low-level questions).

Benefits of questioning:

- Measures student understanding of the material

- Engages students

- Promotes active participation

- Provides opportunities to review, summarize, or emphasize important information

- Fosters critical thinking

Meaningful, well-prepared questioning takes planning, practice, and a clear commitment to knowing every student can respond. Questions can be planned in advance to cover the topics and types of thinking you want students to do. However, questioning also plays a significant role in encouraging participation in the moment. Questioning should focus on eliciting more student engagement, comprehension, and higher-order thinking.

Allow think/wait time

This technique involves giving students time to think, process, and formulate an answer. While we all need time to process our thinking to articulate our thoughts, wait time is especially helpful when asking high-level questions. This is also supportive for English language learners and students who are less verbal than others.

Test Tip

If you see an answer choice that promotes think or wait time, it is probably the correct answer. Think/wait time is on the good words list.

Helping students articulate their ideas

Asking good questions supports students to articulate their ideas. Probing questions can facilitate better responses and inform meaningful discussion.

Respecting students' answers

How you respond to a student's answer is significant. First, always pause after a student answers to allow time for everyone, including the teacher to process what has been said. Second, keep in mind the purpose of the questioning. Positive reinforcement (*good, well said, yes!*) can be easy for simple comprehension questions.

However, if the purpose of the questioning is higher order thinking, then a follow-up question, paraphrasing, or offering a new perspective is more meaningful.

- **Paraphrasing**: *What I hear you saying is….*

- **Follow-up question**: *Can you provide evidence to support your claim? How might another character respond to the same problem?*

- **New perspective**: *Can anyone share another perspective? Have you considered…?*

Handling incorrect answers

Students are not always going to respond how the teacher wants them to. Student answers may be poorly worded, incomplete, repetitive, or incorrect. Good teachers know how to respond to students in respectful ways that probe for meaning and turn incorrect answers into learning experiences. Examples include:

- *Can you say more about that?*

- *What I hear you saying is…*

- *What do you mean by…?*

- *What else could have influenced….?*

Encouraging participation

Encouraging participation means using various methods for eliciting responses. Full participation will come easily to some students and be more challenging for others. Have strategies ready for scaffolding participation. Acknowledge when student responses improve, regardless of whether the content is correct. Examples of ways to improve participation include:

- Respond on **white boards** for short, quick comprehension checks.

- **Stop and jot** answers in their notebooks before sharing in the whole group.

- Talk through their ideas with their neighbor in a **think-pair-share.**

Establishing a non-critical classroom environment

Teacher- and student-led class discussions need norms and rules, also known as consensus statements or discussion expectations. These expectations are explicit procedures for respectful and responsible discourse. Below is an example of the discussion guidelines. To implement these guidelines and expectations, teachers can use role play. Teachers can also refer to the expectations when students make mistakes and when positively reinforcing constructive discussion. Examples of discussion expectations include:

- Ask questions for clarification.

- Respect all perspectives and ideas, even when you disagree.

- Discuss ideas, not people.

- Speak loud enough for others to hear you.

Promoting active listening

Effective discussions require active listening as much as active responses. Active listening means students are processing questions and peer response as they are being shared. They are considering various perspectives and preparing for their own participation. Active listeners are not passively watching while others converse. To promote active listening, teachers can talk to students about what active listening looks like, how it feels, and what it sounds like. Again, teachers can reinforce active listening by reflecting on expectations and giving positive feedback to students demonstrating these behaviors.

Varying the types of questions

Purposeful questioning uses a variety of questioning types to promote thoughtful student responses. Questions are used to clarify, explain, extend student thinking, and to promote reflection, comparisons, categorization, analysis, evaluation and other types of higher order thinking. Sometimes it is useful to begin with questions that are simple to answer to encourage engagement and set the scene for more challenging and thought-provoking questions.

Example question

A class is discussing World War II. A student responds to a question with a claim and supporting evidence. The teacher pauses before responding or letting others share their ideas. What best describes the strategy is the teacher using?

    A. Promoting active listening

    B. Establishing a non-critical environment

    C. Respecting student answers

    D. Allowing wait time

Correct answer: D

While all four choices are important aspects of effective questioning, answer choice D, allowing wait time, is the best way to describe the teacher's strategy. Wait time can come after a question as well as after a student response. The purpose is to give all students time to think and process ideas before moving on.

2. Questioning techniques

Questioning can be used for many purposes. It can be used in direct and student-centered instruction. It can also be used to start a lesson, confer with students throughout an activity, and complete a lesson. For the PLT, you need to be able to explain and provide examples of different purposes for questioning.

Student interest and motivation

Engaging interest and motivating students is consistently part of instructional design and implementation, and that includes crafting and selecting questions. Questions can inspire engagement, trigger new thinking, and influence consideration of diverse perspectives. Teachers can generate interest and motivate students through questioning in the following ways:

- Design questions that are intriguing.

- Select questions that build students' confidence or push them to think in new ways.

- If students are not volunteering answers, begin with questions students can confidently respond to and progress to higher order thinking questions.

Evaluating students' preparation

When beginning a new lesson, teachers need to assess whether students are ready for new learning. Being prepared can mean having appropriate materials on hand, recalling episodic memories from past lessons, and understanding procedures that will be used. Evaluating students' preparation can be a whole class activity.

- **Entry and exit tickets**. For older students, entry tickets are a way to ask students questions to reveal their preparedness. Questions can come from homework problems, prior lessons, or background knowledge the teacher assumes they already know.

- **Thumbs up, sideways and down**. This is an informal and rapid way of evaluating students' preparation by letting them self-assess. Ask questions with background knowledge and let students self-assess what they know. Continue to use this quick assessment strategy throughout the lesson.

Reviewing previous lessons

Questioning can be used to review previous learning in an engaging way. For the PLT, you need to know a few effective ways to do this.

1. Choose 1-2 concepts from previous lessons to connect to the current lesson.

2. Scaffold questions to address different knowledge and skills and allow students to co-construct previous learning.

3. As students discuss questions, list important ideas or draw visual aids to support recall and highlight content that is applicable to new learning.

4. While review questioning may begin with recall, use higher order thinking questions to improve connection and understanding.

Here are some examples of reviewing questions.

- What steps did you use yesterday to simplify a polynomial? Write them down and share with your partner.

- Where did our main character go on her journey? Who did she meet? What do you predict will be his significance in the story?

Setting realistic expectations

Students are still acquiring and practicing self-regulation. When students are not clear about the scope of a task, they can feel overwhelmed. Setting realistic expectations means chunking tasks and mapping out what can be completed in a day, within the week, and before a project is due or a test will be administered. Questioning can support a students' understanding of their feelings and help them build confidence in their capabilities.

Here are some examples of setting realistic expectations.

- **Whole class**
    - What are the stages in the writing process?
    - What is the goal for today's work?
    - What do you believe you can accomplish?
    - Write your goals in your notebook.

- **One-on-one reading conference**
    - What was your goal this week?
    - How did it go?
    - Do you want to change the goal for next week or continue to practice inferencing?

Engaging students in discussion

In many classrooms, teachers do most of the talking. This is not necessarily the best way to engage learners. Questioning can provoke new thinking and prompt students to consider different perspectives articulated by their classmates. Discussions are useful to promote engagement where students are responding to comments from their peers and the teacher. Discussions can happen in a whole group, small group, or between two peers.

Here are some examples of questions to engage students in discussions.

- **Math**
    - What do you think about this equation?
    - Discuss with your partner.
    - Would you solve the problem a different way? Why?
    - How would you teach someone how to solve the problem?

Principles of Learning and Teaching: Grades 7-12

- **Social studies**

  - What do you think about this situation?

  - Have you ever experienced this issue?

  - Do you think there should rules to address this problem?

- **Art**

  - How does this painting make you feel?

  - What do you think the artist was thinking and feeling?

  - How would you have painted this scene?

  - Which materials are you going to use for this assignment? Why?

  - Which colors do you like to use in your paintings? Why?

Determining prior knowledge

Determining prior knowledge is similar to reviewing previous lessons. However, prior knowledge does not always relate to something learned in class. Prior knowledge is what students will use to build new skills and knowledge. As we have discussed in previous sections, determining prior knowledge is critical for deciding how and when new information should be presented.

Here are some examples on how to determine prior knowledge.

- What do you see in this photo? How many plants and animals can you identify? What part of the world do you think this photo was taken? What else could be near, but not in the photo?

- Which two equations on the board belong to the same number family? Why do you think that?

- Who has hiked through a forest before? What did you see and maybe taste along the trail? What did you smell, touch, and hear?

- Name the nouns you see in this photo. Now name the verbs. What about adjectives?

Preparing students for what is to be learned

Questions can be engaging, especially when they connect to students' personal experiences and understanding. Questions can be used to prepare students for new learning by:

- Accessing prior knowledge.

- Reviewing past lessons.

- Previewing what is to come.

To preview upcoming information, teachers can ask questions about a visual or audio example. Here are some examples of ways to prepare students for what is to be learned.

- Conduct a short experiment with elements similar to what students will be doing. Ask students to analyze the steps and determine whether the results matched their predictions.

- Watch a reenactment of an historical event. Discuss what happened and from whose perspective the event is being portraited.

- Listen to the sounds of birds and other life in the rainforest. Ask students to describe what they hear. See if they can predict where the recording is from.

Guiding thinking

Guiding student thinking with questions is a direct teaching method for scaffolding instruction. Guided thinking can happen in whole group, small group, partner, and individual work groups. Questions can be verbal or in writing. They can prompt students to work through a process or provide an opportunity for self-reflection and revision.

Here are some examples using questions to guide thinking.

- Before a writing task, the teacher asks students the steps to writing an essay.
- During a read aloud, the teacher asks students about two of the characters and their relationship to the protagonist.

Developing critical and creative thinking skills

Critical and creative thinking skills can be developed in any subject area and improve comprehension and understanding. Questions can inspire critical thinking such as comparisons to other perspectives, alternative solutions to problems, and other evaluative and analytical thinking. Questions can also inform creative thinking such as inventions and explanation for natural phenomena. Lessons should integrate questions to address higher order thinking skills.

Here are some examples.

- What questions do you have for the author? What does the character's inner dialogue suggest she will do next?
- Why does metal sink in the shape of a paperclip but float in the shape of a cup?
- After learning about the engineering process, what features would you include in a new shoe invention?

Checking for comprehension or level of understanding

Checking for comprehension is important throughout a lesson. Teachers need to know what students understand and where they are struggling. Questioning is an effective way to assess understanding. Teachers can ask questions to the whole group, in small groups, or individually. Questions can be formulated before the class or developed spontaneously in reflection of observations.

Here are some examples of questions that check for understanding.

- A teacher calls out words ending in -nomy. She asks, "What is the ending pattern for each word?" Students write their responses on their white board and hold it up for the teacher to acknowledge.
- In a math lesson, a teacher pulls a small group to work on part of the factoring process. She asks students to tell her what to do next while she illustrates the steps in the problem.

Summarizing information

Summarizing is a higher order thinking skill that is sometimes overlooked. To perform this skill, a student needs to determine what information is important. Then, they need to conceptualize words and phrases to describe this important information. It needs to be done in a clear and concise manner. Questioning can scaffold this process.

Here are some examples of questions to summarize information.

- We have read three different articles on Rosa Parks. Who can summarize the three common themes the authors discussed?
- Can you summarize the main differences between the book and the movie?
- Summarize the main conclusions of the water experiment we did yesterday.

Stimulating students to pursue knowledge on their own

Good teachers recognize moments for all students to explore beyond the content presented in class. This is a way to encourage self-regulation and life-long learning. Many students just need prompting and access to materials to pursue knowledge on their own. Suggesting case studies, questioning what comes next, or simply asking what else students want to know or be able to do can stimulate independent study.

Here are some examples of questions to stimulate students to pursue knowledge on their own.

- What else do you want to know about the Milky Way galaxy?
- Where can you find more information about the construction of skyscrapers?
- What materials and strategies would be useful for building an even stronger bridge?

Example question

Towards the end of a unit on the solar system, a teacher wants to engage her students in more critical and creative thinking. What would be the best question to ask students?

    A. Why do planets orbit around the sun?

    B. If you discovered another planet in the solar system, what would it be like?

    C. What is the difference between meteoroids, meteors, and meteorites?

    D. Why is Pluto no longer considered a planet?

Correct answer: B

While they may be challenging, answer choices A, C, and D are recall questions about the solar system. They have straight forward answers students can recall from the lesson. Answer choice B requires creative and critical thinking. Students have to create a mental image of a new planet in their head and then infer, present, and defend its properties. The question could lead to a culminating task where students actually create models and present a 'new planet' in the solar system.

Example question

A teacher wants to assess what students understand after practicing new concepts, so she can begin to plan for the next day's lesson. What type of questions should she be prepared to ask?

    A. Checking for comprehension

    B. Preparing students for new learning

    C. Determining prior knowledge

    D. Engaging students in discussion

Correct answer: A

The teacher needs to check student comprehension to know what to prepare for the next lesson. Answer choices B and C are tasks for starting a lesson or unit. Answer choice D happens early in a lesson and may not give the teacher a full picture of what students understand and still need practice.

3. **Strategies for supporting students in articulating their ideas**

Helping students to articulate their ideas is a significant part of teaching. Using questioning to prompt, clarify, and extend student's thinking is more effective than simply correcting student answers. Questioning engages students to be self-reflective and encourages analytical thinking. For the PLT, you need to be able to explain and provide examples of strategies for supporting students to articulate their ideas.

Verbal and non-verbal prompting

Using verbal and non-verbal prompts helps students to think deeply and to clarify their responses. This is a more effective alternative than explicitly asking a student to revise their answer. Prompting is a guided learning strategy. For more directed and introductory guidance, use verbal prompts. For less invasive and more facilitated or supportive guidance, use nonverbal prompts. In addition, consider what type of thinking you are trying to elicit to guide what kind of prompts to pose.

Here are some examples of **verbal** prompting.

Category	Example
Remember	Who? What? When? Where? How much? Which ones? What would you choose?
Understand	Can you state it in your own words? Can you read the graph or table please? Can you give an example? What problem are we trying to solve?
Apply	What strategy are we trying to use? What alternatives should be considered? What is wrong with….?
Analysis	Compare and contrast… What can you infer from the photo? What is the author's intent? Whose perspective are we hearing? What is another point of view?
Evaluate	Which is more important? What are your criteria or standards? What are the various perspectives on this issue, and which do you side with?
Create	How would you test that? Can you propose an alternative solution? How would you plan to research that issue? How can we prove or confirm this?

(Walsh, p. 40, 2005)

Here are some examples of **non-verbal** prompting.

- **Signals**: Hand signals can be helpful for encouraging active listening, expanding or wrapping up your statement, focusing attention, and taking time to stop and think about an answer. Signals can also be bells, flags, or other reminders of routines and expectations.

Quick Tip

The questions you ask in the classroom have a huge impact on students' critical thinking. Asking *how* or *why* can increase your question complexity.

- **Connecting words:** Highlight connective words like *"because," "next," and "before"* that promote explanation. For example, write them on index cards and hold them up on popsicle sticks to cue students to continue their explanation.

- **Sentence starters and frames**. You can introduce sentence starters before questioning begins to support student thinking and construction of a meaningful response. Sentence starters can incorporate content-specific vocabulary or be general. Here are some examples of sentence starters for a reading comprehension discussion.

  – I think … because …

  – Evidence that supports my idea is …

  – I inferred that … because I noticed …

  – What I connect to the most is … because …

  – A question I have for the author is …

In addition, any of the verbal prompts listed above can be transformed into non-verbal prompts (like sentence starters and frames) that students refer to on a regular basis to extend and communicate their thinking.

Students read an essay written by an activist of the Civil Rights Movement. The teacher asks questions to engage a discussion about the author and the time period. She asks, "What is the author's intent for writing this essay?" What is the teacher prompting students to do to answer the question?

    A. Remember

    B. Analyze

    C. Apply

    D. Understand

Correct answer: B

Students need to analyze the content of the essay to look for evidence of the author's purpose and synthesize this information into a claim they can defend. Answer choices A and D are lower level cognitive thinking processes that do not describe the breadth of thinking the question asks. Although answer choice C is another kind of higher-order thinking, the question focuses on analysis.

Restatement

What I hear you saying is… Is that correct?

Restating student comments immediately prompts reflective thinking. It gives students the opportunity to hear their exact words or paraphrased ideas. It can help the speaker, teacher, and classmates rethink the stated ideas and the speaker can decide if their words communicated their thoughts. Students can restate what their peers say to reinforce active listening and understanding.

- What I think you're saying is….

- Who can repeat that in your own words?

- Can someone restate or rephrase that?

Restatement or paraphrasing is an important skill for teacher-led and student-led discussions.

Reflective listening statements

"Go on," "interesting," "really?" "I see." These are phrases an active listener might use to acknowledge what the speaker is saying, and signal their attention. Reflective listening statements move beyond acknowledgement to reflect the meaning of the speaker. Reflective listening statements help the speaker process the information they are trying to communicate. Reflective listening is meant to be non-judgmental, supportive, and engaging.

Here are some tips to reflective listening statements.

Statement	Example	Explanation
Reflect the speaker's thoughts	*It sounds like what you are thinking is…*	In this case, the listener reflects what she hears the speaker say. This is a way to check for accuracy and begin the reflective process for the speaker.
Reflect the speaker's feelings	*I hear that you feel…*	This can be trickier because feelings can be difficult to discern from statements. Statements can also be followed with questions to promote clarity and processing of what exactly the speaker is feeling.

Statement	Example	Explanation
Reflect the content in the speaker's response	*So, what you are saying is…What that means is….*	In this case, the listener is focusing specifically on the content and the argument the speaker is trying to convey. For example, if the student is trying to explain why it is going to snow next January, the role of the listener is not to question their statement but to probe the student to examine the facts they have chosen to defend their argument.

Wait time

As mentioned before, maybe one of the best ways to assist students is to simply provide routine time for thinking. Take these steps to give wait time to students that is sufficient and meaningful.

Step	Explanation
Pause after asking a question (3-5 seconds)	Let students know and anticipate this. The more challenging the question, the more time you need to wait.
Call on a student to respond.	If the student needs it, offer support. • Start with non-verbal cues such as pointing to key vocabulary and/or sentence starters. • Continue with other supports, like whisper ideas from a neighbor or more direct prompting.
Pause again after a student's response (3-5 seconds)	This second wait time/think time is important for the speaker, listeners, and the teacher. Students may end up adding to their answers, rethinking without prompting, or asking a clarifying question. Let other enthusiastic students know that you are giving all students time to think. Normalize the active roles of listeners and the idea that wait time is a way to support all learners.

CONTENT CATEGORY II
SECTION C

Example question

A geometry teacher meets with a small group of students to support their understanding of a proof. She writes the steps to the proof on the board and asks the students to explain the proof. A student explains the first step but has trouble explaining the reason for the 2nd and 3rd steps. How should the teacher respond the student's incomplete answer?

    A. Ask a probing question like, "In step 3, what property is represented?"

    B. Tell the student the answer and model how to solve the problem.

    C. Ask another student to answer the question.

    D. Tell the student, "That's a good start!" Then, move on to the next step in the proof.

Correct answer: A

The focus of this guided part of the lesson is supporting student thinking. The student reflected the first step to solving the problem. Probing questions can help the student continue to think through the problem. Answer choices B and D do not extend students' thinking and deters problem solving. Answer choice C is incorrect because the class was not prepared to discuss multiple answers.

4. Instructional methods that promote higher-order thinking skills

Most teachers ask a lot of questions and they tend to focus on basic levels of cognitive thinking: fact, recall, and knowledge. To promote higher levels of thinking, teachers need to ask higher levels of questions (Walsh, 2011) and use various configurations for how students answer questions.

One way to develop the response process for answering questions using higher-order thinking is by using the *think, ink, pair, and share (TIPS) strategy*.

TIPS Strategy

Thinking of answering questions is a process. Students need to learn how to:

1. Listen to a question

2. Understand what is being asked

3. Answer to self

4. Answer out loud

5. Revise the answer

(Gall, 1985 as cited in Walsh, 2011)

Eventually this process is automatized. However, students need support in the beginning (Walsh, p79, 2011). Teachers tend to focus only on step 4. The TIPS strategy encourages students to think through the question multiple times. TIPS is especially useful for higher order thinking questions because each step provides an opportunity for students to process, describe, add on, consider other perspectives, and revise their thinking.

Types of questions to pose to prompt thinking:

- Think of a time…
- Give an example…
- Give a non-example…
- In your own words…
- How does it connect to other things we have been learning?
- Summarize…
- How would you teach it to…?

1. **Think.** Silently, with pencils down, students are given time to think through their ideas and how they want to answer the question(s).

2. **Ink.** Students write or illustrate their thoughts. To scaffold, encourage thinking with supportive prompts such as:

   - Illustrate or draw a diagram of a process.
   - Summarize key concepts.
   - List the costs and benefits or pros and cons.
   - Share a real-life example.

3. **Pair.** Students turn to their assigned partner to listen and discuss their responses and thinking. Students take time to modify their own entry by adding or modifying their answers.

4. **Share.** Students share their completed ideas. The teacher selects a few example responses to share with the whole class.

Methods for encouraging students' higher levels of thinking

Reflect

For the PLT, understand that students need reflection time integrated into every lesson.

The most effective way to routinely promote reflective thinking is the second wait time, after a students' response, that is described above. The routines prompt the speaker and her classmates to reflect on the thoughts that were shared.

Another routine is for students to reflect on discussion norms and participation. Students reflect on how well they collectively listened, responded to questions, and were able to expand and extend their thinking.

Challenge assumptions

We want students to challenge assumptions in what they read and what they learn. Doing so effectively takes practice and vocabulary for identifying and offering alternative perspectives. One of the most effective ways to begin this process is to ask questions about the author or speaker's intent. Students can do this through essay writing, discussion, and debate.

Find relationships

Encourage students to find relationships between ideas and concepts. Relationships are the basis for cause and effect in literature and science, patterns in math, and the impact of historical events. Instead of lecturing about them and depending on rote memory for learning, teachers can ask probing questions to encourage students to discover and describe relationships themselves.

Here is an example of asking questions to help students find relationships.

- Compare and contrast characters, events, and settings in the story. Relate these characteristics to another story, to themselves, or to something happening in the world today.

Determine relevancy and validity of information

While conducting research for a history project, science inquiry, or other learning activity, students need to routinely ask questions to determine whether their sources are relevant to their topic and whether they are a credible source of information.

Here is an example of a list of questions to help students assess information.

1. Who is the author? Is the author objective or do they have a bias on this topic?

2. What is the main purpose of the text?

3. What evidence does the text use?

4. Is the text from a reputable source? Do they have other publications and share a reference list?

Design alternate solutions

To a lot of students, problem-solving means finding the right answer. Questioning can be used to help students generate multiple solutions to the same problem. Designing alternate solutions promotes perspective, creative, and critical thinking.

Here are some examples of finding alternate solutions.

- What is an alternative ending to the fairytale Cinderella?

- What would happen if the ramp was set at a 90-degree angle instead of 60 degrees? How about 120?

- How would our lives be different if women had not earned the right to vote in 1920?

Draw conclusions

Drawing conclusions is making meaning from an assessment and evaluating information. Drawing conclusions requires scaffolding, like most other cognitive skills. Questioning can help students reflect on key concepts such as cause and effect, problem and solution, or the results of an experiment. These concepts help students find meaningful conclusions and articulate the evidence they used to make their decisions.

Here are some examples of questions to help students draw conclusions.

- In the story of the three bears, why did the house have three chairs and three beds?

- Why do we need to understand the difference between weather and climate?

- How will we know when the tomatoes are ready to pick?

Transfer knowledge

Transfer of knowledge or application is an essential part of mastering skills. If students cannot apply what they learn to new scenarios, they need more practice and instruction. Questioning can support transfer of knowledge by suggesting new context, scenarios, and situations. Using operations to solve word problems is a great example.

Here are some examples of how to use questioning to help students transfer knowledge.

- Kara has 5 friends coming to her birthday party and 20 party favors to distribute. What operation would you use to figure out how many party favors each friend will get?

- We discussed variables when we designed our garden experiment. Can you identify the independent and dependent variables in the erosion experiment we conducted today?

Example question

A teacher has planned a lesson for students to determine the validity and relevancy of information they come across as they do research for their class reports. Which TWO questions should be a part of how students assess their sources?

    A.   Does this article address my research questions?

    B.   Have I read anything by this author before?

    C.   Does the article have a clear claim I can use?

    D.   What year was the article written?

Correct answer: A and D

Answer choices A and D address the relevancy of a source. Depending on what is being researched, the date can indicate a primary source or a recent analysis on a topic. It is always important to determine if the source is relevant to the topic being researched. B and C are incorrect because although the questions may indicate something interesting or engaging to read, they do not indicate relevancy or validity.

5. Promoting a safe environment for discussion

Questioning begins with posing an idea and eliciting a response. A discussion implies a deeper connection and examination of ideas. When students begin participating in discussions and debates, they will likely be eager to share their own ideas. It takes explicit instruction, modeling, and practice to develop discussions where students are using higher levels of thinking in their responses.

Techniques for establishing and maintaining standards of conduct for discussions

Guiding meaningful discussions in the classroom requires a clear understanding of roles and responsibilities for teachers and students. Students need support and explicit instruction about how to participate in discussions.

Think about it!

One way to encourage higher order thinking is to build students' capacity for discussion. Here are 4 simple phrases students can learn and use to effectively participate in discussions.

1. "I would like to add…"

2. "I agree with you because…"

3. "I disagree with you because…"

4. "What I hear you saying is…"

Giving students phrases to promote healthy discourse encourages them to challenge ideas respectfully, argue their claims, ask questions, and share differing perspectives. It enables them to engage, and at times, take charge of the conversation.

Engaging all learners

Discussions can take on many forms. To be successful, they need to engage all learners. This means sometimes the teacher calls on students rather than only calling on volunteers. It means providing scaffolds for hesitant speakers such as think-pair-share, letting a friend pass a sticky note with ideas or whisper a response into the speaker's ear. Giving students think time by waiting or asking them to write down their thoughts before speaking also engages all learners. For the PLT, you need to know that a successful discussion means that the teacher is not the primary speaker and that all students can participate in all stages of the discussion.

Creating a collaborative environment

A collaborative environment is one where students are supporting one another's learning. Students are cooperating to practice new skills, cheering each other on, and offering constructive feedback without judgment. Successful discussion skills are developed over time in a collaborative environment. Students need to trust their classmates and work together to build knowledge and understanding. Setting and enforcing expectations for discussion, encouraging cooperative preparation, and constructive feedback all support a collaborative environment.

Respecting diverse opinions

Talk during a discussion needs to be about reasoning. This focus invites diverse opinions and perspectives. Students can demonstrate their respect by how they respond to contrasting ideas. Support students to understand that discussing different opinions actually improves our arguments and help us to better understand people's actions. Even wrong answers are an excellent opportunity to discuss thinking.

Supporting risk taking

A safe learning environment allows students to take risks. Learning involves risk-taking especially when participating in discussions because you might get something wrong or need practice to do it well. To support risk taking, students need explicit feedback to encourage participation, even if their responses are not yet clear, or their thinking can be revised. Risk taking is also supported by clear group rules for discussion.

Here are some examples of how to encourage risk taking.

- Everyone has a chance to participate.
- Everyone feels that they will be respected.
- Everyone can hear what is said and see who is talking.

Discussion roles and responsibilities

The techniques discussed throughout this book should be taught and reinforced though clear expectations.

Here is an example of how to set expectations for discussion and debate in the classroom.

The Norm Form

Students' rights:

1. You have the right to ask questions
2. You have the right to be treated respectfully
3. You have the right to have your ideas discussed (not you personally)

Students' responsibilities:

1. You must speak loudly enough for everyone to hear you.
2. If you cannot hear or understand someone, you must ask the person to repeat what they have said.
3. You are expected to explain why you agree or disagree with someone's ideas.

(O'Connor, 2011)

Example question

Which of the following is not an expectation for class discussions?

A. You are expected to agree and disagree with other people's ideas.

B. Everyone should have an opportunity to talk.

C. Only the teacher should ask clarifying questions.

D. You have the right to be treated respectfully.

Correct answer: C

In a class discussion, students are encouraged to offer differing perspectives, ask questions, and seek clarity from their peers. The more students engage in these types of questions, the more the teacher can become a facilitator rather than a director of the conversation. Answer choices A, B, and D are all important rules for keeping discussions productive and inclusive.

This page intentionally left blank.

D. Communication Techniques

1. Verbal and nonverbal communication

2. How culture and gender can affect communication

3. Communication tools to enrich the learning environment

4. Effective listening strategies

1. Verbal and nonverbal communication

Communication is how we share ideas, opinions, and thoughts with others. For the PLT, you need to be aware that communication is a multi-dimensional process. On the test, you might be presented with a scenario where you will be asked to determine how to modify a teacher's presentation to improve communication. Each of the modes listed below influence how teachers interact with students, colleagues, and parents.

- **Body language.** Posture, stance, how a person holds their arms, what direction they are oriented to, how someone sits, stands, moves, or even holds their shoulders.

- **Gesture.** A specific movement of the head, hands, arms, and body. The movement can be affirming, questioning, indifferent, or hostile.

- **Tone, stress, and inflection.** The way something is said, phrasing, expression, and volume of a question or statement that informs its meaning.

- **Eye contact.** What and how a person looks at someone. Eye contact can cue many intentions including approval, intrigue, understanding, distain, and enthusiasm. Lack of eye contact can cue disinterest.

Think about it!

Effective communication can mean not talking at all. For example, a teacher is ready to end a cooperative learning activity and stands at the front of the room with a hand in the air. This is a signal to the students to stop talking and look to the front of the room for further direction. Because the teacher has communicated what this non-verbal cue means and students have practiced this procedure, students immediately stop talking and focus on the teacher.

- **Facial expression.** The emotions and intentions communicated on a person's face. Through facial expressions, a person can communicate a number of emotions without saying a word. Unlike other nonverbal cues, at least seven facial expressions have been proven to be universal (Matsumoto, 2013).

- **Personal space.** The amount of physical space needed to feel comfortable and confident to communicate with people. This differs depending on relationships, intent of the interaction, and cultures of the people communicating.

To introduce an inquiry activity on the way different types of filters impact water quality, a teacher models how to prepare and test each filter before students break off into small groups. She reads from the directions while preparing the filters. After she is done with the demonstration, she looks up to ask if anyone has any questions. The students seem very confused. Which non-verbal cue would improve her modeling the most?

A. Eye contact

B. More personal space

C. Gestures

D. Tone of voice

Correct answer: A

In this case, she was making little to no eye contact while modeling the behaviors needed to complete the inquiry assignment. She could use eye contact to monitor student engagement and signal important steps in the set-up procedure. Answer choice B is incorrect because we assume from the description that she is standing where all students can see her. Answer choices C and D are important but not as significant as eye contact.

2. How culture and gender can affect communication

A lot of verbal and non-verbal cues differ between cultures and gender. It is important to recognize these differences so someone's cues and intentions are not misinterpreted.

Culture and communication. Student cultures can influence how they react to direction or show deference to authority. Cultural differences can also impact what students perceive as appropriate ways to communicate in class discussions or while a teacher is presenting. In some cultures, background discussion and calling out signifies engagement and interest while in others is it considered rude and distracting.

Creating a classroom culture that supports the background of all students is a big part of the teacher's purpose. Teachers have the power to bring multicultural texts and stories to students. This can be a daunting task for new teachers because many things should be considered when selecting multicultural texts.

Gender and communication. Girls and boys might communicate differently in the classroom. Boys might be more active and likely to speak out of turn. Girls might be better at demonstrating active listening. Boys tend to be more focused on explaining information and girls tend to add tone and phrases to build rapport. There are no rules, however, about how boys or girls communicate in classrooms and you will find all styles.

Think about it!

It is as important to recognize your own bias and tendencies as they relate to culture and gender. For example, research shows most teachers tend to call on boys more often than girls. It is important to notice whether you are doing this and make a plan to counteract this tendency. It is important to self-reflect to identify any other unconscious preferences.

A new student in the class has very limited English proficiency. He does not attempt to answer questions and frequently seems distracted during whole group lessons and independent learning time. What can the teacher do first to help the student acclimate better to the classroom?

    A. Encourage him to follow the model of his classmates.

    B. Have a conference with his parents or family to explain the expectations at school.

    C. Give him warnings and use negative and positive reinforcement to help him learn appropriate behaviors in the classroom.

    D. Walk through class routines to demonstrate instruction and learning, so the student can see the classroom expectations.

Correct answer: D

A student who does not speak English yet will struggle to understand what is happening in the classroom. The teacher needs to explicitly communicate expectations and routines so the student can associate the words with her actions. The student can then emulate what the teacher is modeling. Answer choice A is incorrect because the student needs more explicit instruction. B and C are incorrect because these should never be your first resort.

Example question

Which of the following would be the most effective way to communicate to students and parents about upcoming classroom events and deadlines?

    A. A well-maintained teacher website where students and parents can access information regularly.

    B. A detailed monthly newsletter sent home with students in the students' native languages.

    C. Colorful posters in the classroom that display important information for the semester.

    D. Weekly emails sent to every parent and student.

Correct answer: B

When communicating important information, always send home a physical copy in the students' home language. This is an example of being culturally responsive. Whenever communicating important events or deadlines, it is important for teachers to remember that not all students have Internet access; this eliminates answers choices A and D. Colorful posters are not effective in notifying parents about important events and deadlines.

3. Communication tools to enrich the learning environment

For students to be successful, they must have appropriate oral and written communication skills. It is important for teachers to implement activities that increase and sharpen students' communication skills. It is also important for teachers to model these behaviors.

Teachers have a variety of technologies and communication tools to enrich their instruction. Likewise, students can use many technology tools to enhance their research and communication. For example, researching current events, gathering data, and sharing new perspectives are all ways students can use communication technology and tools.

Teachers need to choose communication tools that support the student-centered learning environment and the standards being taught.

- **Student-centered learning.** Remember, student-centered learning refers to a wide variety of educational programs, learning experiences, instructional approaches, and academic support strategies that are intended to address the distinct learning needs, interests, aspirations, and cultural backgrounds of students.

- **Standards alignment.** Communication tools including software, hardware, equipment, materials, and other resources should always support standards-based instruction. You might find fascinating technology that your students would enjoy using. However, if it doesn't support the standards being taught, it is not the right fit for your classroom.

Audio and visual aids

Because students have different learning preferences—audio, visual, kinesthetic—using different mediums is effective in helping students comprehend text. Audio and visual aids can be used to enhance instruction for all learners. Some examples include:

- Digital images projected during a lesson
- Printed images used for inspiring storytelling
- Primary documents like photos and writing to illuminate an historic event
- Audio books in a listening center
- Podcasts

Again, audio and visual aids should be student-centered and aligned to the standards you are teaching.

Read the scenario below and identify the visual and audio aids the teacher is using to enhance instruction and learning.

The teacher uses a popular song to signal to students their independent work time is over. Students smoothly put away their work materials and return to their desks.

The teacher shows four pieces of art and lists four historical events from ancient China. She asks students to discuss what they see in each piece of art and infer how it is related to one or more of the historical events. The teacher facilitates the discussion by asking questions about the paintings' colors, setting, people, shapes, and symbols. Every time a student makes a connection, she prompts them to explain their reasoning.

Next, the teacher asks small groups to read about the art and associated events. Then each team prepares a presentation on the setting, images, events, materials and any other way the art is a documentation of its time period. Students present their claims and reasoning in as podcasts, presentation slides, dramatic reenactment, and a town hall meeting. The teacher asks prompting questions to understand their thinking and encourage them to defend their claims with clear and meaningful reasoning.

The next week, the teacher uses the art pieces to engage students in a writing lesson. Using a document camera, she models how to plan out the writing task by discussing the colors, symbols, materials, and historical significance of one of the images. Students use this model to guide their own writing process. They publish their work with a photo of the art onto the class blog to elicit feedback from their classmates.

The instructional uses of audio and visual aids in this scenario include:

- The teacher uses music to signal students they are ending one activity and beginning a new one. Music is a great cue for signaling transition times.
- The teacher uses primary documents (period artwork) and asks students to relate them to historical periods when they were made. She is using the images to help students understand the affective and personal experience of people in ancient China. Then, students use text to further explore the connection between the paintings and the time and place they were created.
- The teacher uses audio and visual mediums to differentiate instruction by letting students choose how to present their analysis, claims, reasonings, and examples. When students present, she asks them questions to explain their thinking and develop oral language skills.
- In the writing lesson, the teacher uses a document camera to model writing and refers back to the art. She asks the students to use their presentations and new understanding of the art pieces to plan out their own expository essay.

Text and digital resources

An important part of being a teacher is evaluating and selecting resources for instructional use. The very first thing to consider when choosing materials for the classroom is whether the materials are aligned to the state-adopted standards. Always consult the standards before planning instruction or choosing instructional materials.

It is important to understand how to select appropriate text and digital resources. The table below provides primary and secondary resources for informational text.

	Humanities	Sciences
Primary sources (original source)	• Diaries, journals, letters • Interviews with people who lived during a particular time (e.g., survivors of genocide in Rwanda or the Holocaust) • Songs, plays, novels, stories • Paintings, drawings, sculptures • Autobiographies	• Published results of research studies • Published results of scientific experiments • Published results of clinical trials • Proceedings of conferences and meetings
Secondary sources (interpretation of the original source)	• Biographies • Histories • Literary criticism • Book, art, theater reviews • Newspaper articles that interpret events	• Publications about the significance of research or experiments • Analysis of a clinical trial • Review of the results of several experiments or trials

It is important to evaluate source information for relevancy. This is especially important when using Internet sources. Considerations when evaluating text and digital resources include the following:

1. **Is the research reliable and valid?**

   Validity refers to how sound the research is in both the design and methods. Validity is the extent to which the findings in the study represent the phenomenon measured in the study.

   • **Internal validity** refers to how well a study is conducted.

   • **External validity** refers to how applicable the findings are to the real world.

   Reliability refers to the degree of consistency in the measure. A study is considered reliable when it yields similar results under similar conditions after being conducted repeatedly.

2. **Are the authors authorities or experts in their fields?** Authors who are prolific in their space tend to produce reliable and valid research. Be sure to check the author(s).

3. **Is the research current?** Using research conducted in the last 3 years is more effective than using research from the last 20 years. That doesn't mean that past studies are not important. Plenty of the early research is considered seminal. But when looking for trends and new ways to teach, using current research is best.

4. **Is the research scholarly?** Teachers should consider research that comes from peer-reviewed academic journals. Websites and blogs often contain valid and reliable research. However, to be sure that the research is legitimate, go straight to the academic journal where it was published. Be sure to check the bibliography in the study.

5. **Is the research objective?** Research should be unbiased and objective; it should address questions without opinions or agenda. Often, private companies that sell educational programs will publish research. It is important that teachers differentiate between objective research and research that is skewed one way. You can do this by looking at several studies about a topic. Look for trends and consistencies between and among the studies.

6. **Is the research relevant to the profession?** There are a lot of studies out there with important information. You should be seeking out research in the areas that fit your particular job. For example, if you are a social science teacher in a school with a large population of English language learners, you should seek out research relevant to that area.

(University of Massachusetts Boston, 2019)

Sources	Definition	Examples
Reliable sources	A trustworthy source of information.	• Published results of research studies • Published results of scientific experiments • Published results of clinical trials • Proceedings of conferences and meetings
Unreliable sources	An unqualified and unreliable source to support ideas.	• Online blogs about a particular topic • Chats or discussion forums on the Internet • Websites from private companies

Teachers should also consider diversity when selecting text and digital resources to ensure the materials in your classroom represent all students. This includes considering the following:

- **Accuracy**. Accuracy of cultural representation is a crucial aspect of high-quality, multicultural literature, and books must contain current, correct information to avoid reinforcing stereotypes (Agosto, 2002; Shioshita, 1997).

- **Authentic dialogue**. The dialogue in the text should accurately represent culturally specific oral traditions (Landt, 2006).

- **Presentation of information or issues.** The information in the text should not leave out information that is unfavorable to the dominant culture.

The following was taken from the Urbandale School District (2019) and is a comprehensive outline that should be considered when choosing materials for the classroom.

Instructional materials should provide the following:

- Support the educational philosophy, goals and objectives of the district and the objectives of the curricular offering in which the materials will be used.

- Be appropriate for the age, emotional and social development, and ability level of the students for whom the materials are selected.

- Be diverse with respect to levels of difficulty, reader appeal, and should present a variety of points of view.

- Meet high standards of quality in factual content and presentation.

- Have aesthetic, cultural, literary, or social value. The value and impact of any literary work will be judged as a whole, taking into account the author's intent rather than individual words, phrases or incidents.

- Foster respect for men, women, the disabled, and minority groups and should portray a variety of roles and lifestyles open to people in today's world.

- Foster respect for cultural diversity.

- Be designed to motivate students to examine their own attitudes and behaviors and to comprehend their own duties, responsibilities, rights and privileges as participating citizens in a pluralistic society.

- Encourage students to use higher-order thinking skills and to become informed decision-makers, to exercise freedom of thought and to make independent judgments through examination and evaluation of relevant information, evidence and differing viewpoints.

Students will also need assistance selecting appropriate books, periodicals, reports, and journals in the classroom, media center and online. Students need explicit instruction for accessing and using these digital and text materials.

Internet and other computer-based tools

Before choosing any technology program to implement into the classroom, you must be sure the technology supports the state-adopted standards. In addition to standards alignment, you must be sure research and evidence support the use of the technology. For example, before you decide to use a new reading app on students' handheld devices, you should find research that shows the app or an app like it helped to increase student achievement.

When implementing any technologies in the classroom, teachers should be sure it is age appropriate and within school guidelines. Furthermore, teachers must model appropriate behaviors when using communication technology.

The following are examples of communication technologies appropriate for the classroom.

- **Word processing software**. This software can be used for free writing, essays, and projects. Most students will be required to use word processing software in college and in their careers. Therefore, implementing this communication technology in upper elementary and middle school classrooms is important.

- **Presentation software**. This is best used for whole-group instruction when the teacher is presenting information in the form of short pieces of text and graphics. Students can also create meaningful projects using presentation software.

Quick Tip

Technology can never replace a great teacher. Studies have shown that an effective teacher is more important than technology. Creating a learning environment that is relevant to students' lives can be done with or without technology. For this exam, look for answer choices where technology enhances the learning experience, not replaces the duties of the teacher.

- **Document sharing software**. Document sharing technology allows students to collaborate with each other on a wide variety of projects, editing in real time together in one document.

- **Email**. When teaching communication, focusing on email etiquette is imperative. Students will have to communicate with college professors, team members, and others through email. Showing students how to effectively communicate via email is a skill they will carry into their lives beyond their academic career.

Acceptable use policy

It is important for teachers to clearly communicate acceptable use policies for technology including equipment, software, and the Internet. Each school district and state department of education will have an acceptable use policy that teachers and students are expected to follow. It is important for you to research your state and district's policy and ensure you and your students clearly understand the expectations. It is also important to implement procedures to help students avoid violating the district and state's acceptable use policies.

Acceptable use policies typically include the following provisions:

- Preamble to align the policy with the vision and mission of the school.
- Definitions to help faculty, staff, and students understand the terms in the policy.
- Rights and responsibilities of users including faculty, staff, and students.
- Description of acceptable use.
- Description of unacceptable use.
- Reporting procedures for unacceptable use.
- Consequences of violations of the policy.
- Agreement and acceptance statement.

Derived from National Center for Educational Statistics Sample Acceptable Agreements and Policies retrieved from: https://nces.ed.gov/pubs2005/tech_suite/app_a.asp.

Example question

Some students are struggling with math concepts and number fluency. A group of 9th grade teachers want to use a digital remedial program offered by the district to support these students. They plan to have students practice on the program for 15 minutes a day. What else should they do to support student learning?

A. Rely on the computer software to create reports and monitor student progress.

B. Introduce and reinforce skills through guided instruction in small groups and math centers.

C. Let the parents know students need to use the program at home for 30 additional minutes a day.

D. Let all students use the program to be fair and make planning simpler.

Correct answer: B

Digital tools should be used in conjunction with teaching, not as a replacement. The teacher still needs to support student learning through revisiting lessons, practicing skills, and assessing growth. Answer choice A is incorrect because students need a variety of supportive tools for remediation. Technology can never replace the role of the teacher. Answer choice C is incorrect because it puts the responsibility of instruction on the parents, and it assumes students have access to technology at home. Answer choice D is incorrect because the program should align with the learning objectives for each student. It would not be equitable to have all students use the program.

4. Effective listening strategies

Active listening by teachers and students is a significant part of communication in a classroom. More learning can take place when active listening is occurring. Whether you are integrating active listening into your practice or supporting students to learn better active listening skills, teaching and modeling active listening are important for creating a productive classroom environment. Active listening behaviors also support questioning techniques.

Active listening strategies

Active listening is when the person listening concentrates, understands, responds, and remembers what the person talking is saying. For example, a teacher and a student are discussing the student's semester reading goal.

- **Student:** "I would like to write more essays and complete more writing assignments on time this semester."
- **Teacher:** "You're saying you want to write more and be timely with your work. Let's develop a plan to help you be successful."

The teacher is showing the student that he understands what the student is saying. The teacher appropriately responds by paraphrasing and initiating next steps. The teacher is also modeling good listening skills. Finally, this method helps with clarity because if the teacher misunderstands something the student says, the student can clarify the misconceptions.

The following table provides specific strategies of active listening and with characteristics and examples of scenarios.

Strategy	Characteristics	Example
Attending to the speaker	Eye contact. Receptive body language: shoulders and feet turned toward the speaker.	In a Socratic seminar, the students and teacher sit in a circle so everyone can see one another. Listeners are looking at the speaker, with their feet and shoulders oriented in the speaker's direction.
Restating key points	Paraphrasing, summarizing, pointing out cause and effect, or other patterns in a statement.	• "What I hear you saying is…" • "So, first [this happened], next, you said [this], and finally you wanted [this]."
Asking questions	Questions demonstrate active listening by responding directly to what the speaker is saying. They are not pre-planned or the same for every situation.	• "Can you say more about that?" • "What was the most challenging part?" • "What happened after that?" • "Why do you think she was feeling that way?"
Interpreting information	Reflective acknowledgement: "Yes." "Uh-huh." "Ok, I see." Reflective statements: restating meaning, feelings, or content.	• "It sounds like you felt [this]…" • "That is an interesting response." • "How did that affect your reaction?" • "So, in summary, I hear you saying…"
Providing supportive feedback	Encouraging and non-judgmental gestures, words, and cues.	• "I like how you supported your claim with two reasons." • "You explained the first part of the story well." • "That is interesting because…" • "You and I have different perspectives. I learned a lot from you."
Being respectful	Acknowledging all responses, actions, and participation. Listening even when an answer is incomplete or incorrect. Focusing on encouraging participation and communication strategies.	Helping students to articulate disagreement rather than argue: • "I disagree with you because…" • "I would like to add…" Not immediately correcting a student or cutting off an incomplete or tangential answer: • "What I hear you saying is…" • "Can you say more about [significant part]…"

A teacher is leading a Socratic seminar to discuss how to eliminate the use of plastic at the school. Students have spent several days preparing for the discussion. While the students go around the circle sharing their initial ideas, some students are looking at their notes, fidgeting with pencils, and smiling at one another. What should the teacher say next?

    A. "Your insight is really intriguing. I hope we get to hear more about your ideas."

    B. "Here is a recap of the ideas talked about in this first round."

    C. "Let's review what it looks like and sounds like to attend to the speaker."

    D. "Let's do this over, this time without ignoring the speaker."

Correct answer: C

Active listening needs explicit instruction and practice for students to be able to self-regulate their behaviors with ease. The distracting behaviors of some students may be because they are nervous to share their ideas and are not aware that they are not acknowledging the speaker. Answer choice D is incorrect because the teacher needs to help students monitor their own participation in the discussion. Answer choices A and B are incorrect because they do not address what students can do to be better listeners. Without addressing their actions, students are likely to continue to repeat these actions.

1. Which of the following would be most effective in helping students develop schema or background knowledge? Choose all that apply.

   A. Students discuss what they already know about rocks before reading a passage on different types of rocks.

   B. Students watch a short video about Native American culture before reading Native American poetry.

   C. Before starting a lesson on cells, students fill out a KWL chart.

   D. Before going home for the day, students fill out their worksheets for tomorrow's lesson.

2. Students in Ms. Dwyer's class are participating in a large group discussion where Ms. Dwyer is facilitating the lesson by asking questions about topics discussed. The same 5 students are answering most of the questions. What can Ms. Dwyer do to get more students to participate?

   A. Have students come to the board and write their answer where everyone can see it.

   B. Increase the wait time in between asking the question and calling on a student for the answer.

   C. Encourage everyone to participate so students feel comfortable.

   D. Increase motivation by offering rewards for those who participate.

3. A team of English teachers has just received reading scores on a mid-year benchmark assessment. The team is meeting in their PLC to discuss the data and determine what to do next. What would be the most effective next step the team could take?

Benchmark Reading Scores

   A. Have the teacher of Class D lead professional development on how to increase achievement.

   B. Disaggregate the data to determine the specific areas of need.

   C. Give another exam in the following weeks and compare that data to this benchmark data.

   D. Have the teacher of Class A work with the teacher of Class D.

4. Which of the following would be the opposite of inquiry learning in a science class?

    A. Cooperative learning to follow directions and a checklist for setting up a lab.

    B. Going outside to observe living and non-living things.

    C. Whole-group activity with the teacher using expository instruction.

    D. Using a touch tank so students can touch different shells found on the beach.

5. Students in Mr. Ruiz's class have varying levels of ability. What is the best approach Mr. Ruiz can take when planning instruction to meet the specific academic needs of every student?

    A. Use the state standards to plan differentiated instruction.

    B. Communicate regularly with parents so students are supported in class and at home.

    C. Work with his peer teacher to ensure his instruction is comprehensible.

    D. Attend professional development that will help with teaching struggling students.

6. Students have been immersed in a lesson about genetics for quite some time. Based on assessment data, the teacher feels students are ready to engage in critical thinking. The teacher decides to have the students facilitate class activities based on a set rubric. What is the name of this strategy?

    A. Reciprocal teaching

    B. Socratic seminar

    C. Shared reading

    D. Student take-over

7. The teacher writes on her board:

    • Students will identify parts of a sentence: subject and predicate.

    • Students will understand the difference between fragments and complete sentences.

    These are examples of:

    A. Standards

    B. Objectives

    C. Rules

    D. Rubrics

8. Which of the following would be the most effective way to use interdisciplinary methods during an English lesson?

    A. Allow students to free write in their journals about the Civil War.

    B. Move students through learning centers where they listen to a news broadcast about the 1969 moon landing and answer comprehension questions about the broadcast.

    C. Read stories about space exploration in the 1960s and analyze how the political climate affected the main outcomes of the space program.

    D. Have students work in cooperative groups to analyze a story about Apollo 13 where the characters evolve throughout the story.

9. Which of the following describes backwards design in planning instruction?

    A. Design activities to measure the skills students need to acquire and determine what assessments to use to reach desired outcomes.

    B. Use the textbook to build test questions for the assessment, design activities, and look for standards alignment.

    C. Ask students what they want to learn, look over the standards, and design activities that meet both the students desires and the state standards.

    D. Determine skills the students must acquire, select appropriate assessments to measure desired outcomes, and design activities.

10. Which of the following would be the most appropriate person to collaborate with when planning instruction of special needs students?

    A. The parents

    B. The special education teacher(s)

    C. The school psychologist

    D. The IEP team

Number	Answer	Explanation
1.	A, B, C	Answer choice A has the term *before* in it. Activating background knowledge includes discussing a topic *before* starting the activity. Watching a short video about Native Americans is a way to activate schema before reading Native American poetry. A KWL graphic organizer can be used before reading or an activity to ignite student understanding. The K stands for *know* as in *what do you already **know** about this subject*. The only answer that is not part of building schema is answer D because filling out a worksheet for homework is usually not the correct way to approach learning in any scenario on this exam.
2.	B	*Wait time* is considered a good term on this exam. Using adequate wait time promotes critical thinking and provides the necessary time students need to contemplate questions and provide thoughtful answers. In addition, when students have time to think, they will have more opportunity to participate. If you see *wait time* as an answer choice on the exam, pay attention because it is most likely the correct answer.
3.	B	This is a case where reading the answer choices first helps to focus on the correct answer. Notice answer choice B has the terms *disaggregate* and *specific*. To disaggregate means that to separate the data into specific parts. The graph shows students who are below, who meet, and who exceed the standards. However, it does not say how they did on certain areas of the exam. This graph is just a snapshot of overall scores. To make data-driven decisions, the teachers in this PLC need to disaggregate the data.
4.	C	Expository teaching is the opposite of inquiry learning because in expository teaching, the teacher is modeling or giving students information and they are listening. All of the other answer choices outline some kind of inquiry-based learning.
5.	A	When planning instruction, the state standards should be the number one source teachers use. Modifications, accommodations, and differentiation should be used while aligning instruction to the standards.
6.	A	When students facilitate the class, that is reciprocal teaching. Reciprocal means shared or equal. In this case, the teacher is sharing the responsibility of facilitating class with the students. Socratic seminar is a discussion-based lesson on a text in which the leader asks open-ended questions to the participants. Shared reading is when students share the reading task together. Student take-over is a nonsense answer choice.
7.	B	Objectives are the skills and behaviors students exhibit after a lesson. Objectives are often written using Bloom's verbs. In this case, the objectives are using the verbs *identify* and *understand*.
8.	C	Interdisciplinary means integrating other content areas into the content area you are teaching. This must be done in an authentic way. Answer choice C has students reading (English class) about space exploration (science class) and determining how the political climate was affected (social science class).

Number	Answer	Explanation
9.	D	In backwards design, the educator starts with the desired outcome in mind. In this case, it would be mastery of the standards. Next, the educator should select appropriate assessments to measure desired outcomes. Then the teacher should plan activities.
10.	B	The special education teacher and general education teacher should collaborate to differentiate instruction and engage students. In addition, the IEP team only meets at certain times and may be hard to collaborate with. The parents too are important, but not the most appropriate here.

This page intentionally left blank.

CONTENT CATEGORY

III

Assessment

This page intentionally left blank.

A. Assessment and Evaluation Strategies

1. Formal and informal assessment

2. Various types of assessments

3. Selecting the appropriate assessments to meet instructional objectives

4. Variety of assessment tools to evaluate student performance

   - Rubrics

   - Analytical checklists

   - Scoring guides

   - Anecdotal notes

   - Continuums

5. Students' self and peer assessment

6. Variety of assessment formats

   - Essay

   - Selected response

   - Portfolio

   - Conference

   - Observation

   - Performance

1. Formal and informal assessment

On the PLT, it is important to understand how to use assessments to monitor student progress and use the data to make informed decisions in the classroom. An effective educator consistently analyzes and applies data from multiple assessments to:

- Measure achievement.

- Diagnose students' learning needs.

- Inform instruction based on those needs.

- Drive the learning process.

Assessments are often categorized into two categories: informal and formal.

Formative (informal) assessments

Formative assessments, often referred to as informal assessments, are ongoing and used to monitor student learning. They can provide qualitative data such as anecdotal notes and observations. They can also provide quantitative data like test scores and reading level. The purpose of formative assessments is to measure performance and progress in day-to-day classroom activities. A formative assessment can be as simple as "thumbs-up/thumbs-down" to gauge student understanding. They can also be complex like a planned quiz after a lesson.

Examples of formative assessments include the following:

- Observations

- Exit tickets

- Quizzes

- Running record

- Computer-based knowledge check

Summative (formal) assessments

Summative assessments, often referred to as formal assessments, are at the end of learning and outcome driven. The purpose of a summative assessment is to determine students' proficiency and mastery of material. Summative assessments are used to measure how well the student learned objectives, skills, or other outcomes. Summative assessments typically have evaluation criteria based on standards.

Quick Tip

Summative assessments are most often associated with measuring outcomes. Summative assessments can also be used to assess the effectiveness of a curriculum or instructional program.

Examples of summative assessments include the following:

- Mid-term or final exam

- District benchmark tests

- State assessments

- Performance Assessment like a research paper, digital project, or visual presentation

- Chapter tests

- Science lab at the end of a unit

Example question

Which of the following is the best way to describe a formal assessment?

    A. To measure multiple standards at the same time.

    B. To rank students by achievement level.

    C. To evaluate students' mastery of skills and knowledge.

    D. To measure capabilities against a rubric.

Correct answer: C

Formal assessments, sometimes referred to as summative assessments, are based on the mastery of learning goals and are informed by the content of state standards. You will see questions like this with multiple good answers but only one correct choice on the PLT. While the other answer choices are generally true, they do not describe the core purpose of formal assessments, only individual characteristics.

2. Various types of assessments

Monitoring student progress and making informed decisions based on the assessment is a central theme on the PLT. It is important to understand the different types of assessments and how to use them in your classroom. As previously mentioned, this is done with both formal and informal assessments. For example, a teacher might use a quick formative assessment, such as an exit ticket, to determine if students are understanding a particular skill or concept. A teacher may also use test scores that measure several concepts to measure progress over time, such as a running record or performance assessment.

The following table provides descriptions of different types of assessments and examples of when each is used in the classroom.

Assessment Type	Definition	Example
Diagnostic	A pre-assessment providing instructors with information about students' prior knowledge, preconceptions, and misconceptions before beginning a learning activity. Diagnostic assessments are considered formative assessments because they inform instruction.	Before starting a science unit, a teacher gives a quick assessment to determine students' prior knowledge of concepts in the text. She uses this information to make instructional decisions moving forward.
Informal	A range of informal assessments or checks conducted by the teacher before, during, and after the learning process in order to modify instruction.	A teacher is walking around the room, checking on students as they work through math problems, and intervening when necessary. The teacher uses this observational data to make instructional decisions.
Formal	An assessment that focuses on the outcomes. It is frequently used to measure the effectiveness of a lesson.	A teacher gives a unit exam to measure outcomes and the effectiveness of instructional strategies.
Performance-based	An assessment that measures students' ability to apply the skills and knowledge learned from a unit or units of study: the task challenges students to use their higher-order, critical thinking skills to create a product or complete a process (Chun, 2010).	After reading text about the Civil War, students develop stories about different historical figures in the war. Students then perform these stories in front of the class and answer questions.
Criterion-referenced	An assessment that measures student performance against a fixed set of predetermined criteria or learning standards. Most commonly known criterion-reference exams are state standardized assessments.	At the end of the spring semester, students take the state standardized tests. The state uses the scores for accountability measures.
Norm-referenced	An assessment or evaluation that yields an estimate of the position of the tested individual in a predefined population with respect to the trait being measured. Results are usually communicated as a percentile ranking.	National tests that measure student performance against other students. Advanced placements exams, SAT, and ACT are all norm-referenced assessments.

Assessment Type	Definition	Example
Screening	An assessment used to place students in appropriate classrooms or grade level.	Students are typically screened throughout the year to determine what level they are reading. Placement decisions are made based on the outcomes of the screening.
Portfolio	A purposeful collection of student work that has been selected and organized to show student learning progress over time. Portfolios can contain samples of student work, rubric scores, self-evaluations, reflections, etc.	Over the course of a semester, students collect weekly writing samples and organize them by date in a designated folder. During parent conferences, students show their parents the portfolio and reflect on progress.

Example question

This year, students will take an exam that compares student performances to one another. Students are taking what type of assessment?

A. Formative

B. Norm-referenced

C. Criterion referenced

D. Diagnostic

Correct Answer: B

A norm-referenced assessment yields an estimate of the position of the tested individual in a predefined population with respect to the trait being measured. Use norm-referenced assessments to compare student performances as a percentile ranking.

3. Selecting the appropriate assessments to meet instructional objectives

It is important to understand how to create assessments in various formats that achieve specific instructional objectives. The PLT assesses your ability to select the most appropriate assessment at the appropriate time to measure the appropriate skill. You will be required to understand different assessments and how to use them effectively in the classroom. Remember, assessments are a key step in the backward design process.

Backward design

When creating assessments for lessons, backward design is very effective. The key to backward design is to start with the state standards and work in reverse.

Alignment is critical. Start with the standards, plan the assessments, monitor the students' progress at key intervals, and adjust short-term objectives accordingly.

Steps to Backwards Design

Recall the steps to backward design. Assessments are planned before instruction.

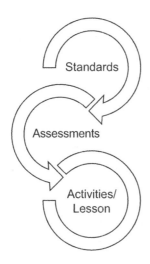

- Start with the state adopted standards. That is the end goal–to have the students master the standard(s).

- Determine how you will know the students mastered the standard and what assessments you will use to measure success.

- Decide what lessons and activities you will have students engage in to work toward standards mastery.

On this exam, you will be required to identify appropriate test questions for formal and informal assessments in different scenarios including:

- Assessments and test questions that you create and use in your classroom.

- Assessments and test questions created by publishers and test makers that you use in your classroom.

- Assessments and test questions that are used in state standardized tests.

It is important that you understand how to create valid and reliable assessments and test questions. You should also be able to identify appropriate test questions created by others. For example, a textbook you are using might have a sample test with several test questions that do not align with the learning objectives of the lesson you are teaching. It is important to recognize which test questions to use and which ones to omit.

Test item analysis

A *test item* is the task the test taker is being asked to perform. In a multiple-choice test, the test item includes the question, answer choices, and any additional stimuli provided like a chart or reading passage. A test item for a physical education lesson on basketball might include demonstrating dribbling or shooting skills. It is important for the test item to assess the skill or objective of the lesson.

A good way for a classroom teacher to evaluate test items is to complete an item analysis after the test. An **item analysis** is a process which examines student responses to individual test items to determine the quality of the test instructions and items.

When many students miss the same test item, the teacher should not automatically assume the students did not study or that they didn't comprehend the lesson material. The test item itself might be poorly written or confusing. Test item quality can be attributed to several factors including:

- The wording was misleading or confusing.

- The skill taught does not align to the skill tested on the assessment.

- There is not a correct answer choice.

- The question is not answerable because there is misinformation in the question.

- The item is too difficult (likewise, an item might be too easy).

The following is an example of how this might be presented on the PLT.

Example question

A teacher wants to be sure that the questions she has developed for a classroom assessment are measuring the appropriate skills. Which of the following practices would be most beneficial in determining if the teacher's questions are performing properly?

    A. Give the assessment over and over again to determine its validity.

    B. Survey students to see how they liked the assessment.

    C. Conduct an item analysis.

    D. Align activities to test taking strategies.

Correct answer: C

Conducting an item analysis will help the teacher determine if the test item is aligned with the lesson, written correctly, and assesses the skill being taught. Be on the lookout for good words attached to bad practices. In answer choice A, *validity* is a good word. However, repeating the assessment over and over without making adjustments is not the best option here. Answer choice B is student-centered, but surveying students will not help the teacher assess the performance of the test questions. Answer choice D includes the good word *align,* but it is attached to *test taking strategies*. In real life, we do help students with test taking strategies. However, on this exam, assessments should be aligned with standards mastery, not test taking strategies.

Assessment sequence

Using assessments in a sequence is very useful to make informed decisions in the classroom. Below is a typical sequence using diagnostic, formative, and summative assessments.

- **Step 1: Diagnostic assessment (pre-assessment).** Before the unit, the teacher gives students a pretest to measure skills, prior knowledge, preconceptions and misconceptions. Based on that data, the teacher makes instructional decisions moving forward.

- **Step 2: Formative assessment (ongoing).** As students move through the lesson objectives, the teacher uses formative assessments—observations, quick checks, writing samples, etc.—to move the lesson along. If any students are struggling with the objectives, the teacher uses targeted interventions to meet the specific needs of all students. The teacher continues to progress monitor throughout the lesson and unit by using formative assessments.

- **Step 3: Summative assessment (end of learning).** After the learning has concluded and the teacher has administered all strategies and interventions, the teacher administers a summative assessment. The teacher uses that data to measure outcomes and make decisions moving forward. The summative assessment also lets the teacher know if the strategies and interventions were impactful.

> **Caution**
>
> When answering assessment questions, try to avoid answer choices that promote using multiple choice (selected-response) tests. In the real-world, teachers use multiple choice tests all the time. However, this test will often require you to choose the *best assessment* to measure progress, which are most often formative. Summative assessments are often associated with multiple-choice tests.

Example question

A math teacher wants to assess whether or not his calculus students understand the concept of derivatives. Which of the following assessments is the best formative assessment for the teacher to use to determine if students understand the concept?

A. A 5-question quiz that includes at least two derivative problems.

B. A pre-assessment on derivatives, limits, and functions.

C. A paired activity where students explain how to find a derivative.

D. A game involving the whole class that includes formulas and functions.

Correct answer: C

The question is asking for the best formative assessment to monitor the understanding of derivatives by calculus students. Answer choice A is monitoring more than just derivatives, so we can eliminate this choice. Answer choice B is a great formative assessment but is not the best option to monitor learning of a particular skill that has just been taught. Answer choice D is a very informative assessment and will provide the teacher with insight, but games are not always the best method for revealing understanding. The best option here is the paired activity. During this activity, the teacher can circulate the room, listen to responses, and answer questions. By collecting qualitative data through this activity, the teacher can determine if students are struggling with or understanding the skill.

Testing environment

On the PLT, you will be required to select appropriate assessments and testing conditions to accommodate all students with varying abilities and learning styles. You will also be required to identify practices that align with testing accommodations for all students, including special education students and English learners.

Students perform better on assessments when they are comfortable with their surroundings. Your test day routine should be the same as your daily activities. The goal is to make students feel as comfortable on test day as they do when they are just taking notes in class. For example, if you turn desks to face the wall and put up big dividers only on test day, you are creating an environment that might induce anxiety for students. This anxiety can have an adverse effect on their test scores.

Controlling the testing environment might be difficult to accomplish during district or state testing. In some cases, providing accommodations might require students to be in different locations with an unfamiliar teacher. You can, however, control how testing occurs in your classroom. Make sure students are in a comfortable and familiar space, and reduce anxiety-inducing distractors.

Accommodations

For day-to-day activities and routine classroom assessments, teachers provide accommodations based on their students' needs. For example, teachers might give students extra time, allow students to use their notes, or permit the use of noise canceling headphones during a classroom assessment. However, on state standardized tests, testing accommodations are only provided if they are specified in the student's Individualized Education Program (IEP).

- **Special education students.** Schools must provide accommodations for students who have an IEP or a 504 plan, as they are outlined in the plan. Examples of these accommodations include:

  - **Flexible presentation.** Test administrators might have to use oral language or sign language to accommodate students who are blind or deaf.

  - **Flexible responding.** Students may have to dictate responses to a proctor if they do not have use of their hands. Students might also use speech-to-text technology.

  - **Flexible setting.** A student may be given the test over short intervals or given the test in a separate testing room. Extended time falls under this accommodation.

  - **Assistive devices and tools.** A student may use varied assistive devices to access the computer (e.g., alternative keyboards, trackballs, joysticks, switch scanning systems, touch screens, mouth sticks, head wands, eye-gaze or head control systems).

- **English language learner (ELL) testing accommodations.** Districts are required to offer accommodations to students identified as ELL. The following are examples of allowable accommodations for ELL students.

  - **Flexible setting.** ELLs may be offered the opportunity to be tested in a separate room with the English for speakers of other languages (ESOL) or heritage language teacher acting as test administrator.

  - **Flexible scheduling.** ELLs may be provided additional time; however, each test session must be completed within one school day.

  - **Assistance in heritage language.** ELLs may be provided limited assistance by an ESOL or heritage language teacher using students' heritage language for directions.

  - **Approved dictionary.** ELLs must have access to an English-to-heritage language translation dictionary or heritage language-to-English translation dictionary, such as those made available to ELLs in an instructional setting

Accommodations in the classroom will be different from the accommodations outlined in an IEP for state testing. If a student is struggling with writing, it is perfectly acceptable to ask them questions orally. Remember, the purpose of your classroom assessments is to determine where the students are in regard to the mastery of standards so that you can adjust your instruction as needed. On the PLT, remember that everything you do must meet the needs of *all* students. If a traditional style test does not accurately measure what a student knows, it is your responsibility to assess the student in another way.

Example question

A teacher has a few students who need specific reading interventions. What would be the most effective way to organize these interventions in the classroom?

A. Have the reading coach work with students who need help and focus instruction to students who have met proficiency.

B. Use a whole-group approach to address the reading deficiencies and apply strategies when needed.

C. Set up a variety of reading centers that target skills students need to practice, use flexible grouping to move students through the centers, and monitor progress by observing students.

D. Group all struggling readers together, apply interventions, and allow grade-level readers to engage in an activity of their choice.

Correct answer: C

Answer choice C accommodates all learners—proficient and struggling. Answer choice C also has good words used the right way: flexible grouping and monitor progress. Answer choice A pushes the responsibility onto the reading coach, which is usually not the correct answer on this test. Answer choice B is not differentiated at all. In fact, it lumps everyone together, whether they need interventions or not. Finally, answer choice D uses homogenous grouping in a bad way; the struggling readers are doing work while the on-level readers get to choose their activities. This is not the most effective approach.

Example question

During class, a sometimes-anxious student answers all of the questions correctly that a teacher asks about a particular topic. On test day, the student seems to freeze up and performs poorly on test items the teacher knows the student should have answered correctly. What should the teacher do to accurately assess the student?

    A. Tell the student they will do better next time and offer the advice to just relax during a test.

    B. Meet privately with the student and reassess the student orally in a less anxious environment.

    C. Retest the student the following day with a similar test that has a few easier questions.

    D. Offer test corrections for partial credit added to the test.

Correct answer: B

Answer choices A and D do not assess the student's mastery of the lesson. Answer choice C is an example of lowering the expectation, which teachers should never do. The question stated that the student is sometimes anxious. If the student froze during the test, it is likely that her anxiety, not lack of knowledge, was the reason she did poorly. In order to accurately assess the student, the teacher should meet with the student in a less threatening environment. Answer choice B is the best option because this approach allows the teacher to accurately assess the student's mastery.

Quick Tip

Providing extra time on state assessments is the most common accommodation for special education and ELL students.

4. Variety of assessment tools to evaluate student performance

Teachers can use a variety of assessment tools to monitor students' progress towards learning goals. An assessment tool is the actual instrument (test, rubric, survey, etc.) that is used to collect data. These tools allow a teacher to monitor student achievement and make informed decisions. Using a variety of assessments is important to collect the most meaningful data about students' progress toward meeting their learning goals.

Rubrics

A rubric is an evaluation tool or set of guidelines used to promote the consistent application of learning expectations, learning objectives, or learning standards in the classroom. Rubrics also measure students' attainment of knowledge against a consistent set of criteria (The Glossary of Education Reform, 2013). Rubrics are typically used for large projects and writing, but they can be used for any assignment.

Rubrics should be used for the following reasons:

1. Rubrics inform students of the expectations before the assignment is started.

2. Rubrics act as a formative self-assessment or peer-assessment tool during the task.

3. Rubrics act as a final evaluative tool for the teacher.

Rubrics can be holistic or analytic.

- **Holistic rubrics.** Best for assessing overall quality, proficiency, or comprehension of content or skills (Suskie, 2018).

- **Analytic rubrics.** Best for giving detailed feedback on a specific set of skills to assess strengths and weaknesses (Suskie, 2018).

Quick Tip

Rubrics across the content areas should include a section for following grade-level English language arts conventions.

Holistic Rubric Example

Score	Description
Meets expectations	• Essay demonstrates complete understanding of the assigned objectives. • Thesis statement is original and clearly stated, and ideas are well-developed. Organization is logical. • Writing is error-free, without ambiguity.
Acceptable	• Essay demonstrates considerate understanding of the assigned objectives. • Thesis statement is stated – somewhat complex and original. • Ideas are stated but sometimes do not support the thesis. • Writing has some errors.
Needs improvement	• Essay demonstrates some understanding of the assigned objectives. • Thesis statement is implied or barely stated. • Writing has many errors and is inconsistent and sometimes confusing.
Inadequate	• Essay demonstrates limited understanding of the assigned objectives. • Thesis statement is missing or too simplistic. • Ideas are missing or unbalanced. • Organization is not clear. • Writing is incohesive and incoherent with numerous errors.

Analytic Rubric Example

Skill	1 – Minimal	2 – Meets	3 – Exceeds
Mechanics	Many spelling, grammar, and punctuation errors; sentence fragments; incorrect use of capitalization.	Some spelling and grammar errors; most sentences have punctuation and are complete; uses upper- and lowercase letters.	Correct spelling, grammar, and punctuation; complete sentences; correct use of capitalization.
Ideas and Content	Key words are not near the beginning; no clear topic; no beginning, middle, and end; ideas are not ordered.	Main idea or topic is in first sentence; semi- defined topic; attempts beginning, middle, and end sections; some order of main idea and details in sequence.	Interesting, well-stated main idea or topic sentence; uses logical plan with an effective beginning, middle, and end; flow of ideas from topic sentence to details in sequence.
Organization	Disorganized and confusing.	Organized enough to read and understand the ideas.	Very organized and easy to understand; uses logical plan with an effective beginning, middle, and end; good flow of ideas from topic sentence to details in sequence.

Analytical checklists

An analytical checklist is a list of what needs to be included in an assignment. Similar to a rubric, analytical checklists should be used throughout an assignment. Teachers and students can preview the assignment, work together to analyze a student's progress through a multi-step task, or reflect on and assess various components of a student's work. Work can be assessed with letter grades or on a continuum. An analytical checklist can also be used to assess prior knowledge and provide feedback on a pre-assessment.

Analytical Checklist Example

Qualities of a Persuasive Paragraph	Yes	Getting Started	Thinking About It
Focus vocabulary used to define and discuss ideas.			
Words create tension for the reader.			
Sentences range in length and depth.			
Paragraph includes details to describe and defend main idea.			
Paragraph has a topic sentence or theme.			
Sentences organized so the reader can anticipate what comes next.			
Punctuation is thoughtful and adds meaning to the paragraph.			

Scoring guides

A scoring guide is a list of specific characteristics for an assignment. Like an analytical checklist, the focus is on whether the work meets the expectation or not. Scoring guides do not have intervals like a rubric. They are frequently used for assessing projects and performance tasks.

Scoring Guide Example

Project Features	Element Description	Points
Map	Map of national park shows physical features and roads and includes a legend with a scale.	/15
Landforms	Landforms are listed and detailed. Includes a complete explanation of how landforms impact the ecology, environment, and livelihood of people in the national park.	/15
Water sources	Water states (ice, liquid, gas) and sources are related to landforms and ecosystems in a model, writing, or activity.	/15
State	A map and other state facts related to the history of the national park.	/12
Places to visit	Provides places on the map for visitors to see.	/10
History of national park	Infographic, paragraph, or a bulleted list describes the history of the park.	/13
Habitats (plants and animals)	Project shows plants and animals and how they support one another to grow and sustain the national park's ecosystems.	/10
Effort	Effective use of time. Positive attitude and used problem-solving skills to ask questions and seek solutions. Respectful to classmates and materials.	/10
Total		/100

Anecdotal notes

Anecdotal notes are clear, concise observations of student learning. Anecdotal notes might describe observations of behaviors, interactions, skills, confidence, questions, or a response indicating growth or mastery of new learning. They can be a useful formative assessment tool. Considerations for anecdotal notes include:

- Have an organizational system for managing notes (i.e., a notebook, organizer, sticky notes).

- Focus on observed learning aligned to goals.

- Use a checklist when useful.

- Compile and organize anecdotal notes for each student to look for patterns over time.

Anecdotal Notes Example

Date	Notes
Student Name:	Shari Valance
1/25	— On time — On task — Using vocabulary in context — Finished assignment ahead of others
1/28	— On time — Somewhat on task – chatting with neighbor twice — Demonstrating skills with ease, using vocabulary — Started working ahead

Continuums

A continuum is an assessment tool that measures student progress toward mastery. It shows where a student falls on the spectrum of development and allows teachers to identify specific evidence of comprehension.

Continuum Example

6th Grade	7th Grade	8th Grade	9th to 10th Grade	11th to 12th Grade
Cites evidence to support explicit and inferred meaning of text.	Cites several pieces of evidence to support explicit and inferred meaning of text.	Differentiates and cites the strongest piece(s) of evidence to support explicit and inferred meaning of text.	Cites strong and thorough evidence to support explicit and inferred meaning of text.	Cites strong and thorough text evidence to support analysis of explicit and inferred meaning of text. Identifies when text leaves ideas and concepts uncertain.
Identifies a theme of the text. Explains the theme through details of the text. Summarizes the text.	Identifies a theme of the text. Explains development of the theme throughout the text. Objectively summarizes the text.	Identifies a theme of the text. Explains development of the theme throughout the text specific to events, characters, and setting. Objectively summarizes the text.	Identifies a theme of the text. Explains the emergence of the theme throughout the text as it is developed and refined. Objectively summarizes the text.	Identifies 2 or more themes of the text. Explains the emergence of the themes – their interactions and their interdependence throughout the text. Objectively summarizes the text.

(corestandards.org, 2010)

Data management

With all of these assessments, teachers can become inundated with data. It is important that teachers organize this information so it can be used effectively when making decisions. This includes:

- State testing scores
- District testing scores (if applicable)
- Classroom assessments and assignments
- Reading levels
- Math levels
- Item analyses
- Learning gains over time
- Standards mastery
- Anecdotal observations
- Notes

Gradebooks, spreadsheets, and databases all provide teachers with ways to organize and analyze data. You are expected to know which method of organization is best for you to evaluate the data and share the findings with students and their parents. For example, an online gradebook provided by the district is the best way for students and parents to track grades. When sharing information about students' grades, make sure you adhere to all applicable privacy laws and policies.

Example question

Which of the following would be the best way to organize student data to be communicated with parents?

    A. Email

    B. Gradebook

    C. Class wiki

    D. Anecdotal notes

Correct answer: B

The gradebook is the only answer that organizes data (student grades). Emails are never the best way to communicate with parents. A class wiki is a nonsense answer. Anecdotal notes are typically used in formative assessments and would not be helpful here. Keep in mind the question is asking you for the *best* method. Choose the *best* answer by eliminating non-answers.

Quick Tip

While teachers can communicate general data with stakeholders, individual student data is confidential and should only be shared with the student and parent or guardian (reference FERPA requirements).

Example question

A high school class is setting up a school store to raise money for a school fundraiser. Ms. Hughes wants to make sure students are applying the math concepts of profit, net cost, and unit cost as they write and submit their plan for the store. What is the best assessment tool for the project?

    A. Holistic rubric

    B. Continuum

    C. Anecdotal notes

    D. Analytical checklist

Correct answer: D

Answer choice D is the best choice because she has specific concepts she wants them to address in their store plan. An analytical checklist will help students before they begin the assignment, provide opportunities for feedback as they work, and give them a clear picture of accomplishment in the end.

5. Students' self and peer assessment

Student self-assessment and peer-assessment apply critical thinking to improve learning and performance. The feedback students generate for themselves and peers informs self-adjustment and revision (Andrade, 2019). Peer and self-assessment are formative assessments. They are most effective when students act on their evaluation to improve their work or performance.

Student self-assessment modes

Self-assessments can be used throughout a lesson. They can be used at the beginning, middle, and end of the lesson. Some common tools for self-assessments include using a traffic light, open-ended questions, reflection journals, checklists, rubrics, and data folders.

Self-Assessment Examples

Mode	Description/Example	Strengths	Limitations
Traffic light	To get a quick idea of student understanding, teachers can ask students to report a red light, yellow light, or green light. The self-assessment allows teachers to modify and adjust their instruction to differentiate for all learners. For example: • Green – I can do this. • Yellow – I'm getting there. • Red – I need help.	Quick, simple, routine, and useful for large and small groups.	Feedback isn't specific. Students are not sharing why they need help or how you can assist them. The teacher still has to make predictions about what instructional strategies to use and what content to review.

Mode	Description/Example	Strengths	Limitations
Open ended questions	One of the simplest ways to promote self-reflection is to ask open-ended questions. For example: • Can you explain how you solved the problem? • What else do you want to know about the topic? • What will you do differently next time?	Informal Can be used with individual students, large and small groups. Teachers can modify questions in the moment to address specific content.	Students might not have the time and space to reflect deeply. It can be challenging to come up with questions that will produce descriptive and transformative responses.
Reflective journal	A qualitative assessment tool where students write about their thinking and learning. They are used to formalize student responses to self-reflection questions, keep track of progress towards learning goals, and to promote metacognition. For example: • Solve 23 X 18. • Explain how you solved the problem. • Why did you choose this method?	Routine Easy to assess student work because all students are participating in the activity.	Challenging to get students to write about their thinking and learning process. Teacher needs to read and respond to student work.
Checklist	Students can use a checklist to assess whether they have included essential elements in their work. They can be used for performance assessments, projects, and group work. A checklist can be written with self-reflective questions. For example: • My graph is clear and easy to ready. • My graph shows data correctly. • My graph has a title, scale, and labels.	Provides a comprehensive overview of assignment elements. Gives clear direction for next steps to complete a learning task.	Takes more time to grade. Does not provide an opportunity to revise for quality. Students do not evaluate their work as they would with a rubric. Takes skill to read, reflect, and adjust.
Rubric	A criterion-based rubric is a good tool for assessing the quality of work. Students can use rubrics to revise and improve certain aspects of an assignment. They can be used at the middle and end of a learning activity.	Encourages ownership of learning. Students evaluate the quality of their work. When used routinely, can build habits of self-reflection.	Components of the skill or knowledge are not outlined in the assessment.

Mode	Description/Example	Strengths	Limitations
Data folder	Students can collect data throughout the school year and review their own achievement and growth. Data folders can contain test scores, learning targets, self-assessment data, and teacher and student assessment of classroom behaviors. Data folders can be used to: • Track progress over time. • Allow students to set their own goals. • Serve as an artifact for parent-teacher or student-led conferences.	Students graph or chart quantitative measures. Students learn to have ownership of their performance and achievement.	Data can be hard to collect and organize. Quantitative focus can limit opportunities for students to include what they know and are able to do.

Think about it!

Students need modeling, guidance, and practice to use self and peer assessment tools effectively. Always begin by modeling with an analysis of example work. Once students are able to effectively conduct self and peer assessments, they have a better model for their own work as learners and assessors.

Example question

A teacher is helping students organize math assessment scores over the course of a semester. Which of the following would be most appropriate in organizing students' scores?

A. School website

B. Bulletin board

C. Journals

D. Data folders

Correct answer: D

Data folders are tools students use to chart their progress over time. Students record their scores and even create graphs to communicate their data to teachers and parents. Student data should remain in a secure place. A school website and a bulletin board are not secure. Also, student data should not be displayed. Finally, a journal does nothing to organize assessment data.

Peer assessment modes

Peer assessments are when one student provides constructive feedback to another student. Self-assessment tools like open-ended questions, criterion-based checklists, rating scale, and rubrics can also be used for peer assessments. Peer assessments require modeling and reviewing expectations so that all students and their work are treated with respect. Peer-assessments are almost always formative assessments.

Use peer assessments to:

- Promote understanding of new knowledge and skills.

- Increase the amount of feedback students receive.

- Promote a culture of support and collaboration.

- Encourage revision and reflection.

- Encourage a deeper understanding of the elements and characteristics of quality work.

Peer scoring and explanation

Peers can give feedback with a rating and explanation system. For example, students were asked to rate their partner's sketch of the water system on a scale of 1-5. Then, they needed to explain the score they assigned. This gives the assessor an opportunity to quantify their feedback and focus their explanation on the strengths and limitations of their peers' work or presentation.

- **Open-ended questions.** Open-ended questions can be used to promote constructive analysis and feedback of peer work. They can also be used by a student to promote discussion and encourage understanding of different perspectives.

- **Checklists.** A checklist is a useful tool for reviewing the process of a writing assignment, project, or presentation. For a peer-assessment, it is typically used for a partnership to stay focused and be sure all elements of the assignment are complete.

- **Rubric.** Using a rubric helps a peer to evaluate their partner's work and provide articulated feedback. Students can be clear about why they chose a 4 or a 5 for a certain aspect of the work. It is a particularly helpful tool for evaluating writing during the revision process.

Peer-assessment strengths:

- Internalizes qualities of good work by helping a peer to emulate those qualities in their own work.

- Promotes collaboration and responsibility.

- Builds oral language skills (presentation, discussion, active listening, respectful response, argumentation, etc.).

- Enhances students' capacity for providing constructive feedback.

- Promotes self-efficacy and independence.

Peer-assessment limitations:

- Takes more time than self-assessment and simply providing feedback from the teacher.

- Assessment and feedback might not be accurate or constructive.

- All students involved need to want to participate.

- Peer assessments work best with constructive, focused pairs which can take time to assign and maintain.

Example question

What is the best mode for a peer assessment of a persuasive essay?

- A. Criterion-based checklist

- B. Analytic rubric

- C. Holistic rubric

- D. Open-ended questions

Correct answer: B

Answer choice B is the best assessment mode for assessing writing because it provides specific areas for improvement. Answer choice A would not be effective because checklists are used to make sure the work includes all of the elements of the assignment. It does not provide feedback to improve the essay. Answer choice C is incorrect because a holistic rubric would provide one score for the essay and not offer enough detailed feedback for the partner to make constructive improvements to the work. Answer choice D is incorrect because open-ended questions are not as efficient as a rubric for providing constructive feedback.

6. Variety of assessment formats

Teachers must be able to select an assessment format that is appropriate for the learning objectives of the lesson. The following table provides uses, strengths, and limitations of a variety of assessment formats.

Assessment Format	Description	Strengths	Limitations
Written assessments	Written assessments are considered authentic assessments because they give a comprehensive view of what a student knows about a particular topic. Written assessments can be as simple as filling in the blank or as complex as writing an essay on a topic. Examples include: • Essays • Lab write-ups • Letters • Journals	Written assessments often yield more information than a multiple-choice test. Teachers should use rubrics to assess written assessments. The main thing to remember when using informal writing assessments is to measure language usage, organization, and mechanics. Then use the qualitative data to make meaningful instructional decisions based on students' individual needs (The International Reading Association, n.d.).	Writing assessments are harder to assess objectively than other assessments and therefore may not be a reliable data point.
Selected response	The most widely used assessment is a multiple-choice assessment, also known as selected response.	Selected response assessments are easy, straight forward, and reliable.	This type of assessment does not always provide the necessary data when it comes to assessing students' abilities and students' needs. Often, an oral assessment or written assessment is more effective than a selected response assessment.

Assessment Format	Description	Strengths	Limitations
Portfolio	Portfolio assessments are where the teacher uses a series of student-developed artifacts to determine student learning.	Portfolios are considered a form of authentic assessment and offer an alternative or an addition to traditional methods of grading. Portfolios are tools to help students establish short-term and long-term goals.	Developing an objective evaluation tool for portfolios is challenging because student samples might have a small or large range of variability. For example, one piece of student work might suggest mastery of content and another suggests the need for growth.
Conference	An oral evaluation of what students know and are about to do. The teacher asks questions related to learning goals, and the student uses their class work, notes, and synthesis to demonstrate their knowledge and understanding. Conferences can be formative or summative.	Conferences emphasize student thinking and understanding. Students are able to demonstrate knowledge and skills in the broadest sense. They are not confined to questions.	Interviewing or conferring with each student, even for 5 minutes, can be overwhelming and outside a teacher's capacity. Not all students need a conference to demonstrate their knowledge. Conferences for assessment purposes are used on a selective basis to support students who will not be able to demonstrate knowledge, skills, and growth another way.
Observation	Observations document student actions. Documentation focuses on demonstration of mastery of content and learning goals.	Observations allow teachers to document growth and learning as it happens. This is especially powerful for younger students or any non-proficient readers and writers.	Not all learning is demonstrated anecdotally and at the same rate by all students. Observations need to be used in conjunction with other analysis.

Assessment Format	Description	Strengths	Limitations
Performance	Assessments where students are required to solve problems demonstrating their knowledge and skills and include: • Participating in a lab or experiment. • Solving and showing work for math problems. • Engaging in roleplay. • Conducting a presentation. • Building picture books.	Performance-based assessments require students to perform a task rather than simply fill in multiple choice bubbles. They are considered authentic assessments.	• Time consuming • Challenging to build objective assessment tools
Informal reading inventory	An informal reading inventory (IRI) is an individually administered diagnostic assessment designed to evaluate reading performance. After reading each leveled passage, a student responds orally to follow-up questions assessing comprehension and recall. The types of questions teachers ask during an IRI are: • Text-based • Inferential • Literal • Main idea • Key ideas • Sequence • Cause and effect • Plot structure	These informal reading assessments are used to measure progress and to make instructional decisions based on a student's individual needs.	Need to be administered one-on-one, students may have different competencies with information and narrative text.

Assessment Format	Description	Strengths	Limitations
Running record	A running record is a way to assess students' oral fluency. These assessments are administered differently depending on what the teacher is trying to measure. However, the basic structure is, a student reads from a passage. The teacher marks any errors or miscues the student makes during the reading. The teacher can also calculate how many correct words per minute (WPM) the student reads.	A running record is helpful because the teacher and the student can go over the miscues, decide on next steps, and set new goals.	Needs to be done one-on-one with students. Some students understand what they are reading better when they read to themselves.
Authentic assessments	Authentic assessments allow students to apply their learning in a real-world scenario or authentic task. These assessments come in all forms and are sometimes referred to as alternative assessments.	Authentic assessments give students an opportunity to demonstrate their capabilities in a real-world scenario. They yield rich, qualitative data that provides a true assessment of students' mastery of skills and capabilities.	A drawback to authentic assessments is that they are time consuming to create and administer. They also produce qualitative data that can be difficult to aggregate.
Oral assessments	In an oral assessment, students show what they know by communicating verbally. Students will often answer questions about a story—sequence, plot, characters, etc. Oral assessments can also be used to measure fluency and comprehension. Oral assessments include: • Oral answers • Performances • Presentations • Roleplay	Oral assessments are helpful when working with ELL students. Often, ELLs will understand a lesson but may be unable to communicate what they know in writing. If the teacher is trying to assess comprehension, ELLs can orally communicate what they have learned. This ensures the teacher is assessing the correct skill—comprehension.	Can be hard to assess because pre-defined objectives may not reflect true strengths of a performance.

Example question

What is the best way to assess student writing over the course of the year?

- A. Oral assessment
- B. Portfolio
- C. Informal reading inventory
- D. Selected-response

Correct answer: B

A portfolio is the best way to track the growth of writing skills and understanding of genre. Answer choices A and C are oral assessments that provide insight to oral literacy development but not written language. Answer choice D is incorrect because a selected-response assessment will not capture student growth or the depth of their content knowledge.

This page intentionally left blank.

B. Assessment Tools

1. Types and purposes of standardized tests

2. Norm-referenced and criterion-referenced scoring

3. Terminology related to testing and scoring
   - Validity
   - Reliability
   - Raw score
   - Scaled score
   - Percentile
   - Standard deviation
   - Mean, mode, and median
   - Grade-equivalent scores
   - Age-equivalent scores

4. Holistic and analytical scoring

5. Interpreting and communicating assessment results

1. Types and purposes of standardized tests

A standardized test is any test that requires all students to answer the same question and is scored in a consistent manner (Education Reform, 2015). Typically, *standardized* describes large scale tests created by testing companies for schools and districts across the country.

- **What they measure.** Standardized tests measure knowledge and skill, students' capacity for learning, and their ability to continue learning. They measure how well students have mastered learning goals and how their performance compares to their peers.

- **How they measure.** Standardized tests are developed using metrics to establish the ability of a question to assess a specific skill or understanding of knowledge. While most questions are multiple-choice, they also include essay questions, true or false, and constructed response questions.

The data from standardized tests is used to inform instruction, report growth and learning, and compare schools, teachers, and students. The data is frequently used as an accountability measure for schools and teachers. You will need to learn what standardized tests are used at your school and what your responsibilities are for administering tests and using the data. Here are three types of standardized tests you need to be aware of for the PLT.

Assessment Type	Description	Use	Examples
Achievement	Assessment of knowledge and skills, and growth overtime.	Measure effectiveness of schools and teachers. Diagnostic tool for academic placement and to understand what students need to learn.	• MAP growth • STAR • Standard 10 (SAT 10) • State standardized test
Aptitude	Measures students' cognitive and physical *aptitude* or ability to learn.	Predict what a student is capable of learning. Placement in gifted programming.	• ACT • SAT
Ability	Measure what students have learned over time both innate ability and learned behaviors (aptitude and achievement).	Allocate special education and English language learner (ELL) services.	ELL: • WIDA • Test of English as a Foreign Language (TOEFL) Special education: • Wechsler intelligence scale for children • Woodcock-Johnson tests of cognitive abilities

(Education Reform, 2015)

Standardized tests produce a tremendous amount of data that teachers use in their classroom to make informed decisions about student learning and instruction.

Data displays

Teachers receive data from various tests and testing platforms that display results in a multitude of formats. It is important that you are able to interpret results based on the test type and the display. It is impossible to cover all types of testing results because each testing platform displays results in different ways. However, results are typically answering one of the following questions:

- *How did my students perform in comparison to other students?*
- *How did my students perform on a particular skill?*
- *How have my students grown over time?*
- *At what proficiency level are my students?*

Quick Tip

All assessment data should be triangulated. That means that when making final decisions about how to report or continue a child's learning, a teacher should consider multiple data points from different kinds of assessments. If there are large inconsistencies, it is possible that one of the measurements is not doing a good job of assessing the student's knowledge and skills.

Learning gains over time

Line graphs are typically used to show students' learning gains over time. Line graphs can include multiple lines so that teachers can compare individual students, class data, school data, or national data. The actual display will depend on the platform from which the data was collected and what type of data is accessible from that platform.

The graph that follows shows a student's progress in overall standards mastery throughout the course of the year.

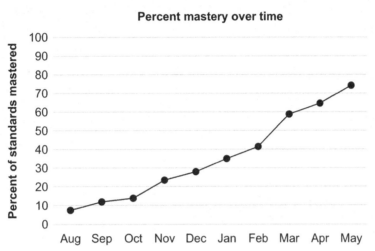

Percent mastery over time

Percentile ranking

Percentile ranking compares how well a student performed in comparison to other students who took the same test. A percentile ranking of 53% can be interpreted one of two ways. Either the student performed better than 53% of those who also took the test, or 47% of those taking the test performed better than the student. Percentile rankings are given as individual student percents and may be shown on a bar graph with 50% highlighted, since 50% is the median ranking.

Proficiency of a skill or standard

Proficiency may be reported in a number of ways, including a percent value, a bar graph, or a box-and-whisker plot. The percent is a number reported out of 100, and a bar graph is a visual of that percent out of 100. Typically, when scores are reported as a percent from an outside testing source, percent ranges are assigned proficiency levels. For example, students scoring 50-70% mastery may be very close to satisfactory but not quite to proficiency.

A box-and-whisker plot is used in the same manner, but the values reported are a little different. A box-and-whisker plot shows a median score, variations of the median, and the lowest and highest values. You need to know that the line in the middle of the box is the median value, or value in the middle of the data collected. Typically, this value is where students are considered proficient.

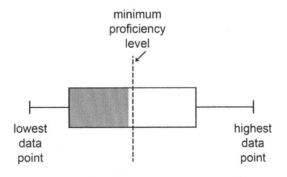

Note that a box-and-whisker plot can be displayed horizontally, as shown, or vertically.

2. Norm-referenced and criterion-referenced scoring

The two most common scoring systems for standardized tests are criterion-referenced and norm-referenced. Teachers need to understand the purpose of each type of assessment and what the scores mean. Looking at student performance and growth on either type of assessment is a good way to inform and measure the effectiveness of classroom instruction.

	Norm-referenced Assessment	Criterion-referenced assessment
Purpose	An assessment or evaluation reporting how well a student performed in comparison to similar students. The questions are designed to find differences in student achievement, not competency. They use a national set of standards (not local curricula). Good for seeing individual student growth overtime.	An assessment or evaluation measuring what students should know and are able to do according to a set of criteria or standards. It is a measure of the knowledge and skills students can demonstrate, not whether a student's score is better or worse than another student. This is in alignment with the philosophy behind state standards and student-centered instruction. State standardized tests are used for accountability measures.
Scoring	**Percent** Student scores are reported as a **percentile** indicating how well a student performed in comparison to the normed group. If a student scored in the 85th percentile, her score is at or above 85% of the people taking the exam; she is at the top. If a student scored in the 25th percentile, she only scored at or above 25% of others taking the same test; she is at the bottom.	**Proficient** Student scores are usually reported on a continuum such as: • Below satisfactory • Proficient • Advanced Scores reflect how well they met the criteria. If a student scored below satisfactory, it means he did not demonstrate proficient understanding of the content on the test. If a student scored advanced, it means he mastered the content and beyond.
Examples	SAT, ACT, MAP growth, STAR The National Assessment of Educational Progress (NAEP) is an exam given every few years for data purposes only to compare students' reading scores across the U.S.	Most classroom assessments created by teachers. At the end of the spring semester, students take the state standardized tests. The state uses the scores for accountability measures. PLT (because it measures your skills against the professional standards for educators)

Think about it!

Normed group. A normed group is formed to create an idea of how similar students score on the same test. The normed group is typically representative of students in the same grade. The normed group can also be selected to compare students with similar age, English language proficiency, socio-economic status, and other characteristics.

Principles of Learning and Teaching: Grades 7-12

Example question

At the beginning of the school year, Ms. Rossi received her students' state standardized test scores from the previous school year. What is the best way for her to use the test results?

   A. Use scores to place students in remedial and accelerated learning groups.

   B. Meet with students individually to create learning goals based on their test results.

   C. Send scores home to families and focus on preparing for the next yearly standardized tests.

   D. Find patterns in areas students need to grow.

Correct answer: D

State standardized tests are criterion-referenced. That means that student scores are based on a set of skills and knowledge that the state has determined they need to know. By looking for patterns of skills and knowledge, the teacher can make decisions about what to emphasize in her instruction. Answer choices A and B are incorrect because the data was collected months ago and will not be specific enough to students' immediate needs. Answer choice C is incorrect because the scores can provide valuable baseline information for instruction.

Quick Tip

An achievement test can be criterion-referenced or norm-referenced. Norm-referenced tests are best for measuring the growth of individual students over time. Criterion-referenced achievement tests can be used to measure the growth of a group of students over time, or they can be used to assess the quality of a school and its teachers.

3. Terminology related to testing and scoring

Standardized tests have a tremendous impact on districts, schools, and students. Teachers need to be able to engage in discussions regarding standardized testing. This includes having an understanding of testing and scoring to interpret, compare, and use data to inform instruction. Below is a list with explanations of terms related to testing and scoring.

Validity. Validity refers to how well the test assesses the skills and knowledge it intends to assess. The assessment is valid if:

1. It is measuring the content it is supposed to measure.

2. It is an accurate measure of that content.

Reliability. Reliability refers to how consistent the test is at giving valid information about a test taker. A test that is valid is almost always consistent.

Think about it!

If a recipe calls for 1 cup of water, you would use a measuring cup to measure the water. The measuring cup is designed to measure liquid, and it is made with material that holds its shape. This makes it a **valid** tool to measure 1 cup of water. If you needed 1 cup of water, but used a 1/3 measuring cup instead of a 1 cup measuring cup, the measurement would not be as valid because it does not accurately measure what you need. If you are using the right size measuring cup, your measurement is also **reliable** because it should consistently measure the same size every time you use it. The same goes for assessments. For a test to be reliable and valid, you must use the proper measurement and be sure you are measuring the intended outcome.

Example question

What is the most important characteristic to consider when choosing or creating a standardized test?

A. Reliability and validity

B. Percentile ranking

C. The bell-curve

D. Criterion-reference

Correct answer: A

Reliability and validity are the most important characteristics of a good standardized test.

Raw score

This is the number of questions a student gets correct on the exam. Raw scores are helpful in determining specific academic strengths and weaknesses. If you received a 45 out of 55 questions, your raw score is a 45.

Scale score

Most state standardized assessments report results as scaled scores with ranges attached to one of five performance levels:

- Inadequate (level 1)

- Below satisfactory (level 2)

- Satisfactory (level 3)

- Proficient (level 4)

- Mastery (level 5)

The scaled scores and levels are reported by student, and levels can be interpreted from a table that lists all grade levels and performance levels. Below is a generic example of how reading levels are reported for state tests.

Level 1	Level 2	Level 3	Level 4	Level 5
Inadequate	Below Satisfactory	Satisfactory	Proficient	Mastery
Highly likely to need substantial support for the next grade.	Likely to need substantial support for the next grade.	May need additional support for the next grade.	Likely to excel in the next grade.	Highly likely to excel in the next grade.

Quick Tip

Each state standardized test is different. The proficiency levels are different, and the terminology is different. You must become familiar with the metrics, format, and language of your state's standardized test scores.

Percentile rank

A percentile rank tells how well a student performed in comparison to other students who took the same test. The percentile rank value is the percent of students the test taker scored better than on the assessment. A percentile rank of 73 means the student scored better than 73% of all the students who took the assessment. The percentile rank does not reflect how well an individual student scored or what they know. It simply compares a student to a much larger group of students to see how their performances compare.

Stanine

A stanine score is a method of scaling test scores on a 9-point standard scale with a mean of 5 and a standard deviation of 2. Stanine allows you to compare scores on a single digit scale. This simplified scale is a way to easily group students from the lowest performers to the top performers. Stanines are another way to compare groups of students, such as percentile ranks and other types of scaled scores. The following table shows how stanine scores are categorized.

Stanine Score	
1, 2, 3	Below average
4, 5, 6	Average
7, 8, 9	Above average

Mean, mode, and median

Measures of central tendency or mean, mode, and median are ways to sort and interpret data. These statistical values are referred to as measures of center because they are symbolic of the values in the data set. They can be helpful for understanding overall performance and deciding the next steps for whole class instruction. The table below provides a description of each measure of central tendency using the following example.

> A group of 7 students took an assessment worth 100 points. These are the scores in order from highest to lowest: 55, 84, 86, 86, 90, 91, 96.

Measure	Description	Calculation	What does it mean?
Mean	The mean is the average of the values.	The mean is calculated by adding all of the scores and dividing by the number of scores in the set. $$\frac{55 + 84 + 86 + 86 + 90 + 91 + 96}{7}$$ The mean is 84. The mean is frequently a decimal or a whole number not included in the set.	Mean is the most common way to manipulate a data set. It tells you the average score which can be an indicator of overall class performance.
Median	The median is the middle number of the data set.	Order the numbers from smallest to largest and find the middle number of the set. If the set has an even number of values, the median is the average of the two values closest to the middle. 55, 84, 86, 86, 90, 91, 96 The median is 86.	The median might be more useful than the average because outliers (like 55 in this set) do not have as much influence on the median number as they do on the mean. Notice that the median, 86, is higher than the mean, 84.

Measure	Description	Calculation	What does it mean?
Mode	The mode is the number that occurs the most frequently.	55, 84, (86) (86) 90, 91, 96 The mode is 86.	Use the mode to find trends in the data and create groups. In this case, the mode is higher than the mean.

Standard deviation

Standard deviation tells you how spread out the scores are. Usually, 95% of scores fall within two deviations of the mean.

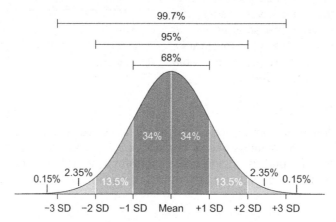

Grade-level equivalency

Scores are often categorized by their grade level equivalency (GLE). You do not need to know how to calculate GLE, you just have to understand what the number represents. Grade level equivalencies match school grade levels K through 12+. They are also assigned a decimal value to pinpoint where in the grade level the student is reading. The decimal allows you to measure small amounts of growth over time. A grade equivalency matches a student's current learning level to its corresponding grade level. For example, a 6th grade student who struggles with reading may be reading on what is considered to be a 4th grade level. Thus, their grade level equivalency, sometimes referred to as reading level, might be a 4.3. A GLE may be below, at, or above a student's actual enrolled grade level. The following are examples of GLE.

- GLE 5.2 – reading at the beginning of 5th grade level.
- GLE 7.8 – almost reading at the 8th grade level.
- GLE 1.5 – reading at the middle of 1st grade level.

Age-equivalent scores

Like grade level equivalency, age-equivalent score is often included on a norm-referenced, standardized test report. It uses age (within 6 months) as a baseline instead of grade. It provides a different insight than other data points because it tells you whether a student performed like others their age or like a student older or younger. It is not considered a great measure for diagnostic or placement decisions for statistical reasons (Frey, 2018). Age-equivalent scores are reported as a decimal value representing years and months.

- AE 6.5 – reading as a typical child at 6 years and 6 months.
- AE 10.75 – reading as a typical child at 10 years and 9 months.
- AE 12.3 – reading as a typical child at 12 years and 4 months.

Example question

Which of the following would be the most beneficial way for a teacher to examine a test score in order to differentiate instruction based on students' specific strengths and weaknesses?

    A. Percentile rank

    B. Scale score

    C. Stanine score

    D. Raw score

Correct answer: D

For teachers to determine specific strengths and weaknesses, a raw score is most appropriate. A percentile rank does nothing to tell the teacher what specific skills students have or do not have. Stanine scores and scale scores are the same thing; they take the raw score and transform it for equating purposes. Stanine and scale scores will not indicate specific skills.

Example question

A teacher receives the information that her 10th grade student has a grade equivalency reading level of 9.8. How should the teacher interpret this score?

    A. The student is reading slightly below grade level.

    B. The student is reading at grade level.

    C. The student is reading 8 points above a 10th grade level.

    D. The student is reading substantially below her enrolled grade level.

Correct answer: A

A grade equivalency level of 9.8 refers to a 9th grade reading level. Because the decimal values range from .0 to .9, a decimal value of .8 is very close to the next grade level. Therefore, the student is reading just slightly below her current grade level, which is 10th grade.

4. Holistic and analytical scoring

Holistic and analytical scoring are the most common methods used for scoring student work. They are frequently used to describe checklists and rubrics, but they are general scoring systems that can describe any numerical feedback on student work.

Holistic scoring. A holistic score (or grade) is one value for the entire assignment. The value may be a percentage, rubric score, or raw point value. In a holistic score, all assignment elements are put together. Holistic scores are used for final grades, to demonstrate mastery for standards, to emphasize the product, and show what a student can do over the learning process. They are often used for large or culminating final projects, rubrics, quizzes, and tests.

- **Advantages:**

  - One score is easy to document and communicate.

  - An overall score takes into considerations the strengths and weaknesses of a performance or product.

  - Scores are more reliable because fewer details are separated for review

- **Disadvantages:**
  - Feedback to students is very general and makes revisions challenging.
  - Criteria cannot be weighted with different values.

Analytical scoring. An analytical score breaks up the components of an assessment to assign scores to various sections and competencies and can include scoring overtime. Analytical scoring is used with rubrics, checklists, and feedback from conferencing. They are also used for a large or culminating final project, when introducing an assignment, or to focus on revisions.

- **Advantages:**
  - Students receive more specific feedback than a holistic score.
  - Feedback is transparent about which elements of the assignment are more important than others.

- **Disadvantages:**
  - Scoring the assignment and analyzing the data is time consuming.
  - Scores are not always reliable.

5. Interpreting and communicating assessment results

In education, **stakeholders** are people who are invested in the success of the school and its students. Students, parents, teachers, administrators, community members, and business owners are all stakeholders. On the PLT, you will be required to identify effective ways to communicate achievement results, in the form of qualitative and quantitative data, to stakeholders. Teachers must be able to communicate achievement data to school leadership, other teachers, students, and parents.

Communicating techniques

Stakeholders want to know about student learning and growth reflected in assessment results. Good communication is done through planning and preparation, maintaining a clear understanding of data, and using appropriate vocabulary to describe student performance.

- **Know your data sources.** Assessment data comes from all of the evaluation tools used to inform instruction. Formative assessments used to drive instruction can also be used to understand students' learning and growth over time.

- **Triangulate data.** Good communication of growth and learning focuses on three or more data points. Teachers should use all data sources available to them when reporting student learning and growth.

- **Know your audience.** When speaking to families about assessments, use common words they can understand and stay focused on their child. When speaking to administration or teaching colleagues, your focus will probably be on overall growth and areas of need.

Scenario

Kevin takes a norm-referenced standardized test 4 times a year. In January, his math scores went down, and his parents were concerned about his learning progress. Kevin's math teacher met with his parents to help them understand the test data. First, she showed them how the report indicated many areas where he had made growth, even if it was small. Then, she pointed out that his scores mainly went down in the area of measurement, a topic not yet covered in class. Next, she shared Kevin's class work and formative assessments to demonstrate ways he was learning and making growth. Together, they contextualized the standardized test scores and made learning goals for the upcoming semester.

Explanation

In this scenario, the teacher used common language to help Kevin's parents read the standardized test report and pointed out strengths and areas of need on the report. She stayed focused on their child. Importantly, she triangulated data; she helped the parents to understand that the test score was only one part of Kevin's demonstrated growth and learning. She used classwork and formative assessments to emphasize how Kevin's learning was improving and used the data to talk about individualized goals for learning in the coming semester.

Quick Tip

Typically, communication between the teacher and stakeholders comes in the form of parent-teacher conferences or student-led conferences. During these conferences teachers, parents and students review and evaluate achievement results, qualitative data, quantitative data at work together to map a plan for success.

Appropriate language

While the technical language presented in this section is important for educators, use everyday language to explain test results and analysis to families and outside stakeholders. Find the simplest way to discuss even the most challenging information. Remember, when communicating with families, it is never okay to compare one student's work with another student's work. Also avoid discussing test scores at an open house or other gathering with school community members.

Family Educational Rights and Privacy Act

It is important to remember that students have privacy rights regarding their education information and data. In U.S. public schools, student rights are protected by the Family Educational Rights and Privacy Act (FERPA). FERPA is the federal law that protects the privacy of student education records. FERPA also gives parents certain rights with respect to their children's education records. These rights transfer to the student when the student reaches the age of 18 or attends a school beyond the high school level (U.S. Department of Education, 2019).

Quick Tip

Student-led conferences are a twist on the old-school parent-teacher conference. In a student-led conference, students are in charge of communicating their progress to their parents. The teacher and parent(s) listen to the student as the student goes over assessments data, portfolios, and progress. This helps the student take ownership of the learning and shows the parents how involved students are in analyzing their own data.

Example question

A teacher is preparing for a data meeting with her principal. She has been asked to bring data on formative classroom assessments in language arts as well as results from students' most recent reading standardized test. What should she study and be prepared to discuss?

- A. Individual student gains and areas of need.
- B. Inconsistencies between test scores and classroom assessments.
- C. How to use all data points to inform instruction.
- D. Specific items from the standardized test.

Correct answer: C

This is an example of a question with more than one good answer. Good words like *assessments, standardized test, gains and areas of need* are in each answer choice. The key to selecting the best answer is choosing which one will describe the overall focus of the meeting rather than just one topic. Answer choices A, B, and D might come up in the discussion. However, answer choice C describes the goal of the data meeting.

This page intentionally left blank.

Content Category III – Practice Questions and Answer Explanations

1. Students are studying a complex topic. For the assessment, the teacher is allowing students to choose among different ways they will show mastery of the skills. Students may choose to conduct a presentation, design a lesson on the topic, or engage in a writing assignment. The teacher is:

   A. Paying attention to multiple intelligences and allowing the students to engage in performance-based assessments.

   B. Using a whole-group approach and requiring students to complete portfolio assessments.

   C. Using cooperative learning and allowing students to engage in criterion assessments.

   D. Paying attention to student interests and allowing students to engage in problem-based assessments.

2. A teacher notices that a student is struggling to read a certain part of the text. The teacher wants to understand what specific skill the student is lacking so the teacher can address it. What assessment type would be the most effective in this situation?

   A. Summative

   B. Criterion-refenced

   C. Norm-referenced

   D. Diagnostic

3. Which of the following is the most effective way to use a criterion-referenced assessment?

   A. To compare student performances.

   B. To drive instructional decisions.

   C. To measure student learning at the end of a lesson.

   D. To decide where to place students for class ranking.

4. A formative assessment is:

   A. ongoing and used as a final grade for students.

   B. static and used as a preassessment.

   C. static and used to compare student performances.

   D. ongoing and used to determine how to move forward with teaching.

5. Which of the following provides rich qualitative data regarding student behavior?

   A. Diagnostic assessment.

   B. Student survey.

   C. Anecdotal record.

   D. Oral assessment.

6. When can teachers provide the accommodation of extra time on a state standardized criterion-referenced assessment?

   A. If the student has permission from a parent.

   B. If a student has permission from the principal.

   C. If the student has an IEP with the accommodation outlined in the plan.

   D. If the student has a doctor's note outlining test anxiety.

7. Which of the following assessment data would be most beneficial when measuring the effectiveness of a new reading program?

   A. Pretest and summative.

   B. Pretest and formative.

   C. Diagnostic and norm-referenced.

   D. Screening and formative.

8. A teacher wants to collect student writing samples over time and have them analyze their performance from the beginning of the semester to the end of the semester. This type of assessment is a _____?

   A. Performance-based assessment.

   B. Portfolio assessment.

   C. Norm-referenced assessment.

   D. Ongoing assessment.

9. What can a teacher do to ensure she is communicating assessment data to all stakeholders?

   A. Invite parents and guardians in for student-led conferences.

   B. Require a parent signature on the quarterly report cards.

   C. Send home progress reports every week.

   D. Remind students to tell their parents about weekly assessments.

10. A teacher wants to be sure that the questions she has developed for a classroom assessment are measuring the appropriate skills. This teacher is concerned with:

   A. Reliability

   B. Validity

   C. Stability

   D. Objectivity

Number	Answer	Explanation
1.	A	All of the assessments in the question are performance-based. In addition, allowing students to choose the different ways they will show mastery is an example of paying attention to multiple intelligences or learning preferences.

Answer choice B sounds good, and the items may be added to a portfolio, but one item does not constitute a portfolio.

Answer choice C is not correct because the assessments are not necessarily completed as a team and are therefore not necessarily cooperative assessments. Because we don't know how the teacher is grading the assignment, the phrase, *criterion assessments*, is simply a distractor phrase.

Answer choice D is incorrect because the assessment types are performance-based, not problem-based. |
2.	D	The teacher is trying to diagnose the issue the student is having. Therefore, a diagnostic assessment is appropriate here.
3.	B	No matter what, assessments should be used to make instructional decisions in the classroom.
4.	D	Formative assessments are often informal, ongoing checks that help a teacher decide how to move forward in a lesson. Remember <u>form</u>ative assessments in<u>form</u> the instruction delivery.
5.	C	For student behavior, observations with anecdotal notes is most effective. The anecdotes provide context and description of the student's behavior.

All other answer choices do not address student behavior, rather they address student learning. |
| 6. | C | The only way a student can receive extra time on a state test is if it is outlined as an accommodation on the IEP. The student must be ESE and have the accommodation documented in the plan. |
| 7. | A | Summative data measures progress when the lesson, strategy, or unit is finished. Determining the effectiveness of a reading program requires student scores at the beginning (pretest) and at the end after the reading program was administered (post-test).

Formative assessments are ongoing, during the teaching, so formative assessments would not be helpful in evaluating the effectiveness of a program. Therefore, answer choices B and D are not appropriate in this situation.

A norm-referenced test does not give specific information about skills learned, so answer choice C also does not fit this situation. |
| 8. | B | Because the teacher is collecting specific student artifacts over time, this is a portfolio assessment. |

Number	Answer	Explanation
9.	A	The term *all stakeholders* means students and parents/guardians. Therefore, student-led conferences are most effective here. Answer choices B, C, and D do not guarantee that both students and parents or guardians are aware of and invested in student performance and progress.
10.	B	**Validity** – the extent you are testing what you intend to test **Reliability** – the extent to which the results are consistent Stability and objectivity are non-answers here.

CONTENT CATEGORY

IV

Professional Development, Leadership, and Community

This page intentionally left blank.

IV. Professional Development, Leadership, and Community

1. Professional development practices and resources
2. Research-based teaching practices
3. Reflective practice and professional growth
4. Support personnel who assist students, teachers, and families
5. Teacher leadership and the community
6. Developing collaborative relationships to support the educational process
7. Major legislation relating to students and teachers

1. Professional development practices and resources

Professional development is driven by state, district, school, and individual professional goals. You will use professional development to:

- Stay up to date on current research.
- Inform teaching methods and practice.
- Explore questions and theories of instruction and learning.

The following section provides descriptions of different types of professional development. On the PLT, you will need to understand how these resources can improve your practice throughout your teaching career.

Professional literature

Professional literature is peer-reviewed publications related to your career in education. Professional literature discusses studies, meta-analysis, new theories, classroom strategies, explanations of legislation, case studies, and other research specific to learning and teaching. Professional literature can be found in digital and text forms. Always consider whether the source is valid and reliable.

Workshops

Workshops are gatherings for educators to explore specific topics and plan or create something to use in their teaching practice. They are organized by publishing companies, education experts, schools, school districts, and state departments of education.

Conferences

Like workshops, conferences are places where educators come together to listen to experts discuss new strategies and theories of practice. Conferences tend to have a wide variety of experts and choices for learning sessions. Conference schedules provide more time than workshops to hear about strategies, theories, and accomplishments. There are also usually opportunities to meet other educators. Many conferences also attract vendors and publishers looking to promote their products.

Professional associations

Professional associations are a great place to find literature relevant to your teaching specialty. Below are just a few professional organizations you can join. These associations have academic journals containing peer-reviewed research, professional development aligned to state standards, and information for conferences and events to collaborate with other content area teachers.

- National Education Association (NEA).
- National Science Teachers Association (NSTA).

- National Council of Teachers of English (NCTE).

- National Council of Teachers of Mathematics (NCTM).

- The Society of Health and Physical Educators (SHAPE).

- National Council for Social Studies (NCSS).

- International Literacy Association (ILA).

- National Association for the Education of Young Children (NAEYC).

- National Association for Bilingual Education (NABE).

- American Association for Applied Linguistics (AAAL).

The important thing to remember is that you should be seeking out the professional development and research provided by professional associations.

Example question

Ms. Picard is a new science teacher. Which of the following would be the most important thing to consider in her planning process?

    A. Choose professional development that is interesting.

    B. Ask the principal about what professional development is available.

    C. Search online for local science workshops.

    D. Identify research provided from the National Science Teachers Association (NSTA).

Correct answer: D

Answer choice D is the best answer because NSTA bases its work on scholarly, peer-reviewed research. All professional learning should be aligned with the standards and grounded in reliable and valid research. The other choices are not as good because they lack specificity. They are also too similar. Answer choices A, B, and C all focus on subjective measures such as interest that are irrelevant if the learning experience will not meet her professional needs. Furthermore, asking the principal is typically never the correct answer on the PLT.

Professional learning communities

Professional learning communities (PLCs) are groups of teachers and professional peers who meet to discuss specific or on-going problems of practice in the classroom. PLCs are organized around a few key questions or a specific investigation. Participants support one another to design, implement, research, assess, and reflect on daily work. Schools typically set routine time aside for PLCs to meet. Participants might read professional literature together, meet with an instructional coach, or collaborate with an administrator. PLCs tend to be assigned to teachers who teach the same students or grade level.

Graduate courses

Graduate courses are usually offered by local colleges and universities. They often provide classes in traditional and online formats. Graduate courses are an excellent way to explore a meaningful topic with guidance and rigor. Graduate courses allow you to earn credits towards certifications or an advanced degree. This can help you become eligible for career opportunities and a salary increase.

Independent research

Independent research is conducted to address a specific question or issue related to your professional practice. For example, a teacher is interested in how to start guided math groups and wants to learn more about this technique. The teacher wants a thorough understanding of how to use guided math groups in his classroom. Independent research is an ideal method for this situation. The teacher can always discuss independent research with an instructional coach or colleague to gain perspective on implementation.

Independent research should follow these guidelines:

- Use articles and text from peer-reviewed journals and other sources.
- Document the origin of any other materials and resources.
- Use a reflective journal or documentation system to:
  - Synthesize notes.
  - Plan instruction.
  - Measure the impact of your work.

Internships

Internships are work experiences for a set period of time where the intern observes, follows, and learns from an expert in the field. Student teaching is a type of internship. You may also consider an internship if you are looking to change your content area or position such as becoming a reading specialist or special education teacher.

Mentors

Mentorships are where veteran teachers mentor new teachers to help them develop goals and plan instruction. Mentor teachers also support reflective teaching practices, which is essential in developing effective classroom instruction. More experienced teachers are frequently asked to mentor new teachers. The specifics of the relationship and arrangements are usually decided by school leaders. When mentor partnerships are not working, it is important to look to the principal for guidance.

- **Formal mentorships** meet for weekly planning, peer observation, and shared reflection time.
- **Informal mentorships** are less structured than formal mentorships. Participants build rapport by asking questions and discussing issues (i.e., school procedures, lesson planning, events). This can be through conversations or emails.

Study groups

Study groups are an excellent way to work with peers to read and understand a new perspective on education. A study group usually follows an agenda to explore a series of articles, a text, or a group of studies to read and discuss. The group meets throughout the school year, communicates online, or meets over the summer.

Example question

A teacher is creating a professional development plan for the year. Which of the following would be most effective when designing the plan?

- A. Find professional development on new technology.
- B. Choose professional development that is aligned to the school's goals.
- C. Collaborate with a peer teacher and attend the same professional development.
- D. Search online for interesting professional development opportunities.

Correct answer: B

All professional development should be aligned to school goals, which are aligned to the standards. Also, *alignment* is a good word. If you see it in an answer choice, it is most likely the correct answer. Answer choices A, C, and, D are not as effective as answer B.

2. Research-based teaching practices

As professionals, teachers are a part of an academic community. They need to be aware of the theories and assertions that support instructional practices. This includes current events and debates surrounding how to implement educational practices. Good teachers engage in discussions about best practices by studying policies related to their field, staying informed about updates and changes in research, and joining professional organizations related to their field.

Accessing available resources

The Internet makes searching and finding resources simple. However, you need to be able to assess the purpose and quality of any resource you use in your professional practice.

Quick Tip

To improve classroom instruction, you should look for articles from peer-reviewed journals and books. These are the most reliable sources and the best answers on the PLT.

Peer-reviewed academic studies and meta-analysis

Academic studies are written in a highly structured manner. They usually start with an abstract, followed by an introduction, literature review, study, results, and conclusion. They may use quantitative data, qualitative data, or both.

When looking for strategies to implement in your classroom, meta-analysis reports can be especially helpful. A meta-analysis compiles all studies that have been done on a specific topic to identify trends or broad conclusions from the data. They tend to be easier to read because they are written for a larger audience, including practicing educators.

The following table provides different types of academic studies and analyses and where to find them.

Source	Description	Uses
Academic journals	Detailed studies using qualitative and quantitative data in a variety of research designs including: • Descriptive • Experimental • Random-control Academic journals are peer-reviewed.	• Teaching a specific skill such as vocabulary, discussion, or reading comprehension. • Comparing methods to determine which will be the most effective.
Articles	Articles can have a variety of topics and perspectives on curriculum, teaching, learning, and policy. Publishers like Edutopia, EdWeekly, and Scholastic tend to have articles that are easy to read and full of information that can immediately be used in the classroom.	• Reading a case study. • Discussing a debate or current issue in education policy. • Learning about a new book or product. • Reading a new theory on instruction.

Source	Description	Uses
Magazines, ePublications, and compiled resources	Many professional associations have publications that are distributed weekly, quarterly, or yearly. SmartBrief is an example of a summary of articles and education topics compiled by an academic association. In these publications you will find, articles, meta-analysis, research studies, book reviews, teacher interviews, and other resources to promote teaching and learning.	• Reading about current trends and studies that have been vetted by a source you trust. • Understanding topics aligned to your teaching specialty and areas of interest.
Books	Never before have there been so many books on teaching theories, how to implement programming in alignment with various teaching philosophies, and ways to improve specific types of learning in the classroom. Make sure books are peer-reviewed and have reliable research sources.	• Reading with peers in a PLC or study group. • Using references as you design and implement curriculum throughout the year.

Social media

Twitter, Instagram, Facebook and other social media platforms have groups of like-minded professionals to collaborate with about a wide range of topics. You can find a social media group on everything from reading instruction to tips on designing an engaging classroom. You can follow education associations, curriculum publishers, and other content area experts. As with any other resource, when using social media, be sure to assess sources for validity, authenticity, and reliability. Social media is a good place to gather ideas and follow informal discussions. However, social media also has misinformation, outdated or incomplete statistics, and biased opinions. This is not the best place to find peer-reviewed, academic research.

Blogs

Blogs are websites or webpages with informal opinion pieces where the author shares her views and ideas about education. Blogs can be written by famous educational leaders and researchers as well as everyday teachers. To assess their credibility, look for citations of peer reviewed research and rational for ideas. Many teachers write blogs part time to share their practice. Be on the lookout for product promotions embedded in the information. Many bloggers are sponsored by companies to promote products to their subscribers.

Caution

Blogs and social media are typically not the correct answers to test questions on the PLT. Social media is not a peer-reviewed, academic source for information, or a formal reference. Blogs and social media are not good sources of reference for instructional design. While the opinions you read online might resonate with you, you still need to seek out academic research to support your practice.

Data, results, and conclusions from research on teaching practices

Teachers must continually seek out peer-reviewed research about the profession of teaching and their content area. On the PLT, you will be required to identify answer choices that support data-informed research. This might also be referred to as researched-based or evidence-based practices. This means that you are evaluating recent studies and applying that research to student achievement.

Interpreting and evaluating research

Follow the same approach to selecting professional development research as you would for classroom materials. As previously discussed on how to select resources for your classroom, consider the following 6 questions:

1. **Is the research reliable and valid?**

   Validity refers to how sound the research is in both the design and methods. Validity is the extent to which the findings in the study represent the phenomenon measured in the study.

   - **Internal validity** refers to how well a study is conducted.

   - **External validity** refers to how applicable the findings are to the real world.

   Reliability refers to the degree of consistency in the measure. A study is considered reliable when it yields similar results under similar conditions after being conducted repeatedly.

2. **Are the authors authorities or experts in their fields?** Authors who are experts in the topic of the study tend to produce reliable and valid research. Be sure to check the author(s).

3. **Is the research current?** Using research conducted in the last 3 years is more effective than using research from the last 20 years. That doesn't mean that past studies are not important. Plenty of the early research is considered seminal. But when looking for trends and new ways to teach, using current research is best.

4. **Is the research scholarly?** Teachers should consider research that comes from peer-reviewed academic journals. Websites and blogs often contain valid and reliable research. However, to be sure that the research is legitimate, go straight to the academic journal where it was published. Be sure to check the bibliography in the study.

5. **Is the research objective?** Research should be unbiased and objective; it should address questions without opinions or agenda. Often, private companies that sell educational programs will publish research. It is important that teachers differentiate between objective research and research that is skewed one way. You can do this by looking at several studies about a topic. Look for trends and consistencies between and among the studies.

6. **Is the research relevant to the profession?** There are a lot of studies out there with important information. You should be seeking out research in the areas that fit your particular job. For example, if you are a social science teacher in a school with a large population of English language learners, you should seek out research relevant to that area.

(University of Massachusetts Boston, 2019)

Example question

Ms. Clarke finds an article online that was published a few years ago. It discusses the profound impact reading at home has on academic achievement. The message resonates with her affinity of independent reading, and she wants to share it with her colleagues. The study was published by a company selling individual readers for young children to use at home and school. Why should she be skeptical of the study?

A. The research is not relevant because it is talking about reading at home, not school.

B. The research might be biased.

C. The article was from the Internet.

D. The research is a few years old.

Correct answer: B

Confirm that a study is peer-reviewed before investing in its results. Watch out for bias when companies do their own research. Even if a company genuinely wants to know if their product works, they are likely to present research in a way that favors the product. Research done by a third party or outside source can be used to promote a product but be free of bias. Answer choices C and D are incorrect because they do not impact the validity or reliability of the article. Answer choice A is incorrect because reading at home is part of a student's literacy development.

Quick Tip

For the PLT, you need to remember that when selecting a text, it is always important to first consider if it is 1) relevant to your instructional context, and 2) can improve the learning of your students.

Relating data, results, and conclusions to educational situations

Here are two examples of how teachers related data, results, and conclusions from research to educational situations. Read the scenarios to identify how the teachers have applied research to their practice. Then, read the explanation and compare your thinking.

Scenario

Mr. Bao received feedback from several parents that they are frustrated by the 8th grade math homework he is sending home. They are confused by the assignments and are unsure how to help their children. He decides to write some example problems and detailed explanations. He also realizes that the parents probably learned to solve these types of problems a different way than how he is teaching it. He prepares some literature to help parents understand why he is teaching math with the new strategies. He then invites the parents to a short meeting after school to walk through the problem-solving methods.

Explanation

In this situation, Mr. Bao needs to overcome two barriers with parents: why and how. First, he needs to explain why they are using the new math techniques. Then, he needs to explain how to employ the new techniques so the parents can help their students. By providing academic references, Mr. Bao can help parents understand why they are using new computation and problem-solving techniques. Citing a meta-analysis and discussing the purposes for "new math" will help parents to understand *why* this approach improves student achievement. Walking parents through the problem-solving steps will help them to understand *how* to help their children. He may also want to offer additional resources for parents to study or meetings to attend if they want more information. Having an article or two references in his hand out will improve his credibility and help parents grapple with any remaining doubts.

Example question

Ms. Schweppe recently went to a conference and attended a seminar about how one-on-one conferring during reading workshops can improve student comprehension. She immediately tried to implement the strategy in her classroom but found it to be very difficult. During the one-on-one sessions, other students frequently interrupted her, and it was difficult to focus on one student at a time. Also, she was not sure what to ask students or how to guide their thinking. It felt like the one-on-one conferring was ineffective and taking up valuable class time.

Which of the following would be the best next step for Ms. Schweppe?

    A. Stop trying to do one-on-one conferring.

    B. Read a book on the theory and how to implement effective one-on-one conferring.

    C. Read meta-analysis on the effectiveness of one-on-one conferring.

    D. Read a blog on conferring and purchase materials from an online store.

Correct answer: B

Answer choice B is the correct answer because Ms. Schweppe needs to understand the theory behind the approach and how to implement it effectively. She can ask a curriculum coach for suggested reading materials on the strategy. She needs to learn how to create a conferring schedule to compliment her guided reading groups. She needs to understand strategies to meet with students, so their time is meaningful and effective. She also needs to learn how to prepare questions and help students craft independent goals. There are a lot of steps she needs to take before abandoning the approach altogether. Reading more data about the strategy or buying products is not going to help her devise a plan to implement the strategy.

3. Reflective practice and professional growth

Looking back and evaluating classroom instruction is an essential step in the professional growth process. When teachers reflect on their practice, they can improve instruction to positively impact student learning. In a reflective practice, teachers analyze their instruction and their students' achievement.

Reflective practice is meant to look back at various aspects of the planning and implementation of instruction. Here are some questions teachers might ask themselves:

- What was the purpose of the learning task?

- How did this activity fit into the larger scope of learning planned in the upcoming days?

- How is this lesson or unit being implemented? What are the challenges?

- How is learning being measured? Do students' self-assessments match teacher evaluations?

Reflective practice should be done formally and informally on a routine basis (daily, weekly, and quarterly). The activities below support the most effective and efficient manner to create and sustain a reflective practice. This will constructively influence instruction and student learning.

Reflective journal

Keeping a journal can be especially effective at the beginning of something new. This could be new content, subject, unit, or lesson, or philosophy of learning. It allows real-time observations, analysis, and note-taking of your professional practice. The key is to write your thoughts down immediately so they are not lost and can be read at a later point. Here are some examples of reflective journal entries:

- "I need to understand the steps of the science experiments better, so I can guide students who are struggling."

- "I can see that since I understood the algebraic concept better today, I was able to explain it more efficiently to students. 21 of 25 students were able to apply the method for solving equations independently."

- "I wonder how I can get students to write for longer periods of time without needing to break."

- "My mini-lessons are still taking too long. Students need more time for independent writing. I will take more time to prepare tomorrow and then really stick to my teaching point."

- "What a great lesson! Students worked in pairs, they gave each other meaningful feedback and revised their work. Taking the time to model, reflect on our actions, and see the benefits of peer review is really working."

Self and peer assessment

Peer assessments are evaluations of your instructional practice provided by peer teachers. Self-assessments are your evaluations of your own teaching practice. Self and peer assessments can be part of a formal evaluation process facilitated by school leaders to improve teaching and learning. They can also be informal and self-directed among colleagues.

Especially when working with a PLC, peer and self-assessment checklists can be useful for understanding the impact of planning and implementing instruction. Assessment checklists should be created based on your instructional goals. They can be used as a reflective activity to self-assess. They can also be used by peer teachers. For example, a peer teacher in your PLC can use the checklist after observing your classroom. Conversely, you can complete the checklist after watching a replay video of your own instruction.

Typically, observation checklists focus on specific aspects of the lesson such as structure, transition times, and formative assessments.

The table below provides a sample assessment checklist for a writing workshop mini lesson.

Goal	Duration	Observation *What did you hear? How was it done? What visuals, audio, learning props were used?*
Learning goals clearly posted and stated		
Connections made to prior learning		
New information stated		
Purpose of new information explained and reinforced		
Thinking about learning is modeled		
Guided practice		

Think about it!

Teachers who struggle to engage in routine self-reflection might want to start by watching a video of themselves with a checklist of attributes they are trying to implement. The checklist will keep the observation focused on student learning and the effectiveness of instruction.

Incident analysis

An **incident** is any unexpected or unplanned challenge in the classroom, you believe to be important. An incident may be a repeated action. For example, a group of students routinely struggle to participate in whole-group learning, or a student cannot keep their work materials organized. A single event can also be an incident. For example, a student is injured in physical education class, or a student is upset for making a bad choice. When an incident happens in the classroom, it is important to document the event, and if necessary, to communicate with student families and administration.

An **analysis** is a systematic reflection on the report to consider the actions that led up to the repetitive action, altercation, or accident. An analysis looks at as many aspects of the situation as possible such as:

- Classroom environment.

- Accommodations being implemented.

- Structure of the learning activity.

- Teacher and student responses.

An analysis is useful because an incident can be complicated and usually has more than one corrective action. Your school should have protocols for incident reporting. It is very important to follow those protocols when communicating incidents to leadership and parents.

The **purpose** of incident analysis is to support new teachers who struggled to identify critical moments of challenge in their classrooms. Incident analysis helps to develop professional judgment that avoids further incidences and provides perspective on what occurred. You should walk away from an incident analysis with new strategies and corrective actions for improving your teaching practices (Tripp, 2012).

Portfolio

A portfolio is a collection of documents and examples of your teaching philosophy, credentials, and impact on student learning. Like student portfolios, teaching portfolios are an excellent means of reflection because you are documenting your learning and growth. You can add artifacts from classroom instruction including peer and administrative observations, recommendation letters, unit designs, student work, and photos.

Peer observation

You might be asked to provide a peer observation for a colleague, or you might ask a colleague to observe your classroom. Either way, it is important to have a rubric or checklist so that you can provide and receive objective feedback based on instructional goals.

- **A colleague observes your classroom.** This is when a colleague simply observes what is happening in your classroom and takes notes to share with you. The observation notes should not be evaluative or analytical. This is challenging because we tend to have an opinion about what we see. The purpose of keeping the observation notes objective is to read the body of observations later to identify trends, patterns, and omissions.

- **You observe your colleague's classroom.** Observing another colleague's classroom can also provide a lot of insight into your own instruction. Following the same protocol, when observing your peers, remember to roam the classroom with your eyes. See the layout for learning, identify the learning goals, notice what students are doing and saying, and recognize how they respond to instructional expectations.

Critical friend

A critical friend can be an instructional coach, a mentor, or a colleague who you meet with regularly to collaboratively reflect on your teaching practice. Critical friends generally receive training to engage active listening skills. The purpose is to support the reflective process rather than offering opinions or advice. Critical friends are focused on your instruction. They do not contrast your work and ideas to focus to their own. A critical friend is supportive, reflective, enthusiastic, and thoughtful as well as constructive and honest with their feedback (Glossary of Education Reform, 2013).

After Ms. Preston spends two weeks on analyzing poetry, she gives students a summative assessment. When she and a mentor teacher look over the data, they observe that many of the students are still struggling with the skill. Together, Ms. Preston and her mentor teacher look back and discuss ways to modify classroom instruction to support struggling learners. The mentor teacher is helping Ms. Preston engage in which of the following?

    A. Evaluation

    B. Reflection

    C. Assessment

    D. Brainstorming

Correct answer: B

The teachers are looking back (reflecting) on the instruction and how it can be improved. This is not simply an evaluation because the teacher is thinking back or reflecting on classroom instruction.

4. Support personnel who assist students, teachers, and families

Schools are made up of professionals who interact with students, parents, and the community to ensure the highest quality education for all students. For the PLT, you will need to know the general roles and responsibilities of typical personnel in the school. You will also need to know the most appropriate and effective way to interact with your colleagues. This might include the IEP team, paraprofessionals, guidance counselors, administration staff, and district leadership staff. The following section provides a description of the different positions and teams you will interact with in your school.

Guidance counselors

Typically, guidance counselors work to support, develop, and maintain students' social and emotional capacity at school. Although this varies from school to school, here are some of the responsibilities of a guidance counselor:

- Manage conflicts at home or at school.

- Make sure students have basic materials and food each day.

- Work with small groups of students to manage emotions or communicate with peers.

- Help process and deal with a crisis at school or in the community.

- Conduct whole-group lessons in your classroom.

Individualized Education Program team

The Individualized Education Program (IEP) team will be different for each student with an IEP. The team members required by law include:

- The student, if appropriate (typically included at 16 years old).

- The student's parent or guardian.

- At least one of the student's general education teachers.

- At least one of the student's special education teachers.

- A school district representative.

- An expert who can interpret the student's evaluation results.

- A translator (if needed).

The IEP team meets at least once a year to review, revise, and update the student's IEP. During the IEP meeting, the IEP team should discuss the following:

- Present level of performance.

- Annual goals.

- Individualized supports and services.

Special education teachers

Special education teachers work in and out of the classroom with students who have IEP accommodations. Collaborating with special education teachers is important so they can support the on-going learning objectives and tasks in your classroom. When making modifications for students in the classroom, discuss how to implement them with the special education teacher.

Speech, physical, and occupational therapists

The three main types of therapy students receive at school are speech, physical, and occupational. Therapists use modeling, interactive games, and play to support student growth. Part of their routine is identifying, treating, and assessing student exceptionalities. They frequently suggest exercises for students to do at school and home. Here are some specific roles and responsibilities for each type of therapist:

- **Speech therapist.** Work with students with speech, swallowing, cognitive and social communication issues, and language exceptionalities.

- **Physical therapist.** Specialize in movement. Their therapy is focused on supporting the development of students' gross-motor skills.

- **Occupational therapist.** Work with students with fine-motor, gross-motor, sensory, and communication exceptionalities. Their focus is improving students' readiness for academic, social, and executive functioning skills.

Therapists play an important role in the education of many students with IEPs. The time they spend with students needs to be protected. They might ask to work with a student during a lesson in your classroom or in another classroom. Therapists might observe a student in your classroom to suggest accommodations to improve learning. Speech, physical, and occupational therapists rarely work at only one school. They might be employed by the district, a school, or by an individual family for specific services.

Library media specialists

The library media specialist works with students and teachers to provide instructional support and enhance student learning.

- **Instructional support.** Support teachers with instructional materials, research, and technology. Media specialists are a great resource when gathering materials for a new unit or searching for differentiated material.

- **Student learning.** Support students with reading materials, research, and technology in both physical and digital formats. Students might have a regular class period scheduled with the media specialist or the media specialist might be available by request.

The library is full of incredible resources for you and your students. Media specialists often collaborate with community libraries and colleges and universities for additional resources. They can help you find the information you and your students are looking for.

"The half of knowledge is to know where to find knowledge." This is inscribed over the entrance to Dodd Hall, which was the original library at Florida State University.

Teachers of the gifted and talented

Some schools have interventionists, or special education teachers, who work with gifted and talented students. The role of the gifted and talented teacher is to engage and challenge gifted students to support their learning to their full potential. In some cases, this resource is district personnel who can support teachers with modifications and scaffolding but has limited time for pullout support. Gifted and talented exceptionalities present differently in different gifted students. You should coordinate with the gifted and talented teacher to develop appropriate instructional materials for these students like project-based learning, independent study, or a specialized STEAM curriculum.

Para educators

Para educators, sometimes called paraprofessionals, support and collaborate with the teacher to plan and implement instruction. For example, they might work with small groups of students to review reading, writing, or math concepts. They might engage with students working at centers while the teacher is leading guided reading groups. Para educators might sit with students during a whole group lesson who need extra support to remain engaged. Some para educators have more specific assignments such as translating for and supporting newcomer ELL students. When a para educator is assigned to your class, always meet together with the principal or supervisor to review their role and responsibilities. You need to be aware of their focus, schedule, and what are acceptable tasks for them to complete.

Test Tip

The para educator should be supporting student achievement, not administrative tasks. When you see test questions about para educators on the PLT, look for answer choices where the para educator is supporting the instructional needs of students. Just say no to para educators grading papers for you.

Example question

A special education student is consistently off-task and when approached she seems startled and shocked that she is not following directions. You have tried accommodating the student by changing her seating and giving her an itemized task list. Who should you contact first for more support?

    A. Principal

    B. Special education teacher

    C. Para educator

    D. Guidance counselor

Correct answer: B

The first person to contact is the special education teacher to observe the student and offer suggestions for accommodations. If additional accommodations are implemented and do not work, the teacher should contact the parents and consider starting an evaluation to better understand what is hindering the student's attention for learning. Answer choices A, C, and D are incorrect because evaluating student engagement is not part of their job.

5. Teacher leadership and the community

Community partnerships are one of the strongest factors to building successful schools. School personnel, parents, and students are the most obvious stakeholders at a school. However, elected officials, school board members, small business owners, cultural and community organizations also have a vested interest in the success of schools in their community. As a teacher, it is important to understand that you are a representative of the education community in and out of school.

Advocating and shaping the profession

Teachers play an important role in shaping and advocating for the education profession. What teachers say socially and politically about the profession can impact students, parents, the school, and the district. It is important to carefully craft what you say on social media and with community members to advocate for education. Here are ways teachers engage socially and professionally with their community:

- Attend school board meetings and prepare statements for board members.

- Understand how policies and laws impact the teaching profession.

- Join unions, community organizations, and professional organizations.

- Lead after-school and enrichment activities.

Perceptions of teachers

Teachers have a tremendous impact on students, families, and the community. Teachers model, mentor, guide, and influence the behavior and participation of students and their families. Teachers are often the only conduit families have for resources and support for their children. Conversely, teachers are often scrutinized or idealized for events and outcomes they may or may not have influenced. As such, it is critical for teachers to be aware of their influence in the lives of their students and the school community. Here are ways teachers can maintain a positive perception in the school community:

- Be mindful of the entire school community when posting messages on social media.

- Maintain positive and constructive interactions with students, parents, and colleagues.

- Adhere to all school and district policies regarding public messaging.

Partnerships with parents and family members

Family engagement is critical to student success. It is so important that district, state, and federal policies emphasize the need for school and family coordination. Furthermore, many teacher evaluation systems assess how well teachers communicate with student families and the broader school community (U.S. Department of Education, 2013).

It is also important to share what students are learning with their parents or caregivers so they can help at home. For example, if you are teaching a specific math strategy, show families how they can help their child to use it to solve equations. Teachers also benefit from hearing feedback from parents and caregivers. Here are some strategies to increase two-way communication between teachers and families:

- Communication folders or message journals for daily classroom updates, homework, surveys, and notifications.

- Parent-teacher organization meetings.

- Weekly or monthly class newsletters.

- Letters home.

- Phone calls and emails.

- Weekly emails.

- "How-to" letters at the beginning of a new unit explaining key concepts and learning goals.

- Classroom presentations and celebrations.

Think about it!

Increasing communication with parents helps increase student achievement. According to the American Federation of Teachers (2010), "Research shows that the more parents and teachers share relevant information with each other about a student, the better equipped both will be to help that student achieve academically." Parents want to hear good things about their children, too. They should not only be hearing from you when there is a problem. It is important to communicate when a student is doing well.

Throughout the school year, you will have a number of formal and informal opportunities to interact with students' families. Back to school night, curriculum nights, and parent-teacher conferences tend to happen at the beginning of the school year. Other formal meetings, like IEP meetings, will happen throughout the school year. You may also communicate informally with parents before or after school, at school functions, or at other places within the community.

Consistency is very important when communicating with students and parents. Communicating in a consistent manner with weekly emails, communication folders, and other tools will help to manage expectations of students and parents. This will cut down on confusion or misunderstandings.

Format is also very important to consider when communicating with parents. Make sure you are providing information to parents in an accessible format. This includes considering students' home languages and potential socioeconomic barriers with electronic communication.

Example question

A teacher is setting up her routines at the beginning of the school year. What is the best way to ensure she has consistent communication with student families?

A. Collect parent email addresses.

B. Create a routine for communication folders to be brought home and returned weekly.

C. Collect parent phone numbers and create a phone tree.

D. Write and distribute a weekly newsletter.

Correct answer: B

While all of these answers are important steps to take to create and maintain communication with parents, a weekly communication folder carried by the student is the most effective way to emphasize routine, two-way communication. Answer choices A and D are important steps because a lot of teacher and parent communication happens through email, and notices can be sent home via email. However, they do not explicitly elicit two-way communication. Not all families have a way to check email on a regular basis, and they may need the newsletter translated to another language. Answer choice C is incorrect because making phone calls is time consuming, not always successful, and you may need a translator. Therefore, phone calls should be reserved for urgent situations.

Partnerships with the community

Community partnerships make schools stronger. Just as teachers and schools should seek out connections within their community to build successful partnerships, a school is generally more successful when outside stakeholders and organizations are invested in student learning. Community partnerships can be built with local businesses, government agencies, and non-profit organizations. Community partnerships can also begin with parents or professionals who work in the community such as doctors, lawyers, artists, and conservationists. It is likely that your school has some existing partnerships. However, it is always advantageous to seek out new ones. Remember to always communicate with the principal about any community partnerships you want to cultivate. School administration will have an important perspective to offer when considering whether the partnership will be constructive.

Engaging with stakeholders for possible partnerships should always align to school goals. If you are using backwards design to develop your lessons, community partners should also align with standards you are teaching in your classroom. Here are some examples of productive community partnerships.

- Guest speakers who are experts in the lesson your students are working on. For example, inviting a scientist from a local lab to explain how she uses scientific theory.

- Local businesses for donations and sponsorships. For example, asking a local newspaper to donate copies of the paper to supplement a social studies lesson on the first amendment of the US Constitution.

- Government and non-profit organizations for ongoing support. For example, asking with the area chamber of commerce to communicate information about the school with their members.

Think about it!

Problem-based and project-based learning are great opportunities to create and build community partnerships. Visiting local a business such as the grocery store, local news station, voter polling center, animal conservation center, nursing homes, and care centers are terrific ways to build community engagement and support instruction.

6. Developing collaborative relationships to support the educational process

It is important to keep in mind the steps for developing collaborative relationships with school stakeholders. Without a clear plan, partnerships may dissolve or become ineffective.

Elements of successful collaboration

There are several key elements to successful collaboration.

- **Purpose.** There needs to be a reason for the collaboration to occur. The purpose of the collaboration should align to school goals and standards.

- **Communication.** There needs to be clear, routine communication to maintain the relationship and achieve the targeted goals of the collaboration. Communication can include the collaboration action plan, meeting notes, follow-up tasks, meeting agendas, and reminders.

- **Coordination.** The people collaborating should be committed to meeting and coordinating with each other to achieve the desired outcomes.

- **Accountability.** People need to be accountable for maintaining their roles and responsibilities of the collaboration.

- **Mutual trust.** The people involved in the collaboration should have mutual trust that builds over the course of the project together.

Developing an action plan

An action plan defines the mission, organization, and roles and responsibilities of a collaboration. Being explicit about these elements provides direction and clarity to the collaborative relationship.

- **Mission.** A mission is an action-oriented concept that often includes a general description of the plan, its function, and its objectives. Especially for building long-term community partnerships, the collaborating group needs to realize how they will benefit from the relationship that promotes success of students and the school (Loria, 2018).

- **Goals.** These are measurable targets that support the plan's mission and align the school's objectives. Goals should be developed using the SMART method. SMART stands for **S**pecific, **M**easurable, **A**ttainable, **R**elevant, and **T**imely.

  - **Specific.** The goal must contain a statement that details specifically what the student will accomplish.

  - **Measurable.** There must be a way to measure progress towards the goal by using assessment data.

  - **Attainable.** The goal must be within the scope of possibility.

  - **Relevant.** The goal must be relevant to what the students are doing.

  - **Timely.** The goal must be completed within a targeted time frame.

- **Organization.** This section of the plan describes how the collaborative relationship will work, the stakeholders involved, the actions that will take place, when these actions will happen, and how will they be documented.
- **Roles and responsibilities.** These are the tasks and duties of all collaborative partners. This explains who will complete each task of the collaboration and when the task will be completed. This holds the partners accountable for participating in the collaboration.

Identifying the stakeholders

Stakeholders are the people working together in a collaborative relationship. For example, a teacher and a para educator worked together to plan literature circles during language arts. In another scenario, a classroom teacher works with the science teacher, media specialist, special education teacher, a local landscaping company, and an administrator to study, grow, and harvest fresh produce for students' lunches as part of an earth science unit.

When you are developing the action plan, one of the first steps is to conduct a stakeholder analysis to identify the best partners to include in the collaboration.

Identifying the purpose of the collaboration

It is critical to make sure the purpose of the collaboration aligns to the standards and school goals. When planning lessons and assessments, work backwards to make sure the collaboration is supporting student achievement toward school goals and state standards. It is very easy to become involved in a collaboration that seems great but doesn't actually align to your instructional goals. Implement the backwards design approach when developing the purpose of the collaboration.

The participating members of the collaboration should also be involved in developing the purpose, goals and objectives of the collaboration. Key stakeholders should be able to articulate the goals of the collaboration.

Supporting effective communication

Effective communication skills are essential to interact and collaborate with students, colleagues, leaders, and parents. Communication occurs in several formats including internal, external, formal, and informal. It also occurs in verbal, written, and non-verbal modes. It is important to understand and use these formats appropriately to ensure the right message gets to the right person in the most effective and efficient way. Important considerations for communication strategies include:

- Identifying who needs what information.
- Identifying who is authorized to access and disseminate that information.
- Identifying when the recipients will need the information.
- Determining where the information is stored and what format it is in.
- Identifying geographical, socioeconomic, and cultural considerations for disseminating the message.
- Identifying the method of communication.
  - Interactive communication – conversation between two or more people.
  - Push communication – information distributed to a group of people.
  - Pull communication – recipients access the information at their discretion.

(Project Management Institute, 2013)

There are norms and protocols for communication in a school environment. This includes verbal, written, and nonverbal forms of communication.

Verbal communication. Verbal communication is the process of exchanging information and ideas by speaking. This includes conversations, voicemail messages, and oral presentations. Verbal communication can be formal and informal. It is important for you to understand how to verbally communicate with peers, supervisors, and other co-workers in an effective and efficient way.

The first step in effective verbal communication is **active listening**. This is the process of listening for comprehension and interacting to demonstrate understanding.

Telephone communication skills are especially important in collaborative relationships with parents and community members. With the advent of text messaging, people often lack the basic skills and confidence to communicate effectively while speaking on the phone. The list below provides techniques for telephone communication.

- Use a positive tone.
- Smile when speaking to help create an upbeat voice.
- Enunciate to make sure the recipient can hear and understand the conversation.
- Sound sincere and genuine, not rehearsed.
- Make a personal connection by using the recipient's name, if provided.
- End the conversation smoothly and politely.
- Understand conference call etiquette.
  - Read the dial in instructions ahead of time.
  - Prepare by reading the call agenda and making notes of talking points.
  - Use mute when not speaking.
  - Do not use hold or call waiting while on a conference call.

Written communication. Written communication is the process of exchanging information and ideas through text. This includes emails, text messages, notes, reports, and memos. Written communication can be formal such as an action plan or informal such as meeting notes. Both formal and informal written communication should follow the rules for standard grammar and punctuation. Other general rules include:

- Spell out common words (e.g., use "you" instead of "U").
- Define acronyms and abbreviations.
- Avoid the use of emojis.
- Avoid slang, jargon, and slurs.
- Provide clear and concise information.
- Use appropriate greetings and signatures in emails.
- State the issue or question in the first sentence of an email.
- Understand the intent of the "To:", "Cc:", and "Bcc:" lines of an email.
- Do not distribute messages that could be interpreted as a violation of the school's acceptable use policy.
- Understand the intent of different communication modes and when it is most appropriate to use written communication.

Nonverbal communication. Nonverbal communication is the process of transmitting information without speaking or writing. This can be achieved through tone, volume, body language, physical cues, appearance, expressions, and touch. It is also important to know and understand when to use nonverbal communication and to recognize inappropriate uses of nonverbal communication in a school environment.

CONTENT CATEGORY IV

Formal communication. Formal communication is the exchange of information and ideas that follows professional standards, rules, and protocols. Formal communication can include a status report, executive summary, or a memo.

Informal communication. Informal communication is the exchange of information and ideas that does not follow formal protocols. Informal communication in a school environment is also referred to as the "grapevine" and includes text messages, instant messages, emails, conversations, and voicemails.

Caution

Communication in a school environment must adhere to the school's policies regardless of format, mode, or method of communication. Inappropriate communication in an informal conversation has the same repercussions as in a formal report. Make sure you are professional in all communication with stakeholders.

Seeking support

As you develop collaborative relationships, you may involve more stakeholders in your projects and instructional design. For example, other teachers, community members, administrators, or parents may be able play a role once a project has started. You may want to seek out parent volunteers to organize your classroom library, ask administrators to be readers or project evaluators, or find donors for a collection of materials you need for an art installation. There are many different ways to engage stakeholders to provide support. The important step in seeking support from others is to conduct a needs assessment so you can identify the specific resources you need.

Action research

When teachers work together to analyze data and design lessons to meet the needs of all students, they continuously improve instruction and increase student achievement. The most effective way to collaborate is through action research.

Action research is when teachers continuously collect both formative and summative data and use that data to differentiate instruction. It is structured around a research question and the disciplined collection of data. Action research is ongoing and part of the teachers' everyday practice. Most of the time, action research takes place in PLCs or department and grade-level teams. The following is an example scenario of effective action research.

Scenario

English teachers at South High School are working together to develop vertically aligned, common language arts assessments. The assessments are based on the state standards and will serve as benchmark tests to measure student understanding of language arts concepts. In addition to common assessments, the teachers develop plans for teaching the language arts concepts. The PLC has developed specific questions to evaluate the impact of their instruction on assessment scores. The teachers meet once a week to review instruction and assessment data to determine what instruction is effective and what should be modified. The teachers regularly engage in this action research.

Explanation

The teachers in this scenario are using action research to plan, develop, implement, assess, and adjust their English language arts instruction. The teachers are evaluating outcomes using data, adjusting their planning by making data-driven decisions, and improving their practice by using reflective thinking.

Which of the following is most effective in planning instruction for struggling learners?

A. Complete professional development

B. Attend PLC meetings

C. Engage in action research

D. Survey students

Correct answer: C

Action research is data-driven decision making, and it can be done in collaboration with other teachers. Answer choice B is not the best answer here because it describes the setting, but it is not specific enough to address the issue in the question. Answer choices A and D are incorrect because they are not going to address the specific needs of the struggling students.

Quick Tip

You will need to differentiate between PLCs and action research on the PLT exam. PLC meetings are meant to inform more student learning through presentations, discussions, and collaborative work. Action research is a formal process for assessing and adjusting classroom instruction to improve student learning.

7. Major legislation relating to students and teachers

The terms *individual freedom and responsibility, equity, social justice, community,* and *diversity* are used frequently when describing effective school environments. However, these terms are rarely explicitly defined. Having an understanding of these distinct terms is valuable for this exam and for your career in education.

Individual freedom and responsibility. Individual freedom in education is the liberty of each student to pursue life and goals without interference from others.

Equity. The terms *equity* and *equality* are often intermingled. *Equality* is associated with treating people the same or people having equal access to resources and opportunities. *Equity* requires leaders to consider the types of resources and supports each individual student needs to succeed in school.

Social justice. Formal definitions for social justice vary, the common themes among them are:

• Equal rights

• Equal opportunity

• Equitable treatment

Community. A community is a group of people who share something in common. In this case, the school and student achievement are what the community members have in common. The school community is made up of stakeholders—teachers, students, parents, administrators, staff, business owners, coaches, etc. Effective leaders cultivate relationships with members in the community to empower students.

Diversity and inclusion. *Diversity* refers to the traits and characteristics that make people unique while *inclusion* refers to the behaviors and social norms that ensure people feel welcome.

Many federal and state education laws and policies have been established to ensure access to high quality instruction for all students. Teachers are held accountable for understanding and implementing all major federal and state legislation.

Equal access

"All students—regardless of race, color, national origin or zip code—deserve a high-quality education that includes resources such as academic and extracurricular programs, strong teaching, technology and instructional materials, and safe school facilities (Department of Education, 2014)."

In 2014 the Office of Civil Rights (OCR) in the U.S. Department of Education updated the federal education policy derived from the 1964 Civil Rights Act. This newest reiteration focuses on providing equitable learning opportunities for all students. Core to the renewed policy is that every student has:

1. **Excellent teachers.** All students have the right to a highly qualified and experienced teacher. This is to address and correct the problem where students of color and students from low economic background were more likely to be taught by "inexperienced, out-of-field, academically weaker, and less effective teachers than are other students (Department of Education, 2014)."

2. **Equitable resources.** Students will have equal access to the resources they need to make their education equitable to their peers. This includes

   – Up to date school buildings.

   – Fully functioning learning facilities with comfortable learning spaces.

   – Current and purposeful technology and instructional materials.

   – Academic and extra-curricular programming.

3. **A safe learning environment.** Schools free of violence with protective measures put in place to maintain an engaging and focused learning environment.

To enforce this updated policy, the U.S. Department of Education set up task forces to increase accountability for implementing policies. This is significant because part of the increased accountability is developing systems for self-assessment within districts. This means school leaders and teachers are a part of ensuring the OCR expectations are being met. (U.S. Department of Education, Office of Civil Rights 2014).

Below is a timeline of specific legislation that impacts K-12 public education.

- **14th Amendment to the United States Constitution in 1868.** The 14th Amendment of the U.S. Constitution guarantees an equal educational opportunity for all children in the United States.

- **Title IX of the Educational Amendments of 1972.** Provides that no individual may be discriminated against on the basis of sex in any education program or activity receiving federal financial assistance.

- **Rehabilitation Act of 1973 Section 504.** States that "no qualified individual with a disability in the United States shall be excluded from, denied the benefits of, or be subjected to discrimination" in any program or activity that receives federal finance assistance.

- **Family Educational Rights and Privacy Act of 1974 (FERPA).** Applies to any educational agency or institution to which funds have been made available under a program administered by the Secretary of Education. Sets out the requirements for the protection of parents and students.

- **Americans with Disabilities Act of 1990 Title II.** Requires that state and local governments give people with disabilities an equal opportunity to benefit from all of their programs, services, and activities, (e.g., public education).

- **No Child Left Behind of 2002 (NCLB).** NCLB introduced accountability to public schools.

  – Title I: Improving academic achievement of the disadvantaged

  – Title II: Preparing, training, and recruiting high quality teachers and principals

  – Title III: Language instruction for limited English proficient and immigrant students

  – Title IV: 21st Century Schools

  – Title V: Promoting informed parental choice and innovative programs

  – Title VI: Flexibility and accountability

- **Individuals with Disabilities Education Act of 2004 (IDEA).** Requires public schools to make available to all eligible children with disabilities a free public education appropriate to their individual needs.

- **Race to the Top of 2009 (RTTT).** Forty-six states and the District of Columbia submitted comprehensive reform plans to compete in the Race to the Top competition. While 19 states have received funding so far, 34 states modified state education laws or policies to facilitate needed change, and 48 states worked together to create a voluntary set of rigorous college- and career-ready standards (The White House, 2018).

- **Every Student Succeeds Act of 2015 (ESSA).** Advances equity by upholding critical protections for America's disadvantaged and high-need students. Requires all students in America be taught to high academic standards that will prepare them to succeed in college and careers. Ensures that vital information is provided to educators, families, students, and communities through annual statewide assessments that measure students' progress toward those high standards (U.S. Department of Education, 2019).

Privacy and confidentiality

Family Educational Rights and Privacy Act (FERPA). FERPA is a federal law that protects the privacy of student education records. The law applies to all schools that receive funds under an applicable program of the U.S. Department of Education.

FERPA gives parents certain rights with respect to their children's education records. These rights transfer to the student when he or she reaches the age of 18 or attends a school beyond the high school level (U.S. Department of Education, 2019).

Student records must be kept private. If you are ever unsure if someone should have access to student records, always ask an administrator. However, on the PLT test, you will need to know that biological parents and guardians do have the right to see student records. The following is how this might look on the exam.

Example question

A local news reporter calls a teacher to ask questions about a student who was arrested the night before. The news reporter asks about the student's grades. What should the teacher do?

    A. Do not disclose student information and refer the reporter to the principal.

    B. Give the overall GPA of the student but not specific grades.

    C. Only disclose the behavior records of the student.

    D. Hang up on the reporter.

Correct answer: A

This is a question that tests your knowledge of FERPA. The best option here is answer choice A. Always refer the media to administration. Also, student records are confidential, no one but the parent or guardian can have access. Hanging up on the reporter is unprofessional and is not the best answer choice. Overall GPA and behavior records are also confidential and should not be disclosed.

First Amendment

Teachers and students' freedom of speech in the school is protected under the first amendment as long as speech is in accordance to the school's educational mission. This generally means that freedom of speech is respected in the classroom – except in the case of political and religious beliefs, and offensive language or opinions that interfere with learning. The following table provides examples of protected and not protected speech for teachers.

	Protected Speech	Not Protected Speech
Actions	Attending a political rally on the weekend. Donating to political campaigns with personal money.	Advocating for a religious or political view in the classroom. For example, talking to students about why you feel strongly about one religion being better than others while studying world religions. Teaching religious concepts, such as creationism, that are not in the school curriculum.
Social Media	Posting a pro Black Lives Matters symbol on personal social media platforms.	Posting about a student on social media – specifically if the post includes a photo or a derogatory characterization of the student.
Writing and art	Writing a letter, published in the local paper, critical of a school board policy being implemented at your school.	Sharing an offensive drawing, essay, or photo at school or in the community. Displaying a poster with a religious mantra.

Discussing issues such as climate change, immigrant rights, and freedom of speech within the context of an instructional unit is acceptable. The best approach to navigate current events or potentially controversial topics is to implement backwards design when developing the lesson and activities. Make sure the discussion topics align with the state standards for the unit.

Quick Tip

In the Supreme Court case *Tinker v. Des Moines*, public school students in Des Moines, Iowa, organized a silent protest against the Vietnam War. Students planned to wear black armbands to school to protest the fighting, but the principal found out and told the students that they would be suspended if they wore the armbands. Despite the warning, students wore the armbands and were suspended. Through their parents, the students sued the school district for violating their right of expression and free speech and sought an injunction to prevent the school district from disciplining them. After several local and state court cases and appeals, the case made its way to the U.S. Supreme Court. In 1969, the high court ruled in a 7-2 decision in favor of the students. The court agreed that students' rights should be protected.

CONTENT CATEGORY IV

Example question

In *Givhan v. Western Line Consolidated School District* (1979) the Supreme Court ruled that a teacher could not be dismissed for speaking up against racial discrimination. The decision protects which category of rights and responsibilities for teachers?

A. Intellectual freedom

B. First amendment

C. Liability

D. Mandatory reporting

Correct answer B

First amendment rights are protected in schools. Teachers can point out inequities, especially when they contradict the mission of the school. In the classroom, it means as long as lessons are in alignment with state standards, students and teachers can discuss multiple perspectives of a current event or social issue. It is also important to teach students to use valid and reliable sources to defend differing opinions and perspectives.

Test Tip

On the PLT, you will see specific court cases such as *Tinker vs. Des Moines* being cited but do not be discouraged. You do not need to know individual case decisions to answer questions correctly on the test. Stay focused on the content of the court case. Chose the answer that makes sense according to what you know about the vocabulary and current rights and responsibilities of students and teachers.

Intellectual freedom

Intellectual freedom means teachers are prepared to select and use materials from credible sources that expose students to a variety of perspectives. For example, a teacher can prepare materials for students to read about various religions currently being practiced around the world. Intellectual freedom also means that students have the right to access and read information from a variety of points of view (American Library Association 2020). It also means that schools cannot censor ideas unless they are derogatory or offensive.

Selection is different from censorship. In fact, most schools select resources to be representative of all cultures, ethnicities, and genders. Schools also select to have firewalls on Internet access and bypass resources with stereotypes or misleading information. Using backwards design when selecting materials for your instruction will help to ensure the resources you are using align with the standards and are appropriate for your classroom.

Mandated reporting of child neglect and abuse

Doctors, nurses, social workers, police officers, childcare workers, and all school personnel are called *mandatory reporters*. That means people in these professions are required to report any suspected child abuse or neglect to authorities. For the PLT, you need to know that educators report any suspected abuse to local child welfare agencies. However, you need to learn the specific agency and procedure for your school. Each state has specific protocols to report abuse. They usually include a hotline to call as soon as you suspect abuse or neglect. Reports are confidential and may require a phone or in-person interview.

Example question

A teacher suspects a student is being abused at home. What should the teacher do first?

   A. Ask the student if she is being abused.

   B. Call the parents and confront them about the abuse.

   C. Talk to the principal about next steps.

   D. Follow school protocols to report the suspected abuse to the child welfare agency.

Correct answer: D

Teachers are mandatory reporters; therefore, reporting abuse is the only correct answer here.

Quick Tip

Your first instinct might be to notify the school principal if you suspect a student is being abused or neglected. However, that is not the correct answer on this exam. The first step to take when you suspect abuse is to report the abuse to authorities. Don't ask the student questions and don't confront the parents. Report it and let the child welfare agency work through the process. In some states, the laws for interviewing children limit the types of questions investigators can ask them and the number of times they can be interviewed. Asking them questions about the abuse might impede a future investigation. Follow the school's protocols for contacting the child welfare agency.

Due process

Due process is a person's rights when an organization is deciding disciplinary actions. This is a right afforded to all school personnel and students, in accordance with the due process clause in 14th amendment to the U.S. constitution. School districts are required to afford these three rights to anyone facing disciplinary action. Due process includes:

1. The right to a fair hearing.

2. The right to appeal.

3. The right to representation.

Parents can also use due process to file a formal complaint against a school concerning their child's education. A formal complaint affords parents and student the right to a hearing or formal process for reviewing and addressing the issues outlined in the complaint.

Example question

A parent has made a complaint about how students are being treated in her daughter's chemistry class. The parent says the teacher hit a student and her daughter is traumatized. The teacher has been asked to leave the school and remain at home on administrative leave until further notice. Which of the following rights is the teacher guaranteed as part of due process? Select all that apply.

    A. Representation.

    B. Continue working in the classroom.

    C. A fair hearing.

    D. An opportunity to discuss the incident with the parents.

    E. An appeal process.

Correct answers: A, C, and E

Answer choice D is incorrect because the teacher cannot talk to the accusing parent or anyone involved in the incident until formal charges have been delivered and due process is complete. Answer choice B is also incorrect because she was put on administrative leave. The teacher has the right to have a fair hearing, have legal representation at the hearing, and the opportunity to appeal if she does not agree with the verdict.

Liability

While students are in your classroom, you are responsible for their safety. In general, schools are not liable for minor injuries. But schools can face legal action for major issues such as sexual harassment, severe injuries, bullying, and wrongful death. Therefore, you need to document and report incidences causing physical or mental harm to students in your care.

Licensing and tenure

Every state has unique requirements for initial and renewal of teacher licensure. Check with your states department of education website in your area for specific requirements. Always check with the certification specialist for your district to confirm licensure requirements for your content area.

- **Licensure.** Generally, there is usually an education requirement (bachelor's degree), no record of child abuse, and no history of felony arrests. All states have unique licensure procedures and certification exams.

- **Tenure.** Tenure implies protection to your position as a teacher. Teachers are typically awarded tenure after a probationary period when they are teaching at the same school or the same school district. Once a teacher earns tenure, they are assured certain protections to their job in addition to due process. If an administration wants to dismiss a tenured teacher from their position, they need a written explanation citing reasonable cause and documentation (AFT, 2020). The specifics of when teachers are awarded tenure and what protections it provides vary from state to state.

Copyright

Teachers must follow copyright laws for all materials used in class. The two exception are for "fair use" and "face to face" use. Here are some guidelines to keep in mind when choosing materials for classroom use:

- Materials must have a clear connection to the instructional objectives.

- Always understand and comply with copyright protected materials including physical books, digital content, and software programs. Be sure the school or district has purchased licenses for students to use digital materials.

- Understand copyright protected artistic works which tend to be more protected than written works.

- Always include the copyright disclaimer in the copy being used for instruction or distribution.

Fair use. This is a doctrine in law that allows the limited use of copyright protected material without the permission of the copyright owner in certain circumstances. This applies to distribution of copyright protected material for educational purposes for students.

Material	Fair use For educational purposes only	Prohibited Without express permission from the author
Written text (Prose, poetry, chapter of a book, newspaper, magazine)	One copy per student in the class if: 1. The copied portion is brief. 2. Copies are spontaneous and not a systemic part of the curriculum.	• Multiple copies used over and over. • Copies to be put into an anthology. • Any copies that avoid purchasing the book or publication.
Art (Graphics, drawing cartoons, diagrams, image from a web page, newspaper, magazine, book)	One copy per student in the class if: 1. 5 or fewer images from one artist. 2. Copies are spontaneous and not a systemic part of the curriculum.	• Multiple copies used over and over. • Copies to be put into an anthology. • Any copies that avoid purchasing the book or publication.

Material	Fair use For educational purposes only	Prohibited Without express permission from the author
Video	Single copy, up to 3 minutes long for in-person use.	• All multiple copies are prohibited without consent from the author. • You cannot copy and distribute music (in any form) or video to students. • Any copies that avoid purchasing the book or publication.
Music (Sheet music, lyrics, musical score, CD, digital software)	Single copy for in-person use only.	• All multiple copies are prohibited without consent from the author. • You cannot copy and distribute music (in any form) or video to students. • Any copies that avoid purchasing the book or publication.
Broadcasts	A recording can be used in full, up to 45 days after it has been aired.	• No specific prohibitions.

(Campos, 2010)

There are specific parameters for what constitutes "brief" and "spontaneous" that are not necessary to memorize for this exam. Copying a portion of a book or periodical is not a substitute for purchasing material that will be used repeatedly, even for educational purposes.

Caution

As a general guideline, the less content you copy and the fewer copies you make, the more you are protected by fair use laws. Photocopies of materials should not be a replacement for buying the book.

Example question

Ms. Lambert has purchased new software for her computer that helps with grammar. She thinks this would be beneficial for all students in her class. What should she do?

    A. Allow her students to use the software by providing them her username and password.

    B. Get permission from the principal.

    C. Let the students use the software only in class.

    D. Contact the publisher and review copyright restrictions on the software.

Correct answer: D

When answering questions about software distribution to students, always follow the copyright. Answer choices A, B and C do not put copyright first and can be considered stealing.

This page intentionally left blank.

Content Category IV – Practice Questions and Answer Explanations

1. A new science teacher is working with a peer teacher to develop a professional development plan. Which of the following would be the most important thing to consider while in the planning process?

    A. Choose professional development that is interesting.

    B. Ask the principal about what professional development is available.

    C. Search online for local science conferences.

    D. Identify research provided from the National Science Teachers Association.

2. Which of the following would be the most effective way to use data in coordination with content area teams?

    A. Compare common assessment data and make instructional decisions as a team.

    B. Assign a team leader to analyze the data and make decisions for the team.

    C. Use common assessment data to give rewards to students who achieve at high levels.

    D. Report common assessment data to the principal for evaluations.

3. Which of the following questions would help a teacher decide what professional development would benefit classroom instruction most?

    A. Is the professional development affordable for the district?

    B. Are colleagues I respect attending the professional development?

    C. Will the professional development enhance my resume?

    D. Is the professional development aligned to the state adopted standards in my content area?

4. Which of the following techniques is most effective when deciding what strategies to use as a department?

    A. Evaluate the research about the strategies to determine their effectiveness.

    B. Google the strategies to see how it is implemented.

    C. Collaborate with colleagues when implementing strategies.

    D. Ask the principal if the strategies are appropriate.

5. Which of the following should a teacher consider when developing a professional development plan for the year?

    A. What professional goals will help the school increase its overall grade?

    B. What professional goals will help increase the chance of being accepted into a leadership program?

    C. What professional goals would strengthen the effectiveness of instruction based on students' needs?

    D. What professional goals do other colleagues use to align professional development?

6. A teacher is organizing a parent night at the school. To help encourage all parents to attend the parent night the teacher should:

    A. Announce parent night on the school website and invite parents and the community to attend.

    B. Send home a newsletter announcing the parent night.

    C. Have students send a personal invitation in their home language to their parents.

    D. Ask the principal to mention parent night in her weekly SAC meeting.

7. A teacher has been trying to implement the school-wide reading strategy. She is having trouble getting students to understand the strategy. What can the teacher do?

    A. Skip the strategy because the students don't like it.

    B. Ask the reading coach to demo the strategy in her class.

    C. Ask her peer teacher how to implement the strategy.

    D. Ask the principal to observe her and provide feedback.

8. What can a teacher do to ensure that cooperative learning will be effective in her classroom?

    A. Check the Internet and see what other teachers are saying about the strategy.

    B. Use research-based strategies when implementing cooperative learning.

    C. Rehearse the strategy at home before implementing it in class.

    D. Use strategies that are predetermined by the district.

9. Which of the following professional development sessions would be most beneficial for a teacher who has a goal of increasing her students' scores in reading by 5%?

    A. Evidence-based strategies to strengthen comprehension.

    B. How to use technology to increase student engagement in reading.

    C. How to use spreadsheets to organize data.

    D. How to use kinesthetic activities to engage learners with ADHD.

10. What should be considered when a team decides what professional development to attend?

    A. Student achievement

    B. Interest

    C. Relevance to the classroom

    D. Technology

Number	Answer	Explanation
1.	D	Remember, professional development includes professional learning, and professional learning should include scholarly research. The National Science Teachers Association provides professional development and scholarly research in its academic journals. Choosing professional development that is interesting is not necessarily the most important thing to consider. Asking the principal is typically never the correct answer on the exam. All professional learning should be aligned with the standards and grounded in reliable and valid research
2.	A	Answer A has all the good words. Common assessments provide important data for teams to compare. In addition, the team is making instructional decisions based on the data.
3.	D	Professional development, first and foremost, should be aligned to the state adopted standards.
4.	A	Staying on top of the research that discusses classroom strategies is the most effective practice here.
5.	C	The professional development plan should always be working towards student achievement. Therefore, C is the best answer here.
6.	C	Personal invitations from students to parents in their home language satisfies many of the important aspects of including all stakeholders in school programs.
7.	B	Reading coaches are there to help teachers implement reading strategies in the classroom and provide support when necessary.
8.	B	Research-based strategies is a good phrase. Be sure to choose this if you see it in the answer choices on the exam.
9.	A	Comprehension is an essential reading skill. In addition, evidence-based strategies are always good to use when teaching reading. All the other professional development sessions address things other than student achievement in reading.
10.	A	Student achievement should always be considered when deciding what professional development to attend.

This page intentionally left blank.

CONTENT CATEGORY V

Analysis of Instructional Scenarios

This page intentionally left blank.

V. Analysis of Instructional Scenarios

Constructed-response questions require you to demonstrate your knowledge in a subject area by creating your own response to particular topics. Essays and short-answer questions are types of constructed-response questions.

For this exam, you will be presented with a scenario that includes several pieces of documentation to analyze. You will also be presented with questions to answer based on the information provided.

Keep these things in mind when you respond to the constructed-response questions:

1. **Answer the question accurately.** Analyze what each part of the question is asking you to do. If the question asks you to describe or discuss, you should provide more than just a list.

2. **Answer the question completely.** If a question asks you to do three distinct things in your response, you should cover all three things for the best score. Otherwise, no matter how well you write, you will not be awarded full credit.

3. **Answer the question that is asked.** Do not change the question or challenge the basis of the question. You will receive no credit or a low score if you answer another question or if you state, for example, that there is no possible answer.

4. **Give a thorough and detailed response.** You must demonstrate that you have a thorough understanding of the subject matter. However, your response should be straightforward and not filled with unnecessary information.

5. **Reread your response.** Check that you have written what you intended. Be sure not to leave sentences unfinished or omit clarifying information.

General scoring guide

- **Score of 2**

  A response in this category:

  - Demonstrates a thorough understanding of the aspects of the case that are relevant to the question.

  - Responds appropriately to all parts of the question.

  - Provides a strong explanation, when required, that is well supported by relevant evidence.

  - Demonstrates a strong knowledge of pedagogical concepts, theories, facts, procedures, or methodologies relevant to the question.

- **Score of 1**

  A response in this category:

  - Demonstrates a basic understanding of the aspects of the case that are relevant to the question.

  - Responds appropriately to one portion of the question.

  - Provides a weak explanation, when required, that is supported by relevant evidence.

  - Demonstrates some knowledge of pedagogical concepts, theories, facts, procedures, or methodologies relevant to the question.

- **Score of 0**

   A response in this category:

   - Demonstrates misunderstandings of the aspects of the case that are relevant to the question.

   - Fails to respond appropriately to the question.

   - Is not supported by relevant evidence.

   - Demonstrates little knowledge of pedagogical concepts, theories, facts, procedures, or methodologies relevant to the question.

No credit is given for a blank or off-topic response.

Writing strategy

1. **Read the questions first.** Use the questions to set up the outline of your response. This will help to keep your response focused on the task you are being asked to do.

2. **Read the prompt and take notes.** Read the case study and the accompanying information. Take short notes that are relevant to the questions. Use the scratch paper you are provided in the exam to make notes and organize your thoughts.

3. **Answer the questions.** Make sure you reread the question and construct your response accordingly. If it is asking for TWO things, make sure you have TWO things. If it is asking you about assessments, make sure your answer is relevant to assessments.

4. **Use specific details.** Include tangible details to support your claim. Make references to the data in the scenario and support materials. Use specific language like, "because only 27% of the students are making gains…"

5. **Proofread.** PROOF, PROOF, PROOF! If you want to be an effective teacher, you better have proper grammar and spelling. Give yourself time to look back through your response to correct spelling and grammatical errors.

Test Tip

When constructing your response, use the language and vocabulary found in the test specifications and throughout this book. Words like *needs assessment, ongoing, progress monitoring, student achievement* will help maximize your score on this task.

Scenario 1 – Students as Learners

Ms. Linder is a new 9th grade social studies teacher. She has several students who have been labeled "challenging" by their previous teachers at the school. Ms. Linder is having a difficult time getting these students to focus and behave in class.

Ms. Linder has submitted an unusually high number of disciplinary referrals to the front office. Her principal has asked her to work with a peer teacher to observe her classroom and provide input on how to better manage discipline in her class.

Document 1 – 9th grade disciplinary referrals

Discipline Referrals: 9th Grade

Teacher	Percent	Quantity
Ms. Albany	19%	13
Ms. Hailey	16%	11
Ms. Linder	46%	32
Ms. Taron	10%	7
Mr. Teller	9%	6

Document 2 – Classroom management observation rubric and notes

	1: Ineffective	2: Needs Improvement	3: Effective	4: Highly Effective
Standards of conduct	The teacher has not established standards of conduct.	The teacher has established standards of conduct but is inconsistent with implementation.	The teacher consistently establishes, communicates, and implements appropriate standards of conduct.	The teacher consistently establishes, communicates, and implements appropriate standards of conduct that instill a sense of self-discipline in students.

	1: Ineffective	2: Needs Improvement	3: Effective	4: Highly Effective
Expectations	Students are often disengaged and unclear about the expectations of the classroom. The teacher must frequently remind students of the expectations more often than what is appropriate for the age and development of the students.	Students are sometimes disengaged and unclear about classroom expectations. The teacher must sometimes remind students of the expectations more often than what is appropriate for the age and development of the students.	Students are usually engaged and understand the expectations of the classroom. The teacher provides few reminders about the expectations that are relative to the age and development of the students.	Students are engaged and clear about classroom expectations. There is no need for reminders about expectations which is appropriate to the age and development of the students.
Learning environment	The teacher does not monitor students' behavior during whole group, small group, independent work, and transitions.	The teacher is inconsistent when monitoring students' behavior during whole group, small group, individual work, and transitions.	The teacher monitors students' behavior during whole group, small group, individual work, and transitions.	The teacher monitors students' behavior during whole-group, small group, independent work time, and during hallway and lunchtime duties.
Classroom management	The teacher ignores misbehavior. The teacher uses an inappropriate voice level when attempting to correct misbehavior. The teacher uses inappropriate language when attempting to correct misbehavior.	The teacher does not consistently address misbehavior. The teacher sometimes uses an inappropriate voice level when attempting to correct misbehavior. The teacher sometimes uses inappropriate language when attempting to correct misbehavior.	The teacher stops misbehavior when needed promptly and consistently. The teacher uses appropriate voice level and language to correct misbehavior.	The teacher stops misbehavior when needed promptly and consistently. The teacher uses appropriate voice level, non-verbal cues, and language to correct misbehavior while maintaining the dignity of the student in a manner that promotes positive behavior and relationships.

Peer Teacher's Notes:

Ms. Linder's room is bright and cheerful with a good use of space. Desks are arranged in groups for small-group instruction. Students' work is displayed throughout the room. However, class rules and expectations are not posted anywhere for reference.

During the first activity of the lesson, Ms. Linder explains the learning objectives of the activity but does not explicitly explain what the students are expected to do in the activity. She does not include behavior expectations in the explanation.

During the activity several students disengage and start talking to their neighbors. Ms. Linder breaks instruction and address the entire class. In an upbeat tone, she chuckles and says, "C'mon guys. You know how you are supposed to behave. Let's all get back on task."

A few minutes later, two students begin to argue over the materials they are using for the activity. The argument distracts the entire class. In a sterner tone, Ms. Linder addresses the whole class and says, "OK guys. That's enough. Let's focus on what we are supposed to be doing right now."

The class settles down for a few minutes and then the chatter and disagreements begin again. At this point, the noise level in the class is too loud for students to hear Ms. Linder provide instruction. Most of the students have disengaged from the activity altogether and two students (Rocco and Tyler) are nearing a physical altercation over the materials. Ms. Linder raises her voice, addresses the whole class, and yells, "That's it! I have had enough! Rocco and Tyler, outside now! The rest of you, open your language arts book and read silently to yourself. The next student who talks will be headed to the office with a referral."

Rating:

- Standard of conduct – 1
- Expectations – 1
- Learning environment – 2
- Classroom management – 2
- Total score – 6

Question 1

- Provide TWO strategies Ms. Linder can use to improve her classroom management.
- Explain how these strategies relate to learning theories.

Question 2

- Provide TWO ways Ms. Linder can help her students develop self-motivation?
- How will this improve teaching and learning in her classroom?

Scenario 2 – Instructional Process

Mr. Haberkern is a 8th grade teacher at Magnolia Middle School which has a diverse student population. Mr. Haberkern is new to teaching and does not have experience with English learners and special education students. Dr. Deacon, the school's assistant principal, is conducting a walk-through of his class to assess his instruction and provide feedback. Provided below is a chart of Mr. Haberkern's class subgroup data. Many of his students fall into more than one subgroup. Also provided are Dr. Deacon's observations from this walk-through.

Document 1 – Subgroup data

Subgroup	Percent	Number of Students
English learner	36%	8
Students living in poverty	65%	14
Special education students	32%	7

Document 2 – Classroom observation notes

Mr. Haberkern begins with a greeting and verbally goes over the schedule for the class period. He starts the lesson by explaining the objectives and instructions for the activity. The activity is a group reading assignment where student's work in their pre-assigned teams to read a text on geography, create posters showing what they learned, and present the poster to the class. Mr. Haberkern walks around the room to support each group.

There are 5 groups each with 4 to 5 students. The groups are assigned at the beginning of the quarter and stay the same until the next quarter. Essentially, the students are in the same group for nine weeks. 2 of the groups have a disproportionate number of English learners and special education students. 1 group consists of students who are the highest performing in the class.

During the activity, the high performing team is surpassing the others with reading the information and creating the posters. Mr. Haberkern spends most of his time with the 2 groups that are struggling with the text.

The reading assignment is from a periodical on geography. While the information is age-appropriate for 8th grade, none of the text selections have visual aids to assist English learners and special education students with the information. Many of the students do not have prior knowledge of the geographical regions they are reading about. One of the texts is about the Sahara Desert. A student from that group says, "I have never heard of this place. Where is it?"

The low performing groups are unable to connect the text with the activity. They begin making posters that do not correspond with the information in the reading. 2 groups are able to finish the text and move on to creating their posters. The high functioning group is finished with their poster far ahead of the others and begin chatting with each other or working on other tasks. At this point, Mr. Haberkern has the students in the high performing group help the two struggling groups. This reinforces the disparity among the groups. The low performing groups become frustrated and disengage from the activity.

Several groups do not finish before it is time to present. The students who are still trying to finish the poster look visibly nervous about presenting to the class. They rush to finish their posters. Their faces are worried, and a student begins to cry. One group gives up entirely and sits quietly.

The high performing group presents first. The poster accurately reflects the reading and is well designed. The presenter speaks fluidly about the information and sits down. Mr. Haberkern provides praise for a job well done. The next group has an unfinished poster that loosely corresponds with the reading. The presenter struggles to find the words and looks down at the floor. Mr. Haberkern helps the student along to finish the presentation. The third and fourth groups present similar posters and struggle to explain the reading. The last group only has a few scribbles on the poster. No one from the group will volunteer to present. A student from the high performing group tries to interject to help the group finish the presentation. Finally, Mr. Haberkern asks a few basic questions about the poster and the reading and then ends the activity.

The students who struggled with the activity look dejected and throw away their poster as they clean up and move on to the next activity.

Question 3

In the observations, Dr. Deacon explains the grouping:

The groups are assigned at the beginning of the quarter and stay the same until the next quarter. Essentially, the students are in the same group for nine weeks. 2 of the groups have a disproportionate number of English learners and special education students. 1 group consists of students who are the highest performing in the class.

- Identify TWO modifications Mr. Haberkern can make so that the groups are more effective.
- Explain how these changes will support the diverse needs of Mr. Haberkern's students.

Question 4

Dr. Deacon notes several instances of students becoming frustrated with the activity and disengaging:

The high functioning group is finished with their poster far ahead of the others and begin chatting with each other or working on other tasks.

The presenter struggles to find the words and looks down at the floor.

The last group only has a few scribbles on the poster. No one from the group will volunteer to present.

The students who struggled with the activity look dejected and throw away their poster as they clean up and move on to the next activity.

- Identify TWO ways Mr. Haberkern can scaffold instruction to support all students.
- Explain how these changes will support English learners and special education students

Scenario 3 – Assessments

Ms. Lewandowsky is a 10th grade reading and language arts teacher, and she is preparing for the upcoming school year. To get a baseline of how her students are performing, Ms. Lewandowsky reviews her students' scores on the state's standardized tests from the previous year. Many of her students performed below their peers when compared to other schools within the state.

Ms. Lewandowsky also receives guidance from the school's principal on the goals and objectives of the school. Reading proficiency scores are at the center of the school's goals.

Document 1 – Standardized test scores

Statewide 10th Grade Reading Proficiency by Competency

Competency	Level 1 Inadequate	Level 2 Below Satisfactory	Level 3 Satisfactory	Level 4 Proficient	Level 5 Mastery
Key ideas and details	3%	25%	37%	19%	16%
Craft and structure	7%	26%	38%	15%	14%
Integration of knowledge and ideas	8%	31%	37%	13%	11%
Range of reading and level of text complexity	11%	36%	35%	10%	8%

Ms. Lewandowsky's 10th Grade Class Reading Proficiency by Competency:

Competency	Level 1 Inadequate	Level 2 Below Satisfactory	Level 3 Satisfactory	Level 4 Proficient	Level 5 Mastery
Key ideas and details	14%	38%	35%	8%	5%
Craft and structure	18%	37%	35%	6%	4%
Integration of knowledge and ideas	17%	42%	34%	4%	3%
Range of reading and level of text complexity	21%	44%	30%	3%	2%

Document 2 – Welcome letter from the principal

FROM: Dr. Clemente

TO: All faculty and staff

RE: Kickoff the New School Year

Team,

As we embark on the new academic year, I want to encourage you all to routinely review the school improvement plan to ensure your instruction aligns with the goals and objectives of the school.

Our school goals and objectives are carefully designed to support the achievement for our unique and diverse student body. We have an opportunity to be a part of the foundation of this evolving school community and build something truly remarkable. That all starts with our goals.

Keep in mind our mission and vision as we kickoff the school year. Our mission is to provide all students with the highest quality education to support them in their academic success. Our vision is for our students to thrive in all aspects of their development.

Please review the school improvement plan so you can implement the goals and objectives into your instruction.

Let's get to work.

Dr. Clemente

Document 3 – School improvement plan: reading goals

This year:

- Collaborate in professional learning communities (PLCs) to identify strategies to increase student reading proficiency in all subgroups from level 2 to level 3.

- Implement interventions to increase the reading proficiency level of English language learners (ELL) from level 2 to level 3.

- Increase student proficiency in reading across all content areas through the implementation of authentic and engaging lessons aligned to the state standards.

Question 5

- In preparing for the upcoming year, identify TWO additional sources of data Ms. Lewandowsky can reference to learn more about her students' capabilities.

- Explain how these sources of data can provide meaningful information about her students' needs to supplement the standardized test scores.

Question 6

- Identify TWO strategies Ms. Lewandowsky can integrate into her planning to support student achievement.

- Explain how these strategies align with the school's goals.

Scenario 4 – Professional Development, Leadership, and Community

Ms. Pache is a new 11th grade English teacher. She is energetic and enthusiastic about her job and is very passionate about teaching high school. She is always looking for new and exciting approaches to help her students learn.

Ms. Pache always comes to PLC meetings with fresh ideas and perspectives on how to support student achievement. She has brought several samples of materials to her PLC meetings that she wants the team to try. However, she has received pushback from some of the veteran teachers in her PLC group. She feels that the veteran teachers are too "old school" and set in their ways. They are not willing to give her ideas a try.

Document 1 – Feedback from PLC team leader

Hi Ms. Pache,

While I appreciate the enthusiasm that you bring to the PLC team, some of the materials you recommended in today's meeting are not on target with what we need to implement in the classroom. The materials you shared are from online sources and lack research-based methods for instruction. Additionally, the instruction in the worksheets is for narrative text and comprehension questions which do not align with 11th grade reading standards for determining key ideas and details.

To reach our reading goals this year, we have to be very targeted in our approach to teaching foundational skills. Please review the standards and goals to make sure your classroom materials align. We want a coordinated approach to teaching and learning so that all 11th grade students are prepared to move on to 12th grade next year.

Ms. Gustav, our media specialist can help you research and find materials for your class that are a great fit for 11th grade. She also has access to other libraries and networks with fantastic materials.

You have great ideas, and I can see how passionate you are about teaching your students. I would really like to help you channel that energy into finding resources that are the perfect fit for your class. Please feel free to contact me for any support or if you have any questions.

Thank you and have a great day.

Ms. Bohn

Document 2 – 11th grade PLC meeting agenda

Action Item	Who?	Time	Notes
Take attendance 1. Ms. Bohn (team leader) 2. Ms. Carlson 3. Mr. Javier 4. Ms. Lewis 5. Ms. Pache 6. Mr. Pearson	Team leader	2 mins	
Review reading goals. 1. Support student achievement in reading by increasing assessment scores by 10% over the next reporting period. 2. Support student achievement in reading by increasing literacy by 5% for ELLs and special needs students over the next reporting period.	Team leader	3 mins	

Action Item	Who?	Time	Notes
Review key ideas and details reading standards. Key Ideas and Details: 1. Cite textual evidence to support analysis. 2. Make purposeful inferences and explain reasoning. 3. Determine themes in a text. 4. Synthesize and write a summary of text. 5. Determine and analyze the author's choice for setting, plot, characters, and events.	Team leader	5 mins	
Review notes and action items from previous meeting.	Team leader	5 mins	
Discuss action research. • What is working? • What are the challenges? • Provide specific data.	All	25 mins	
Assign action items for upcoming reporting period.	All	15 mins	
Open agenda	All	5 mins	

Question 7

- Based on Ms. Bohn's feedback, identify TWO issues with the materials Ms. Pache recommended.

- Explain how these issues affect student achievement.

Question 8

- Identify TWO strategies Ms. Pache can do to find materials that are appropriate for her classroom.

- Explain how these strategies align with the PLC team's goals.

CONTENT CATEGORY V

This page intentionally left blank.

V. Constructed Response Examples

The table below provides examples of constructed responses to the questions after each scenario. There are many different ways to answer these questions. The responses below are provided as one example for each question. Your response will most likely be completely different from the examples provided. However, the goal is to incorporate the main ideas of each response.

Number	Example Constructed Response
1.	Ms. Linder can use positive reinforcement and a cueing system to improve learning and teaching in her classroom. First, she should explain, model, and practice the classroom rules and routines so that students understand the expectations. Then, she can use positive reinforcement by praising students who follow the rules and routines appropriately. This technique of rewards and repetition aligns with Thorndike's connectionism theory. Ms. Linder can also implement a cueing system by using a hand signal or a bell when it is time to quiet down. This method aligns with Watson's conditioning theory. When students hear the bell, they will know to quiet down without Ms. Linder having to raise her voice.
2.	Two ways that Ms. Linder can help her students develop self-motivation are allowing student-centered decisions and providing frequent positive feedback. Ms. Linder is writing 2 to 3 times the number of disciplinary referrals than the other 9th grade teachers. Rather than writing more referrals, she can work with students who struggle to follow the rules and routines to develop a behavior plan together. This will build the students' confidence in their ability to manage their own actions. It will also cut down on the disruptions in class and allow all students to achieve. Ms. Linder can also provide frequent and specific positive feedback to her students when they make good behavior choices. Positive feedback is very effective in building students' motivation to perform well. When they hear they are doing a good job, they are more likely to continue exhibiting that behavior.
3	The first modification Mr. Haberkern can make to the groups is to mix them up or make them heterogeneous. Based on the case study, high-level students are grouped together and ELL students are grouped together, which makes the groups homogeneous. Heterogeneous grouping will allow the high-level and ELLs to balance the activity. The second thing Mr. Haberkern can do is change up the groups more frequently than every 9 weeks. Allowing diverse groups of students to interact with each other more frequently will help students work together to solve problems and complete performance-based assessments.
4.	To help all students in this case study, Mr. Haberkern should scaffold instruction. First, he should support struggling learners and ELLs by providing support during the reading. He can use visuals and videos to accompany the reading, so students have multiple ways to understand the information. Second, before moving on to the presentation part of the lesson, Mr. Haberkern can take time to measure students' understanding and differentiate instruction accordingly. He can work with small groups of students who are struggling while allowing those who understand the content to move onto the presentation.

Number	Example Constructed Response
5.	In addition to the state test scores, Ms. Lewandowsky can look at her students' portfolios of formative assessments from the previous year and anecdotal notes from previous teachers. The portfolio will provide a collection of student work that shows progress over time. Ms. Lewandowsky will see how each student performs on quizzes, homework, diagnostic tests, and project-based learning. The anecdotal notes provide rich, qualitative data that can't be found in test scores alone. This is where Ms. Lewandowsky will find details on each student's interests, background, culture, and diversity. Although the school's reading goals are focused on increasing test scores, these additional sources of data will provide a more comprehensive understanding of each student's needs and capabilities.
6.	Based on the data from the test scores, Ms. Lewandowsky's students are underperforming compared to their peers. Her students are struggling in all four categories of reading proficiency. Two strategies Ms. Lewandowsky can integrate into her planning to support her students are align her lessons to the state standards and collaborate with her PLC team for support. First, Ms. Lewandowsky needs to create lessons that are aligned to the state standards for reading proficiency. This means creating lesson plans that target the four competencies for reading proficiency: key ideas and details, craft and structure, integration of knowledge and ideas, and range of reading and level of text complexity. Next, Ms. Lewandowsky should work in her PLC team to ensure her lessons align with the school's goals and expectations.
7.	While Ms. Pache is very enthusiastic about teaching, her strategies are not appropriate for two reasons. First, the methods she is introducing are not researched-based. To ensure students receive high quality education, Ms. Pache should be using resources that are developed and analyzed through professional organizations or a peer review process. Materials downloaded from the Internet might not meet that standard. Second, the materials Ms. Pache introduced are not appropriate. Ms. Pache should be using grade level text. She should ask questions to supports students' understanding and communication of the key ideas and details as described in the standards.
8.	One way Ms. Pache can find materials for her classroom is to coordinate with the instructional coach at her school. The instructional coach should be able to provide materials from the school library that focus on the specific key ideas and detail goals for 11th grade. She can also help Ms. Pache find peer reviewed research and methods to ensure her instruction is high-quality and standards-aligned. Another way Ms. Pache can find materials for her classroom is to join a professional organization for high school English language arts teachers. These are often non-profit organizations that are focused on helping teachers connect with resources. They routinely publish peer-reviewed research on instructional techniques for improving assessment scores and increasing literacy.

Quick Reference Guides

This page intentionally left blank.

Cooperative Learning Techniques

For this exam, it is important to understand different techniques to differentiate instruction in cooperative settings. The following table provides different learning techniques and how to use them in your classroom.

Cooperative Learning Techniques

Activity	Definition	Example
Jigsaw	A cooperative learning activity in which each student or group of students read and analyze a small piece of information that is part of a much larger piece. They then share what they learned with the class.	Teachers arrange students in groups. Each group reads and analyzes a piece of a text. Group members then join with members of other groups, and each student shares and discusses her section of the text. As the group shares, the entire text is covered. It is referred to as *jigsaw* because students complete the puzzle when they share their individual pieces.
Chunking	A reading activity that involves breaking down a difficult text into manageable pieces.	In a science class, students break down a lengthy and complex chapter on genetics by focusing on pieces of the text. The teacher has planned for students to read and analyze the text one paragraph at a time.
Think-pair-share	A cooperative learning activity in which students work together to solve a problem or answer a question.	**Think** – The teacher asks a specific question about the text. Students "think" about what they know or have learned about the topic. **Pair** – Students pair up to read and discuss. **Share** – Students share what they have learned in their pairs. Teachers can then expand the "share" into a whole-class discussion.
Reading response journals	A writing activity where students use journals to react to what they read by expressing how they feel and asking questions about the text.	After reading a chapter of a book in class, the teacher asks students to use their reading response journals to reflect on the story emotionally, make associations between ideas in the text and their own ideas, and record questions they may have about the story.
Evidence-based discussion	The teacher sets the expectation that students use evidence in the text to support claims they make during the discussion.	The class is discussing World War II. Students are asking and answering questions. When making claims, students identify support for those claims in the text.
Literature circles	A small-group, cooperative learning activity where students engage and discuss a piece of literature or text.	In their cooperative groups, students read and analyze text together. Each student contributes to the learning. There is an administrator who decides when to read and when to stop and discuss. There is a note taker who writes down important information. There are 2 readers who take turns reading the text based on the administrator's suggestions.

This page intentionally left blank.

When I write study guides, I identify *good words* you should look for in the answer choices to determine correct and incorrect answers. Good words are terms and phrases taken from the test specifications that highlight best practices. If you see these words in answer choices on the exam, slow down and have a closer look. There is a good possibility these words are in the correct answer choice. I have also included a list of bad words and phrases to avoid. These are typically not the correct answer choice on the exam.

Good Words and Phrases

Accommodations. Modifying instruction or using supports to help special education students achieve. Accommodations do NOT involve lowering the standard or delaying learning.

Action research. The process of evaluating data in the classroom to identify issues and implementing effective and quick actions to solve problems.

Allocating resources. Portioning resources so all students have equal opportunity and time while balancing curriculum and instruction.

Assessments. Using formative and summative data to monitor progress and measure outcomes.

Authentic instruction. Providing students with meaningful, relevant, and useful learning experiences and activities.

Balanced literacy. Reading and writing instruction that uses a variety of literary genres including literary and informational texts.

Bilingual instruction. Helping students use elements of their first language to support learning in English.

Celebrate culture. Finding materials and resources to celebrate the different cultures represented in your classroom.

Classroom management. A variety of skills and techniques that teachers use to keep students organized, orderly, focused, attentive, on task, and academically productive during class.

Collaborative learning. These are strategies that are student-centered and self-directed rather than led by the teacher. Collaboration can also be working with colleagues or stakeholders to improve, create, or produce something.

Communicating data with stakeholders. Stakeholders include students, parents, teachers, administrators, community members, and local business owners.

Comprehensible education. Making information and lessons understandable to students by accommodating and using ancillary materials to help with language barriers.

Concept map. Visual representation of content. Especially useful for illustrating concepts like cause and effect, problem and solution, compare and contrast, etc.

Consent Decree. Protects students' right to a free, comprehensible education. It addresses civil and academic rights of English language learners (ELLs) and requires instruction be delivered in a comprehensible manner so all students can fully participate.

Controversy. Some topics in science can elicit controversy from students, teachers, and parents. Make sure all instruction is aligned to the standards to mitigate controversy.

Concrete representation abstract (CRA). Components of math fluency where students evolve in their learning from concrete concepts, then to representation, and finally to abstract concepts.

Critical thinking. Higher-order thinking skills that involve evaluating, analyzing, creating, and applying knowledge.

Cultural responsiveness. Instruction as a pedagogy that empowers students intellectually, socially, and emotionally by celebrating and learning about other cultures. This includes recognizing the importance of including students' cultural references in all aspects of learning and designing a productive learning environment.

Data driven decisions. Using scores, writing samples, observations, and other types of qualitative and quantitative data to make instructional decisions.

Depth of knowledge. Framework that is used to identify the cognitive complexity of a problem.

Developmentally appropriate instruction (DAP). Choosing text, tools, activities, and experiments that are appropriate for the students' grade level.

Differentiated instruction. Providing all learners in a diverse classroom with different methods to understand instruction.

Diversity as an asset. Seeing diversity in the classroom as an opportunity to learn new things through the perspectives of others.

Evidenced-based. Providing instruction using materials with the best scientific evidence available.

Follow the IEP. A student's individualized education program (IEP) is a legal document. If you see IEP in the answer choices, it is most likely the correct answer.

High expectations for ALL learners. Holding all students to high academic standards regardless of the students' achievement level, ethnicity, language, socioeconomic status.

Horizontal alignment. Organization and coordination of standards and learning goals across content areas in the same grade level.

Inclusive. Providing students with resources and experiences that represent their culture and ethnicity.

Informal learning. Supporting students with self-directed, collaborative learning outside of the classroom.

Inquiry-based. Science instruction should foster students' inquiry and encourage students to ask, "why?"

Interactive activities for reading. Seek out activities in content area reading that are interactive and real-world based. Making content reading interesting is key.

Interdisciplinary activities. Activities that connect two or more content areas; promotes relevance and critical thinking.

Intrinsic motivation. Answers that promote autonomy, relatedness, and competence are ways to apply intrinsic motivation. Be on the lookout for these answer choices.

Manipulatives. Manipulatives are used to represent counting, patterns, operations, physical attributes of geometric figures, and formulas.

Metacognition. Analysis of your own thinking.

Modeling. Demonstrating the application of a skill or knowledge.

Modifications. Changes to the curriculum and learning environment in accordance to a student's IEP. Modifications change the expectations for learning and the level of assessment.

Outcomes. The results of a program, strategy, or resources implemented in the classroom.

Performance assessment. An activity assigned to students to assess their mastery of multiple learning goals aligned to standards.

Primary resource. These are materials and information in their original form like diaries, journals, songs, paintings, and autobiographies.

Prior knowledge. What students know about a topic from their previous experiences and learning.

Progress monitor. Keeping track of student or whole class learning in real time. Quantifiable measures of progress, conferring, observing, exit tickets, and student self-assessments.

Questioning. Students should be encouraged to continue to question, research, and test phenomena.

Relevance, real-world, and relatable. Be sure to choose answers that promote real-world application and make learning relatable to students' lives.

Reliable. Consistent. Producing consistent results under similar conditions.

Remediation. Correcting or changing something to make it better.

Rigorous. A word used to describe curriculum that is challenging and requires students to use higher-order thinking skills.

Scaffolding. Using supports to help students achieve a standard that they would not achieve on their own.

Scientific method. The techniques for investigating phenomena: observe, classify, predict, hypothesize, investigate.

Secondary resource. These are materials and information derived from the original like newspaper articles, history textbooks, and reviews.

Specific and meaningful feedback. More than just a grade at the top of a paper, effective feedback includes positive aspects and how students can apply those positive aspects to improving. In addition, feedback should contain specific things the student should do to improve.

Standards-aligned. Ensuring that curriculum and instruction is aligned to the state-adopted standards.

Student centered/learner centered. A variety of educational programs, learning experiences, instructional approaches, and academic-support strategies that address students' distinct learning needs, interests, or cultural backgrounds.

Thematic unit. An interdisciplinary study typically organized around a social studies or science theme.

Validity. Accuracy. How accurately knowledge or skills are measured.

Vertical alignment. Organization of standards and learning goals across grade levels. Structure for which learning and understanding is built from grade level to grade level.

Vocabulary in-context. Always teach vocabulary in context. It helps to relate the vocabulary to the real-world.

Wait time. Time between a question and when a student is called on or a response to a student's reply.

Bad Words and Phrases

Bias. Inserting personal beliefs, stereotypes, and assumptions in the learning process. This can also include learning materials developed from the perspective of the dominant culture that exclude minority perspectives.

Call the parents, principal, district, etc. You are expected to effectively manage your classroom without deferring responsibilities to others. In real life, teachers will often need to call the parents or principal. But on this exam, avoid answer choices that defer responsibilities to someone other than the teacher.

Extra homework. On this exam, students should be getting all of the instruction they need in class. In real life, we all assign homework. However, on this exam, extra homework is not the correct answer choice.

Extrinsic motivators. These are rewards of extrinsic value like pizza parties, recess time, etc. Students should be motivated by intrinsic motivators like self-confidence, sense of accomplishment, and feeling successful.

Hiring a contractor or external vendor. Anytime the answer choice includes using an outside resource like a contractor or a vendor to provide instruction or classroom management, this is typically not the correct answer choice. You are expected to be able to manage your own classroom using your own skills and capabilities.

Homework. Assigning homework is not a preferred strategy on this exam, especially when students are struggling with the material.

Homogenous grouping. Grouping by gender, English proficiency, or learning level is never a best practice on this exam or in your classroom. Homogenous groups should only be used in special circumstances and on a temporary basis.

Punitive solutions. Avoid answer choices that sound like punishments. For this exam, teachers are expected to be implementing positive behavior support methods so avoid any answer choices that sounds punitive.

Student aides. Using students as translators or support for special education or ELL students is never a best practice in the classroom.

This page intentionally left blank.

Landmark Legislation and Court Cases

For this exam, you will need to know how significant legislation and court cases have impacted public education policy throughout U.S. history. The following timeline provides an overview of the legislation and court cases you might see on the PLT.

U.S. Legislation

- **14th Amendment to the United States Constitution, 1868.** The 14th Amendment of the U.S. Constitution guarantees an equal educational opportunity for all children in the United States.

- **Title IX of the Educational Amendments, 1972.** Provides that no individual may be discriminated against on the basis of sex in any education program or activity receiving federal financial assistance.

- **Rehabilitation Act of 1973 Section 504.** States that "no qualified individual with a disability in the United States shall be excluded from, denied the benefits of, or be subjected to discrimination" in any program or activity that receives federal financial assistance.

- **Family Educational Rights and Privacy Act of 1974 (FERPA).** Applies to any educational agency or institution to which funds have been made available under a program administered by the Secretary of Education. Sets out the requirements for the protection of parents and students.

- **Americans with Disabilities Act of 1990 Title II.** Requires that state and local governments give people with disabilities an equal opportunity to benefit from all of their programs, services, and activities, (e.g., public education).

- **No Child Left Behind of 2002 (NCLB).** NCLB introduced accountability to public schools.
  - Title I: Improving academic achievement of the disadvantaged
  - Title II: Preparing, training, and recruiting high quality teachers and principals
  - Title III: Language instruction for limited English proficient and immigrant students
  - Title IV: 21st Century Schools
  - Title V: Promoting informed parental choice and innovative programs
  - Title VI: Flexibility and accountability

- **Individuals with Disabilities Education Act of 2004 (IDEA).** Requires public schools to make available to all eligible children with disabilities a free public education appropriate to their individual needs.

- **Race to the Top of 2009 (RTTT).** Forty-six states and the District of Columbia submitted comprehensive reform plans to compete in the Race to the Top competition. While 19 states have received funding so far, 34 states modified state education laws or policies to facilitate needed change, and 48 states worked together to create a voluntary set of rigorous college and career ready standards (The White House, 2018).

- **Every Student Succeeds Act of 2015 (ESSA).** Advances equity by upholding critical protections for America's disadvantaged and high-need students. Requires all students in America be taught to high academic standards that will prepare them to succeed in college and careers. Ensures that vital information is provided to educators, families, students, and communities through annual statewide assessments that measure students' progress toward those high standards (U.S. Department of Education, 2019).

U.S. Court Cases

- **Plessy v Ferguson (1896).** Supreme Court ruling that upheld racial segregation of Black people and established the "separate but equal" doctrine. This ruling became constitutional justification for very restrictive Jim Crow Era legislation based on race. With this decision, the Supreme Court sanctioned segregation which became commonplace throughout the country for the next 60 years.

- **Brown v Board of Education (1954).** Overturned *Plessy v Ferguson* and established that separate education facilities are NOT equal. This ruling mandated that segregated public schools be integrated to include Black students.

- **Engel v Vitale (1962) and Abington School District v Schempp (1963).** Two court cases involving school prayer where the Supreme Court ruled prayer in school is a violation of the 1st Amendment.

- **Tinker v Des Moines (1969).** Students protesting the Vietnam War wore armbands to school to express their dissatisfaction with the federal government. The arm bands were then prohibited by the school district's dress code. The students argued that the ban was a violation of their 1st Amendment rights. The court ruled in favor of the students which extended free speech protections to students.

- **San Antonio Independent School District v Rodriguez (1973).** A lower court found that the Texas school financing system was unconstitutional under the equal protection clause because it discriminated on the basis of wealth. The system was based on property taxes where wealthy communities had better schools than poorer communities. The supreme court reversed the decision of the lower court and established that poor schools in underserved communities are not unconstitutional.

- **Givhan v. Western Line Consolidated School District (1979).** Supreme Court ruled that a teacher could not be dismissed for speaking up against racial discrimination.

- **Plyler v Doe (1982).** This Supreme Court decision established that all children living in the U.S. are protected by the equal protection clause of the 14th Amendment regardless of their citizenship status. This established that children living illegally in the U.S. are entitled to a free and public education.

- **New Jersey v TLO (1985).** This court decision allows school administrators to search students' belongings if the administrator has a reasonable suspicion of criminal activity.

Theorists

Name	Major Contribution
Albert Bandura	Social learning theory (SLT), students learn from what they observe.
Benjamin Bloom	Bloom's Taxonomy, levels of complexity and specificity for learning objectives.
Jerome Bruner	Learning is an active process where learners construct new ideas based on current or prior knowledge.
John Dewey	Learning by doing hands-on activities, inquiry-based, experiential learning.
Erik Erickson	8 psychological stages of learning.
Lawrence Kohlberg (photo not available)	Stages of morality development.

Name	Major Contribution
Abraham Maslow	Hierarchy of needs, basic needs must be met before moving to high-order needs.
Jean Piaget	4 stages of cognitive development.
B.F. Skinner	Operant conditioning theory, changes in behavior are a result of response to events.
Edward Thorndike	Connectionism theory, emphasizes rewards, repetition, and readiness.
Lev Vygotsky	Zone of proximal development (ZPD), social interaction is critical to cognitive development.
John Watson	Conditioning theory, students can be conditioned to associate positive feelings with classroom routines.

Practice Test

This page intentionally left blank.

Practice Test

1. A teacher is standing in the front of the room presenting information as students take notes. This type of instructional method is called:

   A. Simulation

   B. Expository

   C. Reciprocal

   D. Experiential

2. Ms. Jackson believes students bring their own experiences and background knowledge to their learning. She often has classroom discussions before starting a unit to help students activate their prior knowledge. Ms. Jackson is most closely aligned to this theorist.

   A. Piaget

   B. Vygotsky

   C. Thorndike

   D. Bandura

3. A new teacher is developing objectives for an upcoming lesson. Which of the following would be helpful for her to align objectives to the skills necessary for standards mastery?

   A. Maslow's Hierarchy of needs

   B. Vygotsky's ZPD

   C. Bloom's Taxonomy

   D. Piaget's stages of cognitive development

4. Research shows that classroom management policies are most effective when:

   A. Students are offered rewards for good behavior.

   B. Teachers regularly call home to share positive news with parents.

   C. Students have the opportunity to plan and practice classroom routines.

   D. Teachers allow students to work in cooperative groups.

5. Ms. Schaffer has several students in her class who are special education students with varying exceptionalities. What would be the best way to help these students achieve at their highest potential?

   A. Group the students together so they can support each other during learning.

   B. Read each student's IEP to target interventions and accommodations.

   C. Request meetings with each student's parents to determine specific needs.

   D. Request that a paraprofessional be placed in her classroom to assist students.

6. Which of the following workshops would be most effective in helping a new 8ᵗʰ grade teacher with classroom management?

A. A guide to teaching emotional intelligence to middle school students.

B. How to structure cooperative learning groups in the classroom.

C. A guide to increasing parent involvement.

D. How to collaborate with teacher teams to increase student success.

7. Mr. Rodriguez is planning instruction for several of his gifted students. In terms of cognitive characteristics, what should Mr. Rodriguez consider?

A. Gifted students have high expectations for themselves and others.

B. Gifted students work most effectively in groups.

C. Gifted students like to help tutor other students.

D. Gifted students have the ability to generate original ideas.

8. Sarah is a student under the "least restrictive environment" provision. Sarah has ADHD and has a short attention span during class. In the goals section of her IEP, it states that Sarah will take notes for 5-10 minutes during whole-group instruction.

Which of the following strategies would be most effective in beginning this type of accommodation for Sarah?

A. Provide Sarah first with an outline structure she can use to guide her notetaking.

B. Have Sarah first record the lesson and then copy down her notes.

C. Have Sarah work with a partner and mimic how her partner takes notes.

D. Allow Sarah extra time after the lesson is over to finish her notes.

9. A teacher is helping students design short-term goals based on their reading data. Students are thinking about realistic milestones and how reaching these goals would help them in their overall achievement. The teacher is helping students with:

A. Metacognition

B. Aptitude

C. Comprehension

D. Self-efficacy

10. Which of the following is not related to intrinsic motivation?

A. Autonomy

B. Rewards

C. Relatedness

D. Competence

11. A social studies teacher leads her 15 and 16 year old students in a forensic investigation of artifacts and primary sources. Students then use their observations to develop a claim about the cause of past events that can be supported with reasoning and examples. The deductive reasoning students are using -- to connect reasoning and examples to their claims -- indicates what stage of cognitive development?

    A. Sensorimotor

    B. Pre-operational

    C. Concrete operational

    D. Formal operational

12. A science teacher has students read through a short passage on their own. The passage contains one high-level vocabulary word and two complex concepts the students may have not known before the reading. After they read, she has them work in their cooperative groups to discuss how they approached the passage. Below are a couple of the students' comments.

    • *"I didn't know what that word was there, so I looked it up in the dictionary to figure it out."*

    • *"This part was confusing, but then I reread it and focused on figuring out the main idea."*

    • *"I tried to understand this word, but I was running out of time, so I skipped it."*

    In what type of activity are these students engaging?

    A. Concrete operational

    B. Schematic

    C. Metacognitive

    D. Recall

13. A 5th grade advanced student will be absent from school for several weeks as she recovers from surgery. To be sure she is not penalized for missing school and that she receives necessary academic accommodations while recovering, which of the following should be put in place for this student?

    A. An IEP.

    B. A behavioral plan.

    C. An IEP team.

    D. A 504 plan.

14. Students are beginning a short novel in their reading block. The teacher begins the lesson by asking students what they know about the Bermuda Triangle. She asks the following questions:

    • **Teacher:** *Have you ever heard about the Bermuda Triangle?*

    • **Student 1:** *Is that where all the planes crash?*

    • **Student 2:** *What? I thought Bermuda is where all the cruise ships go for vacation.*

    • **Teacher:** *Those are great questions. Let's put those two concepts on the board, so we remember them as we read. Has anyone else ever heard of the Bermuda Triangle?*

    The teacher is focusing on this cognitive process:

    A. Schema

    B. Mapping

    C. Modeling

    D. Scaffolding

15. Ms. Jefferson, a brand new 9th grade teacher, is beginning to plan a math lesson. What should she do first?

   A. Consult her peer teacher.

   B. Reference the state-adopted math standards.

   C. Bring her lesson to the team meeting for review.

   D. Review the lesson with the assistant principal.

16. Which of the following is most effective when using questioning techniques in a 12th grade classroom?

   A. Focus on recall questions, so all students are engaged.

   B. Allow students to use their notes if they need to.

   C. Allow 5 seconds of wait time before students can answer.

   D. Have students use hand-held devices to answer questions.

17. A teacher is temporarily grouping 7th grade students based on their reading levels, so she can prescribe targeted interventions. What type of grouping is this?

   A. Homogeneous

   B. Heterogeneous

   C. Interest

   D. Multi-age

18. Which of the following activities would be most effective in increasing students' critical thinking?

   A. Cooperative groups to identify difficult words in text.

   B. Partner reading to work on fluency.

   C. Flashcard activity to work on sight word memorization.

   D. Think-pair-share to analyze text structure.

19. Which of the following would be most effective for a whole-group lesson where the teacher models how to edit sentences based on specific grammar concepts?

   A. Hand-held clickers

   B. Document sharing software

   C. Plagiarism software

   D. Document camera

20. Which of the following is NOT an effective active listening technique?

   A. Restate what the student is saying.

   B. Form a counter argument.

   C. Make eye contact.

   D. Asking questions.

21. Which of the following would be most effective in increasing students' intrinsic motivation to read?

    A. Allow students extra time in the library if they finish their daily reading.

    B. Call home to praise students' progress in reading.

    C. Provide students with a safe and engaging space to discuss the books they're reading.

    D. Have students complete reading worksheets in groups.

22. A new teacher is planning a science unit. Which of the following sequence of steps would ensure that the students are meeting objectives?

    A. Reference the state standards, plan classroom activities, design assessments, execute instruction, assess learning.

    B. Plan classroom activities, reference the state standards, design assessments, execute instruction, assess learning.

    C. Assess learning, plan classroom activities, reference the state standards, design assessments, execute instruction.

    D. Reference the state standards, design assessments, plan classroom activities, execute instruction, assess learning.

23. Which of the following practices in education ensures that teachers are holding students with varying levels of understanding to high academic standards?

    A. Remediation

    B. Differentiation

    C. Modeling

    D. Assessment

24. Ms. Jones, a high school science teacher, wants to help her students increase critical thinking by making connections between science and social science events around space exploration. Which of the following practices would be most effective in this situation?

    A. Use an integrated curriculum that includes elements of the 1969 Moon Landing.

    B. Use reciprocal teaching so students see the lesson from various perspectives.

    C. Use cooperative learning to explore a variety of topics regarding the Solar System.

    D. Guide students through a semester-long research project exploring the Solar System.

25. A new teacher is spending a lot of time on redirecting inappropriate behavior, transitioning to activities, and cleaning up after activities. She has both the classroom expectations and the steps for moving through transitions and cleaning posted clearly on the wall. However, students are often unfocused, and the classroom is very chaotic. What would be the best approach the teacher can take in this situation?

    A. Call home to students' parents and ask them to intervene.

    B. Ask the principal to come in and speak with the students.

    C. Revisit and practice classroom procedures before doing any more activities.

    D. Ask a peer teacher to observe the situation and offer support in this area.

26. A teacher is adjusting group size and composition to accommodate and reflect student progress and instructional objectives throughout the lesson. The teacher is using what type of grouping?

   A. Homogeneous

   B. Heterogeneous

   C. Flexible

   D. Continuous

27. Which of the following would be most effective in creating an engaging learning environment for students in an 8th grade math classroom?

   A. Integrate technology in the classroom.

   B. Allow students to pick what type of activity they will engage in.

   C. Bring in guest speakers to share their knowledge on topics.

   D. Use relevant information and relate content to students' lives.

28. Which of the following is most effective in increasing student engagement and critical thinking during a whole-group discussion activity?

   A. Allow students to discuss their thoughts first with their partners and then answer questions.

   B. Ask students to write their questions down before answering.

   C. Have students answer questions on their hand-held devices.

   D. Ask higher-order questions and increase wait time in between questions.

29. What can a teacher do to ensure students are gaining the most out of every lesson?

   A. Work with a peer teacher on lesson plans and objectives.

   B. Encourage family members to discuss lessons at home.

   C. Organize resources and time by planning instruction for various environments.

   D. Develop a well-defined syllabus outlining expectations

30. A teacher is working on her weekly lesson plan. On which of the following should she focus the most?

   A. Rewards for students who complete tasks.

   B. The state test happening at the end of the month.

   C. The state standards and scope and sequence of learning objectives.

   D. The school-wide initiatives for at-home reading practice.

31. A high school Spanish teacher is using the gradual release or the I do, we do, you do method. Which theory is this practice aligned to?

   A. Stages of cognitive development

   B. Zone of proximal development

   C. Taxonomy of skills

   D. Hierarchy of needs

32. Which of the following would be most effective for measuring students' understanding at the end of a lesson?

   A. "Using thumbs up or thumbs down, how do you feel about today's lesson?"

   B. "Use your exit slips to write down 2 things you've learned and 2 questions you still have.

   C. "If you have any questions, write them down and put them in the question box."

   D. "Did everyone understand the lesson? Raise your hand if you didn't or see me after class."

33. Which of the following is the primary purpose of using inquiry learning in a science classroom?

   A. Inquiry-based activities make it easier on the teacher to assign grades to students.

   B. Inquiry-based activities are the most interesting for students.

   C. Inquiry-based activities promote critical thinking and curiosity.

   D. Inquiry-based activities help students achieve on state tests.

34. The objectives of a lesson should include:

   A. The supplies needed for the lesson.

   B. The skills the students will have acquired in the lesson.

   C. The page number in the textbook.

   D. Ancillary resources students can use to supplement activities in the lesson.

35. Ms. Jones is working at a diverse school. Students come from different socioeconomic and cultural backgrounds. Which of the following practices would be most effective in this diverse classroom?

   A. Celebrate Black History Month in February.

   B. Engage in a unit on tolerance at the beginning of the year.

   C. Allow students to speak their home language during certain times of the day.

   D. Read and analyze literature told from different cultural and economic perspectives.

36. A new teacher is trying to decide what reading strategy she will use in the next unit. What would be her best course of action before implementing the strategy?

   A. Determine if there is research to support the use of the strategy.

   B. Consult with her peer teacher about the strategy.

   C. Search online to see if other teachers are using the strategy.

   D. Survey the students to see if they want to use the strategy.

37. While the teacher is walking around and monitoring the class during their individual work, she notices that only 2 or 3 students out of 15 get number 7 correct. What should the teacher do?

   A. Stop the class and go over the concept again before having students move on.

   B. Allow the students to finish and go over it another time.

   C. Grade the assignment as is because students should have gotten the concept by now.

   D. Tell the students the correct answer for that problem and move on.

38. 12th grade students read a newspaper three days per week as part of class. At the end of the week, in their cooperative groups, students design and simulate a play summarizing what they read throughout the week in the paper. This type of activity is:

A. Performance-based

B. Problem-based

C. Inquiry-based

D. Research-based

39. After students have spent a week on a science unit, the teacher decides to have students facilitate an activity. In cooperative groups, they will use what they have learned over the last week to design and implement a learning activity of their choice. Each group will guide the rest of the class in the activity. They will debrief after the activities are over. This technique is:

A. Socratic seminar

B. Reciprocal teaching

C. Literature circles

D. Whole-group presentation

40. An effective strategy to use with a child who struggles with finishing work in a timely fashion is to:

A. Send all incomplete work home with the student to finish as homework.

B. Call the parents to urge them to get a psychological evaluation.

C. Write the student referrals for non-compliance until they learn better time management.

D. Set a stopwatch for the student's work periods and determine goals to be achieved in that time.

41. A teacher is using math and science together during instruction to relate the learning to everyday life. This approach is called:

A. Cognitive

B. Interdisciplinary

C. Behavioral

D. Gradual release

42. Ms. Summer notices that some students in her class are struggling with study strategies, as evidenced by their low test scores. What is the most effective strategy for her to employ?

A. A targeted, small-group differentiated strategy session during the school day.

B. A whole-group lesson on the various study strategies.

C. A worksheet on study strategies.

D. An after-school program.

43. On a norm-referenced exam, a student scored in the 75th percentile. This means the student scored:

A. At or above 25% of the students who took the test.

B. At or above 75% of the students who took the test.

C. Above 75% of the students who took the test.

D. Below 75% of the students who took the test.

44. Over the course of 3 weeks, 11th grade students have worked through a whole unit on genetics. Students have completed activities, classwork, and assessments. The teacher wants to measure student mastery through a performance-based assessment. Which of the following would be the most effective way to do this?

   A. Work through a DNA extraction lab, follow procedures, record findings, and communicate results.

   B. Complete a multiple-choice test on all the vocabulary presented in the genetics chapter.

   C. Complete a worksheet on genetics.

   D. Engage in a group discussion on genetics.

45. Which of the following assessment tools would be most effective when grading a project or writing assignment?

   A. Criterion-referenced

   B. Norm-referenced

   C. Rubric

   D. Diagnostic

46. Which of the following approach is most appropriate for assisting a special education student who is taking a state standardized assessment?

   A. Allow the student extra time.

   B. Provide the student assistive technology.

   C. Have the student test in a separate room.

   D. Follow accommodations outlined in the IEP.

47. Which of the following assessments would be most effective for students to use in their student-led conferences with their parents?

   A. Diagnostic

   B. Formative

   C. Summative

   D. Portfolio

48. A math teacher collected samples of student work, test scores, and surveys. The teacher should use this data to:

   A. Communicate with parents.

   B. Make instructional decisions.

   C. Show the principal.

   D. Rank students.

49. A teacher is using a variety of assessments in the classroom. Which of the following assessment sequences would be most beneficial to students?

   A. Formative assessment, diagnostic assessment, summative assessment

   B. Diagnostic assessment, formative assessment, summative assessment

   C. Summative assessment, formative assessment, diagnostic assessment

   D. Diagnostic assessment, summative assessment, formative assessment

50. This type of assessment is used to place students in certain classes or grade levels.

   A. Norm-reference

   B. Screening

   C. Post-assessment

   D. Rubric

51. Which of the following data would be the most helpful for a 10th grade teacher who is planning lessons for the first quarter of school?

   A. Student scores on the previous year's state assessment

   B. Student behavioral records

   C. Teacher-made tests

   D. Parent surveys

52. A teacher is administering informal assessments periodically throughout the semester. The teacher is most likely using these assessments to:

   A. Rank students

   B. Grade students

   C. Communicate with parents

   D. Monitor progress

53. Which of the following types of scores would a teacher use to evaluate individual performance on certain standards?

   A. Scale score

   B. Curved score

   C. Raw score

   D. Combined score

54. Which of the following is an effective way to communicate achievement data with stakeholders?

   A. Share individual student data at the school reading assembly.

   B. Share individual student data with parents during student led conferences.

   C. Post reading challenge results on the classroom bulletin board.

   D. Email parents the results of the state assessment.

55. Which of the following question formats would be most appropriate in assessing the following standard?

Determine two or more main ideas of a text and explain how they are supported by key details; summarize the text.

A. Extended response

B. Multiple-choice test

C. Fill-in the blank

D. True/false

56. Which of the following is the most common type of assessment accommodation for special education and ELL students?

A. Quiet room

B. Screen reader

C. Extended time

D. Dictation

57. An ELL student is progressing very well and is making huge gains in class. The teacher would like to communicate this clearly with the student's parents, who have limited English language proficiency. What would be the most effective way to communicate to parents of an ELL student?

A. Send home a weekly newsletter with the ELL student's progress report attached to it.

B. Schedule a parent teacher conference and be sure to enlist the help of an interpreter to attend the conference and translate.

C. Call the parents on the phone and try to speak Spanish as best as she can to show them she is trying.

D. Have the paraprofessional assigned to the student call the parents and explain the student's learning gains.

58. According to this law, school districts must provide accommodations for each qualified student with a disability who is in the school district's jurisdiction, regardless of the nature or severity of the disability.

A. Section 504

B. Race to the Top

C. No Child Left Behind

D. FERPA

59. When developing a professional development plan, the teacher must ensure the plan includes:

A. Measurable goals

B. Interesting research

C. Technology application

D. Peer teacher evaluation

60. Which of the following is the most effective way to engage in professional learning communities?

    A. Discuss changes needed on the administration team.

    B. Reflect on the current curriculum and textbook.

    C. Engage in action research to improve student performance.

    D. Develop a department newsletter for parents.

61. A math teacher wants to implement new strategies to help students engage with algebra. Which of the following approaches would be most beneficial to students' learning needs?

    A. Search online for engaging activities and strategies.

    B. Consult peer-reviewed academic journals for research on current learning trends in algebra.

    C. Meet with a peer teacher to go over strategies that work in the classroom.

    D. Survey students to determine what strategies they like and dislike.

62. Which of the following should teachers consider most when choosing professional development?

    A. Is the professional development interesting?

    B. Is the professional development aligned to school goals?

    C. Is the professional development affordable?

    D. Did the principal approve the professional development?

63. A new PE teacher has several ELL students in class. The teacher wants to be sure to meet the specific learning needs of these students. What should the teacher do?

    A. Ask a peer teacher for help.

    B. Request a paraprofessional.

    C. Ask another student to translate when needed.

    D. Reference National Association for Bilingual Education (NABE).

64. What should a teacher do before attending an online training called Using social media in the classroom to engage and motivate students?

    A. Reference the district acceptable use policy.

    B. Consult with a peer teacher.

    C. Survey students.

    D. Contact parents.

65. Which of the following would be most beneficial to a new reading teacher who is looking for current trends in reading education?

    A. Reading teacher social media group

    B. District library

    C. International Literacy Association

    D. State statutes

66. This law focuses on standards and accountability for schools, teachers, and students.

    A. No Child Left Behind (NCLB)

    B. Every Student Succeeds Act (ESSA)

    C. Family Educational Rights and Privacy Act (FERPA)

    D. Individuals with Disabilities Education Act 2004 (IDEA)

67. A teacher notices a bruise on a student's arm. She suspects abuse but isn't sure. What should the teacher do?

    A. Schedule a meeting with the school counselor to discuss the situation.

    B. Call the parents to investigate.

    C. Ask the student if he or she is being abused.

    D. Report the abuse to the child abuse hotline.

68. Mr. Reese sees a teacher harassing another teacher in the teachers' lounge. Mr. Reese reports the harassment to the principal. Which of the following obligations is Mr. Reese adhering to?

    A. Obligations to the student.

    B. Obligations to the public.

    C. Obligations to the code of conduct.

    D. Obligations to the profession.

69. Once a student turns 18, the student's FERPA rights:

    A. Continue with the biological parents.

    B. Are transferred to the student.

    C. Are transferred to the school.

    D. Are terminated.

70. A teacher wants to share software with students so they can work with the software at home. What should the teacher consider?

    A. Copyright

    B. Cost

    C. Reading level

    D. Accessibility

Number	Content Category	Answer	Explanation
1	I.	B	Expository teaching is when the teacher is giving information to the students and the students are receiving information usually during whole-group instruction. Expository learning is often referred to as the "sage on the stage" approach. **Quick Tip** In education, the *sage on the stage* approach is when the teacher is standing in the front of the room delivering information. This method should not be the main mode of delivering instruction. Ideally, teachers should be the *guide on the side*, allowing students to facilitate and engage in their own learning.
2	I.	A	Piaget, a constructivist, found that learners use schema/schemata (a cognitive framework) to make sense of new experiences. When you see the words schema and prior knowledge, think Piaget and constructivism.
3	I.	C	Bloom's Taxonomy is a hierarchical model used to classify educational learning objectives into levels of complexity and specificity. The higher up the pyramid, the more complex the thinking skills. The skills are represented as verbs on the pyramid.
4	I.	C	Effective classroom management requires teachers and students to plan and practice routines to ensure time is spent on learning and not on behavior and management. Answers A and B offer extrinsic rewards, which you want to avoid on the exam. Answer D is not necessarily effective in this scenario.
5	I.	B	Whenever special education is mentioned, look for answer choices that outline the practice of reading each IEP and accommodating for each individual student's needs based on the goals of the IEP.
6	I.	A	When students have emotional intelligence, they have a self-awareness, which enables them to recognize feelings and manage their emotions. Teaching students about emotional intelligence is effective in classroom management.
7	I.	D	The key word in the question stem is *cognitive*. Answer D is the only answer choice that involves the cognitive process. Beyond that, only answer A is a characteristic of gifted students, but answer A is about emotional characteristics of gifted students, not cognitive.

Principles of Learning and Teaching: Grades 7-12

Number	Content Category	Answer	Explanation
8	I.	A	Answer A is an accommodation the teacher can use to help introduce Sarah to notetaking. As she gets better, she can start her own notes without the premade outline.
9	I.	D	Self-efficacy is essential in goal setting. Metacognition and comprehension are used in reading instruction. Aptitude is what a person is capable of doing, which is not part of the goal-setting process.
10	I.	B	Autonomy, relatedness, and competence are all part of intrinsic motivation. Rewards are part of extrinsic motivation.
11	I.	D	Refer to Piaget's stages of cognitive development for this question. The age of the students is the first indication of their stage of cognitive development. 15 year olds are capable of formal operational thinking. In the formal operational stage, students understand abstract concepts and use abstract thinking to solve problems. Students can use deductive thinking to hypothesize and systemically defend their argument.
12	I.	C	Students are thinking about their thought process and discussing it with other students. This is a metacognitive activity.
13	I.	A	Students who are home bound or hospitalized for an extended period of time are considered students with a disability. In accordance with IDEA, an IEP must be created and services provided for these students.
14	I.	A	The teacher is activating students' background knowledge or building schema before they read about the Bermuda Triangle.
15	I.	B	When planning instruction, the first thing any teacher should do is reference the state-adopted standards. The standards should be the main point of reference. Later she can go to her peer teacher. However, the standards supersede all answer choices on this exam. If you see state-adopted standards in an answer choice, it is most likely the correct answer.
16	I.	C	Allowing for think or wait time is essential in questioning techniques because it allows time for all students to participate, which increases engagement. It also allows students to think critically about complex concepts. None of the other answer choices are effective for questioning. Think or wait time is on the good words list, so if you see it in the answer choices, it is most likely the correct answer.

Number	Content Category	Answer	Explanation
17	I.	A	Homogeneous grouping involves grouping students who all have the same situation. In this case, she is grouping them based on ability level, so everyone in the group is the same level. **Quick Tip** Homogeneous grouping should only be used temporarily for intervention purposes. Leaving students in homogeneous groups for too long can have a negative impact on their learning.
18	I.	D	Think about Bloom's Taxonomy in this scenario. Critical thinking is a higher-order cognitive skill. The verb used in answer choice D is *analyze*, which is at the top of the Bloom's pyramid, which aligns to critical thinking.
19	I.	D	A document camera allows the teacher to project the document in the front of the room and model how she edits sentences. This is the best tool for the lesson scenario.
20	I.	B	All of the techniques listed are effective active listening skills teachers should model except answer B. If someone is formulating an argument, he or she is not actively listening.
21	I.	C	Answers A and B are extrinsic motivators. Answer C is an intrinsic motivator and aligns with Maslow's hierarchy of needs. Answer D is not an effective answer and does not fit this scenario. Worksheets are usually in the incorrect answer choices on the exam.
22	II	D	When planning instruction, use backwards design. Always start with the standards because they outline what is expected of students. Then design the assessments because you have to determine how you will assess learning. Will you use a writing assignment, multiple choice test, project, or observation? Plan and conduct the lesson, then assess student performance.
23	II	B	Differentiation is when teachers analyze data (qualitative and quantitative) and modify their instruction to meet the needs of every student. In addition, differentiation keeps the standards high for all students and allows the teacher to accommodate based on students' varying abilities.
24	II	A	Helping students make connections between science content and social science content is using an integrated curriculum. In this case answer A is the best choice.

Number	Content Category	Answer	Explanation
25	II	C	In this situation, the teacher and students have procedures in place. However, they are not using them properly. Therefore, the best decision is to stop all activities and practice the procedures, so students can clearly understand expectations. Calling home and asking the principal are not effective classroom management tactics when answering questions on the Praxis PLT. Asking a peer teacher is effective, but revisiting the plan and practicing the procedures should come first.
26	II	C	The term *adjusting* in the question stem is a good indication that the teacher is using flexible grouping. Flexible grouping strategies often employ several organizational patterns for instruction. Students are grouped and regrouped according to specific goals, activities, and individual needs.
27	II	D	Integrating relevant and real-world activities into the classroom helps students make connections from the learning to their lives. This is effective in engaging students. Remember you are looking for the *most effective* way, as stated in the question stem.
28	II	D	Effective questioning includes asking higher-order questions (increase critical thinking) and giving ample wait time between questions (increases engagement). *Wait time* is on the good words list.
29	II	C	Using appropriate techniques for organizing, allocating, and managing the resources of time, space, and attention in a variety of learning environments ensures student learning is taking place in all classroom situations. Answer choices A, B, and D are all good classroom practices, but organizing time and resources and managing environments is essential in effective lesson planning.
30	II	C	The most important part of teaching is aligning objectives and lessons to the state-adopted standards and the scope and sequence of the academic plan.
31	II	B	The gradual release method is most closely aligned to Vygotsky's zone of proximal development (ZPD).
32	II	B	The exit slip is the best answer because it is specific enough to measure student understanding and provides data for the teacher to analyze and use. Answer choice C is incorrect because most students won't participate. Answer choice D is incorrect because students will usually not follow-up on their own if they didn't understand.
33	II	C	Promoting critical thinking is the most important practice in this question. Inquiry-based activities help students think critically about concepts.

Number	Content Category	Answer	Explanation
34	II	B	Objectives detail what a student will be able to do by the end of the learning activity. Objectives should be measurable because teachers have to determine if the objectives of learning were met before moving on to the next lesson.
35	II	D	Being culturally responsive should be ongoing. In addition, choosing stories that represent different cultural and economic perspectives is an effective way to help students see themselves in stories. Answer choices A, B, and C all take place at a certain time.
36	II	A	Remember, evidence-based and research-based are good words on this exam. This is one of those questions where all 4 answers could be beneficial in this situation. Because she is a new teacher, it makes sense that she would consult her peer teacher. In addition, using the Internet to see how other teachers feel about the strategy is something teachers do all the time. Finally, surveying students is also a good way to decide whether to use the strategy. However, the first and most important thing she should do is see if the strategy is researched-based.
37	II	A	Remember, when a teacher is observing students, the teacher is collecting valuable qualitative data. The teacher can make immediate decisions using observation data. This is a formative assessment. The teacher notices only a few students got a question correct. Therefore, she makes the decision to stop and revisit the concept which is data-driven decision making.
38	II	A	Students are applying what they learned as they perform a play. This is a performance-based activity
39	II	B	In reciprocal teaching, students facilitate the learning. This requires a deep understanding of the material. It also requires critical thinking, teamwork, proper planning, and creative thinking. Socratic seminar is a questioning and discussion method. Literature circles is a cooperative learning activity where students read and analyze text together. Whole-group presentation is when students present information to the class.
40	II	D	Notice that the only answer choice that is positive is answer choice D. In addition, answer choice D focuses on a specific and tangible task and goals.
41	II	B	The teacher is using two different disciplines—math and science—in the lesson. This is interdisciplinary.
42	II	A	Because only some students struggled, small group is most appropriate here. In addition, this answer choice contains good words: *targeted* and *differentiated*.

PRACTICE TEST

Number	Content Category	Answer	Explanation
43	III	B	If a student scored in the 75th percentile, the student is at or above 75% of all the students who took the exam.
44	III	A	A performance-based assessment measures students' ability to apply the skills and knowledge learned from a unit or units of study. The only performance-based assessment in the answer choices that does this is a DNA extraction lab.
45	III	C	Rubrics are used to communicate expectations and outline a set of standards for student work. Rubrics are typically used for large projects and writing, but they can be used for any assignment.
46	III	D	The question stem does not name the specific exceptionality the student has. Therefore, following the IEP for accommodations is the best answer here. There are many different accommodations available to special education students. Students who have learning disabilities may receive extra time on exams or may be permitted to test in another room. Students with physical disabilities may be provided with assistive technology. Following the IEP and accommodating accordingly is almost always going to be the correct answer on the Praxis PLT.
47	III	D	Out of all the answer choices, portfolio would be most beneficial for a student-led conference. Students can show their parents samples from the portfolio and reflect on their learning over time.
48	III	B	Remember, the number one reason for assessing students and analyzing data is to drive instructional decisions. Teachers do use it to communicate with parents and other stakeholders. However, using data to make instructional decisions is always the best answer on the Praxis PLT.
49	III	B	A diagnostic assessment is a pre-assessment and often occurs before learning takes place. Formative assessments are ongoing and typically happen during the learning. Finally, summative assessments occur at the end of learning to measure outcomes. If you know that summative happens at the end of learning, you can immediately eliminate answer choices C and D.
50	III	B	Students are typically screened throughout the year to determine what level they are reading. Placement decisions are made based on the outcomes of the screening.
51	III	A	State assessment scores will give the teacher scale scores of students in reading and math from the previous year. This is the best data to use at the beginning of the year because it gives the teacher an idea of where the student will be as they start the school year.

Number	Content Category	Answer	Explanation
52	III	D	Periodic, informal assessments are formative assessments. Formative assessments are used to monitor progress and make instructional decisions. The effective teacher uses formative assessments to monitor student progress and performance.
53	III	C	A raw score shows how many questions a student got correct. This is most beneficial when looking at individual student performance. A scale score is not specific enough for this situation. Combined score and curved score are nonsense answers.
54	III	B	The best answer choice is to share the data in student led conferences. Student data is private; therefore, sharing it at a reading assembly or posting individual scores on a bulletin board is inappropriate. Finally, emailing assessment data is never the correct answer on this test for two reasons: not all parents have access to email, and assessment results should be kept secure. Email is not a secure way to send assessment results.
55	III	A	Out of all the answer choices, an assessment where students can explain by writing is best. The standard says: …*explain how they are supported by key details; summarize the text*. This requires the student to write. Fill in the blank, multiple choice, and true/false cannot be used to properly assess this standard.
56	III	C	Extended time is often provided for special education and ELL students. The other accommodations are not used as frequently as extended time.
57	IV	B	This is important communication and must be presented in a comprehensible manner. Therefore, answer B is the best choice.
58	IV	A	Section 504 of the Rehabilitation Act requires schools to provide accommodations. In fact, these accommodations are often called a 504 plan.
59	IV	A	The purpose of a professional development plan is to outline the teacher's professional goals for the year. Like student learning, goals should be measurable. Interesting research is irrelevant. Technology application and peer-teacher evaluation might be included in a plan, but they are not required. However, measurable goals must be included in the plan.
60	IV	C	Action research is by far the most effective way to collaborate with colleagues in a PLC.
61	IV	B	Teachers must always use strategies that are researched based. In addition, research from peer-reviewed academic journals is likely to be the most reliable and valid. Answer choices A, C, and D are all things teachers do in the classroom. However, using research-based strategies and referencing peer-reviewed academic journals is the best approach.

PRACTICE TEST

Number	Content Category	Answer	Explanation
62	IV	B	Alignment to school goals also means alignment to the state standards because school goals must be aligned to the standards. In the real-world, answers A, C, and D are all things teachers consider when choosing professional development. However, alignment is most important.
63	IV	D	The National Association for Bilingual Education (NABE) will have professional learning, research, and other resources for this teacher to use when helping ELL students. Asking a peer teacher is not as effective as referencing the association. Requesting a paraprofessional not appropriate here. Finally, never ask other students to translate for ELLs.
64	IV	A	Before enrolling in an online training in technology, the teacher must determine if social media is even permitted in the district. If it is permitted, the teacher must determine what restrictions the district has on the technology. The teacher should not waste time or money on professional learning that cannot be applied because of district policy.
65	IV	C	Professional associations will often have conferences for professional development. They will also have journals where teachers can find peer-reviewed academic research. In this case, the International Literacy Association is the best resource.
66	IV	A	NCLB introduced accountability to schools. FERPA is about student records and confidentiality. ESSA is concerned with equity. IDEA governs ESE students.
67	IV	D	Educators are mandatory reporters, and teachers must, by law, report suspected abuse immediately. Teachers should not contact parents or students about the suspected abuse. Scheduling an appointment is delaying reporting.
68	IV	D	Reporting harassment falls under obligation to the profession. Teachers shall make reasonable effort to assure that each individual is protected from such harassment or discrimination.
69	IV	B	FERPA gives parents certain rights with respect to their children's education records. These rights transfer to the student when he or she reaches the age of 18 or attends a school beyond the high school level (U.S. Department of Education, 2019).
70	IV	A	The teacher must determine if the copyright allows her to share the software with multiple students. Copyright supersedes all other answer choices.

This page intentionally left blank.

Bibliography

This page intentionally left blank.

Bibliography

Agosto, D. E. (2002). *Criteria for evaluating multicultural literature.* Retrieved from http://www.pages.drexel.edu/~dea22/multicultural.html

Akerman C., (2020). Retrieved from https://positivepsychology.com/positive-punishment/

American Library Association (2020). Retrieved from http://www.ala.org/aboutala/offices/oif

Andrade, H. (2019). A *critical review of research on student self-assessment.* https://doi.org/10.3389/feduc.2019.00087

Bandura, Alfred (1971). *Social learning theory.* General Learning Press, New York. Retrieved from http://www.asecib.ase.ro/mps/Bandura_SocialLearningTheory.pdf

Boynton, M., & Boynton, C. (2005). *The educator's guide to preventing and solving discipline problems.* Alexandria, VA: Association for Supervision and Curriculum Development.

Campos, A. (2010). *What copyright laws affect teachers or students? What are the implications and possible consequences?* Education Technology Center, University of Iowa. Retrieved from https://wiki.uiowa.edu/pages/viewpage.action?pageId=42017025

Common Core Standards (2020). Retrieved from http://www.corestandards.org/

Donovan S., Bransford J. & Pellegrino J., (Eds). National Research Council. (1999). *How people learn: bridging research and practice.* Washington, DC: National Academy Press: U.S. Dept. of Education

Frey, B. (2018). *Age-equivalent scores.* The SAGE Encyclopedia of Educational Research, Measurement, and Evaluation. Retrieved from https://dx.doi.org/10.4135/9781506326139.n31

Glossary of Education Reform. (2013). *Critical friend.* Retrieved from: https://www.edglossary.org/critical-friend/#:~:text=A%20critical%20friend%20is%20typically

Glossary of Education Reform. (2015). *Standardized tests.* Retrieved from https://www.edglossary.org/standardized-test/

Glossary of Education Reform (2017). *Standards-based.* Retrieved from https://www.edglossary.org/standards-based/

Glossary of Education Reform. (2018). *Portfolios.* Retrieved from: https://edglossary.org/portfolios/

Hattie, John. (2012). *Visible learning for teachers: maximizing impact on learning.* London; New York: Routledge

Kahlenberg, R. (2015). *Tenure: How due process protects teachers and students.* American Educator. Summer 2015.

Kohlberg, L., Levine, C., & Hewer, A. (1983). Moral stages: A current formulation and a response to critics. *Contributions to Human Development, 10,* 174.

Landt, S. M. (2006). Multicultural literature and young adolescents: A kaleidoscope of opportunity. *Journal of Adolescent & Adult Literacy*, 49(8), 690-697.

Loria R. (2018). A *how-to guide for building school-community partnerships.* Retrieved from https://www.edweek.org/ew/articles/2018/03/23/a-how-to-guide-for-building-school-community-partnerships.html

McDevitt, T.M., & Ormrod, J.E. (2010). *Child development and education* (4th Ed, pp. 24-25). Columbus, Ohio: Merrill

Matsumoto, D., Frank, M. G., & Hwang, H. S. (Eds.). (2013). *Nonverbal communication: Science and applications.* Sage Publications, Inc.

National Association for Gifted Children (2019) Retrieved from https://www.nagc.org/sites/default/files/Position%20Statement/Definition%20of%20Giftedness%20%282019%29.pdf

National Center for Educational Outcomes, (2020) retrieved from https://nceo.info/Resources/publications/TopicAreas/Accommodations/Accomtopic.htm

Next Generation Science Standards, 2020. Retrieved from https://www.nextgenscience.org/

Northern Illinois University Faculty Development and Instructional Design (n.d.). Instructional scaffolding to improve learning. Retrieved from https://www.niu.edu/facdev/_pdf/guide/strategies/instructional_scaffolding_to_improve_learning.pdf

O'Connor, C, Ruegg, E, Micheals, S. (2012) Norms for productive discussion. Retrieved from http://pankotai.weebly.com/uploads/4/1/0/1/41019291/ngsx_overview-classroom_norms_for_productive_discourse_and_discussionmco_final.pdf

Piaget, J. (1975). *The equilibration of cognitive structure*. Chicago, IL: University of Chicago Press.

Poole, I., Evertson, C., & the IRIS Center. (2017, rev. 2020). *Effective room arrangement: Elementary*. Retrieved from http:// iris.peabody.vanderbilt.edu/case_studies/ICS.pdf

Project Management Institute (2013). *Project management book of knowledge, fifth edition*. Project Management Institute, Inc.

Reading Recovery (2019). Retrieved from https://readingrecovery.clemson.edu/home/reading-comprehension/lesson-structure/guided-practice/#:~:text=Guided%20Practice%20is%20the%20transition,support%20them%20easily%20and%20quickly.

Responsive Classroom (2018). *The joyful classroom*. Center for Responsive Schools, Inc.

Rycus J., Hughes, R. (1998). The field guide to child welfare volume III: Child development and child welfare. *Child Welfare League of America Press*.

Sanders, C (2006). *Kohlberg stages of moral development*. Britannica. Retrieved from https://www.britannica.com/science/Lawrence-Kohlbergs-stages-of-moral-development

SEDL and U.S. Department of Education. (2013). *Partners in education: A dual capacity-building framework for family–school partnerships*. SEDL publishing. Retrieved from https://www2.ed.gov/documents/family-community/partners-education.pdf

Seifert, K. and Sutton, R. (2009) Education psychology. *Center for Open Education*. Retrieved from https://courses.lumenlearning.com/suny-educationalpsychology/chapter/gender-differences-in-the-classroom/

Stone, S. & Burriss, K. (2019). *Understanding multiage education*. Routledge Books.

Sutton, R., Hornsey, M.J., & Douglas, K.M. (Eds., 2011). *Feedback: The communication of praise, criticism, and advice*. Peter Lang Publishing: New York.

The IRIS Center. (2012). *Classroom diversity: An introduction to student differences*. Retrieved from https://iris.peabody.vanderbilt.edu/module/div/.

Thorndike, E. (1932). *The fundamentals of learning*. New York: Teachers College Press.

Tripp, D. (2012). Critical incidents in teaching: Developing professional judgement. United Kingdom: Routledge.

University of Massachusetts Boston (2019). *Evaluating sources*. Retrieved from https://umb.libguides.com/c.php?g=351182&p=2367584

Urbandale Community School District (2019). *Instructional materials: Selection, inspection, and reconsideration*. Retrieved from http://www.urbandaleschools.com/policy/article-600-educational-program/627-instructional-materials-selection-inspection-and-reconsideration/

U.S. Department of Education (2015). *Disabilities discrimination: Overview of the laws*. Office for Civil Rights. Retrieved from https://www2.ed.gov/about/offices/list/ocr/disabilityoverview.html

U.S. Department of Education, National Center for Education Statistics. (2019). *Digest of education statistics, 2018* (NCES 2020-009), Chapter 2.

U.S. Department of Education, Office of Civil Rights. (2014). *Fact sheet: Ensuring students have equal access to educational resources without regard to race, color, or national origin*. Retrieved from https://www2.ed.gov/about/offices/list/ocr/docs/dcl-factsheet-resourcecomp-201410.pdf

Walsh, J. A., & Sattes, B. D. (2011). *Thinking through quality questioning: Deepening student engagement*. Thousand Oaks, Calif: Corwin Press.

Weiner, B. (1976). An attributional approach for educational psychology. *Review of Research in Education, 4*, 179-209. Retrieved September 21, 2020, from http://www.jstor.org/stable/1167116

Wood, C (2018) *Yardsticks*. Center for Responsive Schools, Inc.; 4th Edition

Yudin, Michael K. and Musgrove, Melody (2015). *IDEA topics area least restrictive environment*. Retrieved from https://www2.ed.gov/policy/speced/guid/idea/memosdcltrs/guidance-on-fape-11-17-2015.pdf

BIBLIOGRAPHY

This page intentionally left blank.

Made in the USA
Coppell, TX
17 January 2025

44529759R00155